A NEW COLLECTION OF MORE THAN 400 FAVORITE
RECIPES FROM THE WORLD'S TOP RAW FOOD CHEFS

THE COMPLETE BOOK OF

RAW FOOD

VOLUME 2

HEALTHY, DELICIOUS VEGETARIAN CUISINE
MADE WITH LIVING FOODS

LISA MONTGOMERY, EDITOR

 hatherleigh

The Complete Book of Raw Food, Volume 2

Text Copyright © 2014 Hatherleigh Press except where noted

Library of Congress Cataloging-in-Publication Data is available.

ISBN: 978-1-57826-431-5

Cover and Interior Design by Carolyn Kasper and Barbara Balch

Printed in the United States

10 9 8 7 6 5 4 3 2 1

www.hatherleighpress.com

Contents

PART III: APPENDIX & RESOURCES

Dedication

The Complete Book of Raw Food, Volume 2 is dedicated to the memory of Linda Mer-rylees, who passed away in April 2013. Linda, the Operations Manager at Lionville Natural Pharmacy, used to work at Kimberton Whole Foods. Years ago, when I found out that I had food allergies and candida and initially didn't know what to do, Linda was the person who took me around the store and showed me what I could and couldn't eat. I am, and will always be, eternally grateful to Linda.

Thank you, Linda, for being a blessing to me and so many others.

Acknowledgments

A very special thanks to those of you who have contributed to *The Complete Book of Raw Food, Volume 2*. The folks who have contributed to this book are not only amazing in their own areas of expertise; each and every one has touched my heart and my life. I pray they will touch yours as well.

A very special thanks to Donna Batman (who was the visiting nurse to both my mom and my dad) for lending me her son, Josh Batman, who I like to call my "rent-a-son." Josh came to my rescue when I broke my leg two years ago and couldn't drive, but still needed to attend physical therapy. He needed a summer job, and I needed a lift. Then, while I was on crutches from the spring through to the fall and needed extra help, I was able to count on him for support. Whether it's cleaning out the chicken yard or assembling some new gadget I got (and couldn't for the life of me figure out how to put together), and even helping me with my computer skills (or lack thereof), Josh has been an enormous help. Two years later, Josh is still helping me—this book would not be possible if it weren't for his computer prowess. Thank you, Josh. If I had had children, I would want them to be just like Josh.

Introduction

The Complete Book of Raw Food, Volume 1 was the book that many of us used as our "go-to" resource when we were getting acquainted with and developing our raw food lifestyles. It taught us what tools to use, how to set up a raw food kitchen and how to sprout greens. The contributors were (and are) prestigious raw food chefs from around the world; people who we looked to and learned from as we started out.

Now we are the next generation, and I look forward to the day when we will pass on the baton to those who will succeed us. *The Complete Book of Raw Food, Volume 2* presents an all-new collection of the recipes we love to share; quick, simple, easy to make, and good for you—recipes that you can easily make as part of your daily life; and addresses new topics like GMOs, the importance of raw, living water, and much more.

Living in the real world, too often we find ourselves juggling multiple jobs, balancing family commitments, and somehow trying to find time for ourselves, all while trying to maintain healthy eating habits, and live a healthy and realistic lifestyle. Some of the contributors in this book are world-renowned chefs with raw restaurants or markets of their own, all of which help support our healthy lifestyles. Others support our healthy journey in different ways, such as acupuncture, permaculture, and herbalism. No matter what their background, all of the contributors in this book have carefully selected delicious, nutritious raw recipes that will make it easy to live the raw lifestyle.

While a healthy diet is vitally important, we are more than just the food we put in our mouths. We need to remember to not only eat healthy, but to *live* healthy. If you have unhealthy emotions and relationships, or an unhealthy work environment and lifestyle, eating organic heirloom vegetables will not be your savior. But when we change our diets and begin to take more care of what we put into our bodies, it becomes apparent what areas we need to work on to improve the rest of our lives. We can work together to learn what tools we need to have a better relationship with ourselves and others. Be discerning in what you put in your mouth; be discerning in what you let into your life.

Your journey begins now…

GOOD LUCK!

—Lisa Montgomery

PART I

The Raw Kitchen

1 Living a Raw Lifestyle

There are many benefits to the raw lifestyle, but you will come to find that we each have our own personal reasons for making the switch. When I attended the Institute of Integrative Nutrition (IIN) in New York, New York several years ago to become certified as a Holistic Healthcare Practitioner, my diet was already predominantly raw. During my studies at IIN we were introduced to many different eating styles including South Beach, Ayurvedic, Atkins, and, of course, raw. Although my diet was predominantly raw, I chose to eat the way we were being taught at the time. So if we were being taught Atkins, I would eat an Atkins diet. If we were being taught microbiotic, I would eat a microbiotic diet. However, I soon came to realize that these eating styles were *diets*, not lifestyles. The raw diet is a raw *lifestyle*. When I tried the other diets they made me physically sick. On the other hand, the raw lifestyle resonates down to my soul. When I eat this way I feel at peace, which is a gift that no money can buy. Once you begin to feel that peace in your heart and notice how your body works for you on a daily basis, you will come to understand the answer to the question, "why raw foods?"

Raw foods include fruits, vegetables, nuts, grains, and seeds that are uncooked. Because raw foods are never heated above 118°F, they retain all of their nutrients, allowing your body to get the most out of your food.

While a raw diet is a lifestyle change, it's much easier to follow than you may think. For me, a typical day starts with juicing wheatgrass in my Tribest® Green Star juicer. Sometimes I also make a vegetable juice in my juicer and store it in a glass jar to drink throughout the day. For breakfast I also have a smoothie which I make in my Vitamix® high-speed blender. Lunch usually consists of a salad of greens, sprouts, fermented sauerkraut, chopped vegetables, and a pâté. Many times, I don't even eat dinner as I find that I'm not hungry. Instead, I usually have a vegetable juice or watermelon juice in place of dinner. If I do feel like I need more than just a drink, I will have a handful of almonds or a few raw crackers. As you can see, my raw diet is really very simple—and yours can be, too!

THE RAW LIFESTYLE: NOT JUST A DIET

For some, "raw" means more than just changing your diet—it can also be a powerful lifestyle transformation. The quest to grow emotionally, spiritually, and physically is a lifelong endeavor. I am always striving to expand and grow beyond my current limitations; in my mind, there is no ceiling on what you can accomplish. Once I started to live a healthier lifestyle with raw foods, I grew so much emotionally and

TRANSITIONING TO A HEALTHY WAY OF EATING

Many who have heard me speak have heard me say, "Set yourself up for success, and take it one step at a time." Start by making smoothies for breakfast. If you do nothing more than make smoothies for one month, then so be it. For people without allergies or dietary restrictions, it may be easier on your head, your body, and your family if you take it one step at a time.

Another great way to incorporate healthy foods into your diet is, contrary to what your mother always said, by starting with dessert. I have made raw chocolate mousse pie at many events, and no matter what the guests' eating preference was, the dish was always a hit. Try to add a new dish each week, or even just each month. Don't overwhelm yourself. Look at it as an exciting adventure; a chance to try something new. In a perfect world, try to get the entire family involved. If not, start by just bringing in one dish at a time. If your kids like to help you prepare meals, then get them on board. Let them change their diet and watch them have their own awakening. It will happen, and when it does, everyone benefits.

spiritually. You would not believe how much bad food choices and an unhealthy lifestyle can hold you back from reaching your true potential.

But in order to reach that potential, you must learn to be selective of what you put into your body and into your life. Discernment is important in *all* aspects of your life. You must be discerning when you choose what foods you put in your mouth. Ask yourself, "Will this food support my body? Will it give me more energy? Will it build me up or tear me down?" My oldest sister passed away from cirrhosis of the liver. Some folks say wine is good for you. What are my thoughts? After watching a loved one die from excess alcohol, you can't ever convince me that it's good for you—excess of anything can be harmful to the body and to the mind.

Beyond switching to a raw diet, part of the raw lifestyle is to take a look at your life to see where you can make positive changes. Perhaps you can benefit from reassessing who you associate with, breaking some bad habits, or creating better boundaries for yourself. If I had not changed my diet and got my body healthy, I would not have been able to make better emotional and spiritual choices.

Start your journey today by taking baby steps to transform your life. Below are five simple steps that every person can take to improve mental and physical health and prevent disease. I'm happy to say I follow each one in my day to day life, with wonderful results:

1. Don't smoke or drink.
2. Exercise daily.
3. Promote a healthy diet.
4. Manage your stress and mental health with release activities.
5. Sleep eight hours a day, in a regular sleep pattern.

If it works for you, also try keeping a food diary to write down everything you eat over a two-week span. Then, try and revise your diet so that you can eat better and live better. Once you clean out the unhealthy food in your life, it is amazing how easy it becomes to clean out the *other* unhealthy parts of your life.

Study these five steps and determine whether you're on target, or whether you need to make some changes in your lifestyle. Remember: change isn't bad—it's *good*. We are always growing and changing. Don't stay stuck.

2 Essential Ingredients for a Raw Kitchen

L ike anything in life, following a raw diet is a whole lot easier if you are prepared. Stock your kitchen with the ingredients you use regularly so that you have them on hand. If possible, also try to have some basic ingredients prepped ahead of time. This advance planning will help to set you up for success and will make it so easy to prepare healthy, raw meals every day. In the following pages, you will find a selection of common ingredients for a raw kitchen.

RAW NUTS AND SEEDS

For people who ask where protein comes from in a raw food diet, the answer is simple. While in reality there is protein in virtually everything, nuts and seeds are full of protein, in addition to being incredibly useful ingredients. I always have raw nuts and seeds on hand. My favorites are:

- almonds
- walnuts
- macadamia nuts
- pine nuts
- Austria's Finest, Naturally® Pumpkin Seeds
- cashews

- Brazil nuts
- pistachios
- flax seeds
- sunflower seeds
- chia seeds
- hemp seeds

Almonds, Brazil nuts, walnuts, cashews, macadamia nuts, sunflower seeds, and pumpkin seeds are great for making nut milks, pâtés, crackers, crusts, breads, croutons, granola, trail mixes, snack, candies, and desserts. I store them in plastic containers in a cool area of my house and/or freezer.

SEA VEGETABLES

Sea vegetables have 10 to 20 times more useable minerals than vegetables grown on land. I buy my sea vegetables dried from Rising Tide Sea Vegetables®. You can rehydrate them and they are ready to use. They are great in salads, soups, raw sushi, and pâtés. My favorite sea vegetables are:

- **Arame:** Mild in flavor. Great in salads and veggie burgers.
- **Dulse:** Extremely salty. I use this in making un-tuna pâtés or a sea-inspired veggie burger.
- **Hiziki:** This is my favorite sea vegetable. Hiziki is a great source of calcium. It's great as a standalone salad or in a salad with other ingredients.
- **Irish moss:** Used as a thickener in smoothies, pâtés, and some desserts.
- **Nori:** Everyone who eats sushi (raw or not) is familiar with nori. Nori are the sheets used to roll up the vegetables in the nori rolls.
- **Sea Palm:** A great snack eaten dried or rehydrated. I like to make sea palm salads for an Asian flair.
- **Wakame:** Another popular sea vegetable as it is used in miso soup. Whether you eat raw or cooked soup, it adds flavor, minerals, and vitamins.

SPICE OF LIFE

Many of you probably already have a cabinet full of spices, which is great. You can use these spices to help perk up your food. I also grow my own herbs in the summer and eat them fresh or dry them when I can no longer grow them. This year I started growing medicinal herbs as well. One of the many helpful tips from my Herbalism teacher, Sue Hess, (from Farm at Coventry) is to dry herbs by simply placing the cut dry herbs in a brown grocery bag and placing the bag in the back of your car on a hot summer day. Within a couple of days, the herbs will be dried.

OILS

Cold-pressed olive oil, raw pumpkin seed oil, and coconut oil are among the most common oils that I use in "un-cooking" my food. Coconut oil is also great to use on your skin!

SWEETENERS

Dates, raw honey, and stevia are healthy sweeteners. Some folks use maple syrup which isn't really raw. Others use raw agave, which has also sparked some controversy over whether or not it is raw. Whichever sweeteners you choose, use them sparingly.

YOUNG THAI COCONUTS

Young Thai coconuts are great for a base for smoothies, or to be used in desserts like raw puddings and cheesecakes. You can also cut the meat into strips and create noodles. The juice is super healthy, as well. I give the shell to my African Grey Parrot, Tweety, as a chew toy. Once he is done with it, I burn it in the fireplace. One of the best things about raw foods is that they are the foods that keeps on giving… to me, my parrot Tweety, and to the fireplace to heat my house.

Coconut Fudge, page 285.

FRUIT

I always have bananas, assorted berries, oranges, and apples on hand. I buy the fruit by the case so it is more economical and handy. I try to buy the berries in season and freeze them so when they are out of season and the cost goes up, I have a freezer full. Dried Fruit is also great to have on hand as you can rehydrate it and incorporate it in your food dishes like crackers, on top of a salad, or in a snack mix. I also have dried fruit like raisins, cranberries, goji berries, and blueberries that can be great as snacks, in smoothies, on salads, or in dressings.

RAW WATER

(courtesy of MJ Pangman)

Raw water is defined as unprocessed, natural water found in the environment. This can be ground water, spring water, or the water found in lakes and rivers. If we lived in a perfect world, raw water would *also* be living water—a liquid crystalline matrix full of vital minerals and healthful organic acids. Unfortunately, most of our water has been mistreated; it no longer has crystalline properties, nor does it carry the life-supporting patterns and frequencies it was intended to carry. Thankfully, there are ways to return the living qualities to the water you drink; and, just like living *food*, the consumption of living *water* can make a big difference in how you feel. Combined with a raw diet, living water can bring a new dimension to your health and well-being.

Water and salt are obvious companions; neither is complete without the other. Water without salts is empty, and likewise, salt without water is incapable of delivering the energy it holds. Water's taste is also affected by the minerals/salts it carries. Natural, unprocessed salt contains all the elements, and in the same proportions that exist organically in the ocean. And yet, most Americans suffer from a lack of salt. At the same time, they are literally poisoned with *refined* salt. Refined salt (sodium chloride) is empty, unnatural, and aggressive. It causes imbalances because it lacks balancing counterparts. In nature, alkaline minerals such as calcium, magnesium, and potassium balance the sodium.

The deficit of natural salts, with its balance of minerals, causes salt cravings which can never be satisfied by refined salt. The more refined salt people eat, the worse off they are. If you are in the habit of using processed "table salt," you may want to consider replacing it with some kind of unprocessed salt. There are many wonderful unprocessed salts, including Celtic sea salt, Himalayan pink salt, Redmond real salt, and salts from many islands including Bali, the Philippines, and Hawaii. However, note that most salt sold as "sea salt" has been refined to some degree and should be avoided.

SEA SALT

In place of iodized salt (what we know as regular table salt), use Himalayan pink salt or Celtic sea salt, which has 133 minerals. Iodized salt is not healthy for you and is even full of chemicals.

DATES

Medjool dates are my favorites. They are great as a snack, or as a sweetener in smoothies and in desserts. I buy dates by the case, just like I do for all of my fruits.

LEGUMES AND GRAINS

Beans, buckwheat, chickpeas, lentils, quinoa, and natural wilderness rice are also staples for my raw kitchen. You can store them easily. Soak, blossom, and use them in soups, granolas, side dishes, salads, or in veggie burgers.

WHEATGRASS AND SPROUTS

Wheatgrass and sprouts are the foundation of a raw, live foods lifestyle. The sprouts are live food which is where the name "living foods" came from. Wheatgrass is full of vitamins and minerals, which makes it cleansing, healing, and detoxifying. Wheatgrass is a great stand-alone juice. I start almost every day by juicing several ounces. Remember: you should not drink wheatgrass quickly. Instead, sip and swish a mouthful at a time. Wheatgrass is available pre-cut and packaged, or can be bought uncut on a mat, which is typically a more economical option. To cut wheatgrass from the mat, use either a straight edge blade or a sharp knife or shears. Place the wheatgrass in a large re-sealable bag with paper towels to soak up the moisture and store it in your refrigerator.

There are a lot of varieties of sprouts such as sunflower, mung beans, lentils, broccoli, and green pea to name a few. You can grow sprouts in jars, bags, soil, sprouting machines, or hydroponically. See Chapter 4 for more details on sprouting.

3 Raw Kitchen Tools

Just as important as having the right ingredients on hand, a well-stocked raw kitchen needs a few pieces of essential equipment. Whenever I speak or teach a workshop the attendees always ask me what brands I use for my kitchen equipment. I share these brands because it took me five juicers to get to the Tribest® Green Star Elite Juicer. It is my favorite juicer and once I find something that works, I stick with it. I also went through three brands of dehydrators until I tried the Tribest® Sedona Dehydrator…I love it! I lucked out when my first high-powered blender was a Vitamix®. I have had my first Vitamix® for 15–20 years. It appears Consumer Report and I both feel the same about Vitamix®. Did you know they did a consumer report on the top 50 blenders and Vitamix® was number 1 for the past 17 years? Plus, it is made in America.

In this chapter I include an overview of the tools I use in my healthy kitchen. I have been using these products for years and they hold up well. The companies stand behind their products and they are nice people. I have a sign in my kitchen that says, "because nice matters". I like the fact that the people behind the products that I use are nice people and people of integrity, which shows in their products as well.

THE BASICS

There are three basic tools that use regularly: a high-speed blender, a juicer, and a dehydrator.

Juicer

Believe it or not, I have five different juicers (Walker, Omega, Champion, Jack LaLane™, and Tribest), but I would not expect you to go out and get all five juicers. After trying all of these juicers, my favorite has been the Tribest Green Star juicer, because it does everything. When I started my raw diet, I was told that the Omega juicer was the best, but I found that it could only do half of what I needed. The Omega would juice the wheatgrass and greens, but was not good for hard fruits and vegetables like apples, carrots, and red beets. Plus, while it was easy to clean, I had to run the pulp through the machine several times, which was time consuming and warmed the pulp. Then I was told that the Champion juicer was the best ever,

Image courtesy of Tribest.

but found that it too could only handle half of what I needed (although it is great for making banana whips). Then someone told me that the Walker would be the end-all. It was huge, expensive and cumbersome. I got the Jack LaLane™ juicer at the suggestion of raw chef Dan of Quintessence, because he told me that it would create the perfect "crab-like" texture for the pulp of his "un-crab cakes,"

and that no other juicer would make the pulp texture look like crab cakes. So, I now use my Jack LaLane™ juicer whenever making raw crab cakes. I held off for the longest time in getting the Tribest Green Star juicer, because I heard that it had so many parts and was hard to put together. I am not very good with mechanics or technology, but I can put the Green Star together with no trouble, and I do like it best in terms of function. I can run the pulp through once, and it extracts more juice than any other juicer and is simple and easy to use. I also love that the folks at Tribest stand behind their products, and are nice and easy to work with. I have spent so much of my life taking care of others that I really love when people take care of me and stand behind their products.

Reproduced and reprinted with the permission of Vita-Mix Corporation
(www.vitamix.com).

High-Speed Blender

There are several high-speed blenders out there, but my favorite is the Vitamix®.
I have tried the Blendtec® and the Montel Williams™, and I still came away loving
my Vitamix®. When I was in California for a book tour for my first book *Raw
Inspiration, Living Dynamically with Raw Food*, I stayed at a friend's house. She had
a Blendtec® and absolutely loved it. She tried my Vitamix® and I tried her Blend-
tec®, but by the end of the weekend, we still loved our own blenders. Another
great aspect about Vitamix® is they stand behind their equipment. If something
breaks, you simply call them, and they will verify your warranty and send you a
shipping label to return the blender for service, and then ship the repaired blender
back to you. The Vitamix® has the speed and power to blend nuts, seeds, and ice
quickly. If you attempt to make nut pâtés (or even simply juice a watermelon) in
a regular blender, it just does not have the power or speed to do the job like the
Vitamix® does. When traveling, the Tribest Personal blender is great, because it fits
in my suit case so I can take it with me anywhere, and it has the power to make my
smoothies, dressings, and pâtés in a compact container.

Image courtesy of Tribest.

Dehydrator

The dehydrator is the raw foodist's version of an oven. It is used in much the same way, save that the temperature doesn't go above 118°F. I tend to set my dehydrator at 105°F for the best results. The Tribest® Sedona Dehydrator keeps a consistent temperature, and I use it for making crackers, croutons, and scones. I also use it for sprouting wild rice, quinoa, and unroasting vegetables, and it's great for melding flavors when you make a lasagna or veggie burgers.

Spiralizer

The spiralizer is another very cool gadget that I didn't know about until I started taking raw cooking classes. Spiralizers take zucchini, red beets, yams, and other similar vegetables and "spiralize" them, turning them into angel hair pasta or spaghetti-like vegetable noodles. There are a wide assortment of spiralizers on the market, so make sure to do your homework.

OTHER HELPFUL TOOLS

Below are some additional tools for a healthy kitchen; some of which you probably already own:

- Food processor
- Chopping board
- Knives, spatulas, spoons
- Grater
- Glass dishes
- Storage containers
- Mandoline
- Ice cream scooper (used for cleaning out coconut meat from young Thai coconuts and also good for scooping out seeds from various vegetables)
- Parchment paper, wax paper, aluminum foil, plastic wrap, assorted Ziploc® bags
- Cheesecloth (used when making fermented cheese and sauerkrauts)
- Canning jars with lids (great for storing your nut milks, juices, soups, sauces, dressings, and sauerkraut…I even freeze food in them)

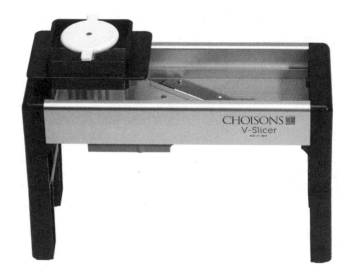

A mandoline slicer—like this Choisons V-Slicer—is a handy kitchen tool for the raw chef. Image courtesy of Tribest.

4 Sprouting

Sprouting is one of the fundamental ingredients in the raw food lifestyle. One of the reasons the raw food lifestyle is even called raw, *living* food is because of sprouting. Sprouts *are* living food; the energy that is in living sprouts when you eat them has a way of revitalizing your health.

JAR SPROUTING

For me, the easiest way to sprout is in jars. Sprouting doesn't take up much space, so if you live in a small apartment or a hotel room, this method is convenient and effective.

Supplies needed:
- Seeds
- Jars
- Clean pure water (non-chlorinated)
- Rubber bands
- Mesh cloth, screen

Place the seeds in the jar, cover with water and place mesh cloth to cover the jar. Use the rubber band to hold the mesh cloth to the jar. The next morning pour out the water, keeping the mesh cloth on the jar. Rinse the seeds/sprouts with water two to three times a day. Each time after rinsing the seeds, making sure you have drained out all of the water, lay the jar on its side on the counter. You will notice some seeds sprouting right away, while others will take a little longer.

SOIL SPROUTING

This takes more space. You need either a racking system or table with growing lights or even a heated green house for best results.

Supplies needed:
- Soil—organic or compost
- Seeds
- Lunchroom trays
- Heavy weights

Place seeds in a jar or bowl. Cover with water and soak overnight. The next day spread a half inch of soil over the tray. Spread the soaked seeds over the soil. Place an inverted tray on top of the tray. You can continue to do multiple trays or you can just plant one tray. Place weights on top of trays. When the living sprouts are strong enough, move them to trays. Remove the top tray and place in the sun or under grow lights. Make sure you water the sprouts each day.

Image courtesy of Tribest.

Some people use a water bottle to spray their sprouts, while other people have actual watering systems in their greenhouse.

Mung Beans: Probably the easiest plants to sprout. If you are trying to get your family to start eating sprouts, the mung bean might be the easiest place to start.

The optimum length is 1 inch, with a growth period of 3–5 days. Mung beans are full of Vitamin C, iron, amino acids, and potassium.

Sunflowers: Probably my all-time favorite sprout. You can sprout in just a couple of days, though if you plant in soil and want full-grown sprouts, it can take a week to 10 days. Sunflower sprouts are full of Vitamin B, amino acids, calcium, phosphorous, iron, magnesium, and potassium. Sunflower sprouts keep longer than most other sprouts after they are harvested. When you harvest the sprouts from the soil, you can cut them with a straight edge blade, a sharp knife, or scissors. Place sprouts in a Ziploc® bag with paper towels. The paper towels will soak up any moisture so the sprouts won't rot so quickly. Leaving the bag open can also help prevent this.

Alfalfa: After mung beans, alfalfa is probably the sprout that everyone is most familiar with. It seems to be in most salad bars and sandwiches in public restaurants and cafeterias. Plus, if you are making nori rolls and wraps it fits in the wraps nicely. The best length is 1 inch. It takes 3 to 5 days to sprout, and contains a wealth of vitamins and nutrients: Vitamins A, B2, C, D, E, niacin, minerals, zinc, iron, magnesium, amino acids, and chlorophyll.

Broccoli: ½ inch is the best length, with a harvesting time of three to five days. These sprouts are amazing. They are full of Vitamin A, B, C, E, and K; calcium; iron; magnesium; phosphorous; potassium; zinc; carotene; chlorophyll; amino acids; trace elements; antioxidants; and sulforaphane. The broccoli sprouts are said to stimulate the body's natural defenses against cancer.

Fenugreek: ½ inch is the preferred length. These sprout really quickly: just 2 to 3 days. They are good as a lymph, blood, and kidney tonic, and contain Vitamins A and C, iron, and phosphorous.

Chickpeas: These only take 2 to 4 days to sprout, with ½ inch being the preferred length. Chickpeas contain Vitamins A and C, amino acids, carbohydrate, fiber, minerals, calcium, magnesium, and potassium. So for those of you who don't like bananas, chickpeas are another great source of potassium. Although I can't imagine anyone not liking bananas!

Lentils: It only takes 2 to 3 days for lentils to sprout to their optimum length of ½ inch. They are full of Vitamin C, iron, and amino acids.

MICROGREENS

After sprouting, microgreens are the next step of a seed's development. You can grow microgreens in your own trays and soil. You don't have to be an industrial grower. Microgreens are seeds that are grown in soil after establishing root systems and their first set of leaves.

Supplies needed for growing microgreens:

- Cafeteria trays or black greenhouse trays
- Soil
- Seeds—heirloom, organic
- Seed press—can be made out of cardboard or board and is used to create a flat seed bed
- Cover—you can either cover the seeded tray with dirt or with moist paper/cloth towels
- Watering—spray bottles, hose, and watering cans
- pH test kit
- Lids
- Heat mats

Test Kit for pH: Just as we as humans function better when our pH is at the optimum of 7.4, so microgreens also need their appropriate pH. You need to test the water to see if it is acidic or alkaline. If you need your water to be more acidic, add lemon juice to lower the pH. If you want to raise the pH, add baking soda, powdered oyster shells, or dolomite lime. They also have pH test strips to test the water, similar to what we use to test our own pH levels.

Let's get started.

Fill your trays with soil. Spread your seeds over the dirt. Spread evenly with the wood or cardboard. Cover your seeds with moistened towel or a thin layer of dirt. Water your plants so that the entire tray has been gently soaked. If you are not growing in a greenhouse, cover with a lid to speed up the germination process. I have also grown microgreens right in the dirt in my greenhouse in the summer. Be sure to check your microgreens every day to make sure the soil (and the towel, if using this method) is moist. You don't want them to dry out; nor do you want to flood them either. Balance is key. You don't need grow lights to grow microgreens. Find a sunlit window sill or porch. Once the seeds start to germinate, remove the towel and the plastic lid. Microgreens grow at varying rates . . . some take only a few days whereas others need a few weeks.

You can harvest your microgreens after the first set of leaves have popped out or wait until the second set have come on the scene. Using scissors, straight edge, or very sharp knife, store them in a Ziploc® bag left open lined with paper towels to soak up the water. Water will rot the microgreens, just like it does the sprouts. Some people even put a fan on their greens to dry them.

STORAGE

I store my sprouts and wheatgrass in open Ziploc® bags lined with paper towels. I leave the bags open to let the air in, and I line the bag with the paper towel to soak up any moisture that may leak. Sprouts, if grown long enough, can grow into plants with leaves. With sprouts, you eat everything, roots and all; with greens, the roots are discarded. Please note that you discard the seed shell when growing sunflower sprouts.

If you don't want to grow your own sprouts, you can buy them at your local healthy market or from your local sprout grower.

5 Dehydrating

When I first began my raw food journey, I used to think that dehydrating was just good for drying fruits, nuts, and vegetables, or making raw crackers. But one of the greatest abilities of a good dehydrator is the way in which it can meld your flavors, adding new dimensions to "unroasted" vegetables, casseroles, and salads. For a raw foodist, a dehydrator does so much more than act as an oven.

Dehydrators are great for making crackers, breads, croutons, and scones. You can soak nuts and seeds, dry them in your dehydrator, and then jar them and have them ready to go whenever you need them. You can also dry vegetables and bag them to hydrate later to use in soups, snacks, or as accents on salads. You can even marinate vegetables in a glass dish in your dehydrator or warm a dish to meld the flavors in a glass dish in your dehydrator. And the important thing to remember is that none of this is time-consuming. Many non-raw foodists think that making raw crackers, cookies, pizza crusts, granola, and flax wraps takes forever. When I make raw crackers or granola, I make enough to fill up my nine-tray dehydrator—that means I am making enough for a month!

RAW NUTS

After soaking nuts like raw almonds, walnuts, or pumpkin seeds overnight, pour off the water and place them in the dehydrator at 105°F until they are totally dry. Store them in a glass canning jar with a lid. By soaking, drying, and storing in advance, you set yourself up for success—they are ready to use when you need them.

SUN-DRIED TOMATOES

I make my own sun-dried tomatoes in my Tribest® Sedona dehydrator. When my tomatoes come in season, one of the ways that I harvest them is to slice them thinly, place on the racks of my Tribest® Sedona Dehydrator, and dehydrate them until dry. I store the tomatoes in air-tight, Ziploc® bags or canning jars with screw-on lids.

HARVEST TIME

A great way to use your harvest is to dehydrate your vegetables. You can make your own vegetable and/or fruit snack by slicing the vegetables and placing them in the dehydrator until dry. Remember that 118°F is the magic number for a raw foodist. If the temperature is above 118°F, the food loses it nutritional, enzymatic value. I use the Tribest® Sedona Dehydrator, which holds its temperature beautifully. There are some dehydrators on the market that can't hold their temperature and have power

DEHYDRATED SOUP

One way to store your vegetables from your garden is to dehydrate them. I use Tribest's Sedona Dehydrator, or either of my two solar dehydrators, which were built as referenced in Eben Fodor's book, *The Solar Food Dryer*. I like the idea of a solar dehydrator so I can tap into our natural resource: the sun. Plus, if the electricity goes out, I can still use a solar dehydrator. Dehydrated vegetables can be rehydrated with water to create a soup. Pull out your slow-cooker and set it at the lowest setting, so it is below 118°F. Throw the dried vegetables into the slow-cooker, along with fresh, sliced mushrooms and frozen corn, tomatoes,  or any of your favorite frozen vegetables. Add a dash of salt and pepper to taste. When I freeze corn and tomatoes, I make sure to still keep it raw. My Mom and I would freeze our corn and tomatoes together, and she would always cook hers for the full length of time, as she was not into raw foods. I would instead only cook mine for a quarter or half of the required time, so it would still be considered "raw," but cooked enough to preserve. When I serve my soup, I also top it with croutons (remember to save your almond pulp when you make almond milk, so you can make your own croutons). The croutons, besides being great on soups and salads, make a great snack.

surges, which is why you will see many raw foodists setting their dehydrators at 105°F.

Dehydrating your herbs or vegetables for preserving is really quite simple. For vegetables like tomatoes, start cutting them into slices, place them on a dehydrator tray at 105°F, and dehydrate until dry. I also dehydrate my tomatoes with various seasonings and eat them as a snack or crumble them on top of a salad. When dehydrating herbs, you would use the same principle, making sure to first remove any stems. Herbs typically take very little time to dehydrate, so be sure to keep an eye on the dehydrator. Dehydration is a great way to preserve, and you can also rehydrate any dehydrated vegetables by simply adding water.

6 Fermentation

(courtesy of Annmarie Cantrell)

Fermented foods are created when the starch or carbohydrates in whole foods are broken down and changed by microorganisms into smaller, more digestible components. Fermentation serves several purposes:

- **To preserve:** The nutrients are preserved and you prevent the spoilage of perishable raw materials.
- **To enhance flavor:** Fermentation brings out unique and tangy flavors found in thick cheese, wine, and sauerkraut.
- **To salvage:** Foods that would otherwise be wasted are made usable again through an easy and inexpensive process.
- **To reconnect:** Shared activity and food preparation with each other allows us to develop relationships and build community.

Fermented foods also aid in digestion, as the presence of digestive enzymes breaks down and predigests the foods. For example, the phytic acid present in grains is deactivated through fermentation. Fermentation also increases nutrient availability by elevating the bioavailability of beneficial nutrients such as amino acids, minerals, and vitamins B and C. It even has the ability to enhance the production of certain vitamins, particularly the B vitamins and vitamin K2.

GETTING STARTED

Fermenting your own food is rewarding, easy, and economical. Once you have the basics set in place, you will find that it is as much an art as it is science. There are general guidelines for fermenting, but intuition plays a large role in creating your final product. You will learn to ferment according to taste and feel, and by connecting with your instincts. People following the same sauerkraut recipe will see different end results based upon the microbes in their environment and the intentions put into it.

There are several types of fermentation (alcohol ferments, acetic acid ferments, alkaline ferments, and lactic acid ferments). Most raw foodists will concern themselves primarily with lactic acid fermentation, the process that results in sauerkraut, kimchi, kefir, yogurt, and various chutneys and relishes.

There are basically two ways to achieve lactic acid fermentation. One method is wild fermentation, which uses a salt brine to control the organisms that naturally occur in the vegetables (and in the air) by inhibiting the putrefying bacteria and promoting the lactic acid-forming bacteria. These good bacteria transform the vegetables into a relatively stable, delicious, and health-promoting food. The other method involves adding bacterial cultures that produce lactic acid to the food, which can result in yogurt, kefir, and vegetable ferments.

FERMENTATION EQUIPMENT

- Sharp chef's knife
- Cutting board
- Food processor (optional)
- Mason jar (or similar)
- Fermentation crock: Make sure your fermenting vessel is clean before using; after washing the jars well, rinse them out in hot water.
- Salt: I prefer to use a mineral rich sea salt, such as Celtic sea salt (another option is Himalayan salt).
- Water: When making brined vegetables, be sure to use clean, filtered, non-chlorinated water. Chlorine inhibits the growth of the beneficial bacteria.

A BASIC GUIDE FOR SALTING VEGETABLE FERMENTS

When using the dry salt method described on page 26 to make sauerkraut, you can use about 3 tablespoons of salt for every 5 pounds of vegetables (or roughly 1½–2 teaspoons of salt per pound of vegetable). For brining vegetables whole (like pickles), you would use salt equaling about 5% of the weight of the water, or 3 tablespoons of salt per quart.

Time

The time it takes for the fermentation process to begin varies based on the temperature and the amount of salt used. Vegetables that ferment for a longer time produce a tangier flavor and have more beneficial bacteria than a ferment that is only 3–4 days old.

The best judge of time is your palate. If you prefer ferments that are tangier, let them sit for 2–3 weeks at room temperature and put them in colder storage. Cold storage, either refrigeration or a root cellar, will *slow* the fermentation process, not completely *stop* it.

The amount of salt used also affects the fermentation process. Recipes that use more salt take longer to ferment and those that use less, take less time to ferment.

Temperature

The ideal temperature for fermentation to take place is approximately 70–72°F. During the summer months, temperatures warmer than this will produce a more quickly fermented product. To offset the hot temperature, you can opt to add more salt when fermenting in the summer in order to slow down the fermentation a bit. Conversely, in cooler weather, it will take longer for the product to ferment, and you can opt to use less salt in the recipes during the winter months.

You can find recipes using fermentation techniques on pages 64, 88, 123, 124, 137, 139, 142, 144, 147, 181, 182, 184, 209, 239, 242, 263, and 304.

WHAT TO FERMENT

Vegetables: Essentially any vegetable can be fermented: cabbage, cucumber, carrots, beets, kale, turnips, cauliflower, broccoli, etc.

Fruits: Fruit can also be fermented. I add fruits as additions to my vegetable ferments (for example. I use apples in my sauerkraut, oranges in my beets, etc.). Note that to ferment fruits on their own requires heavier salting or a culture starter. When left to ferment on their own, fruits will ferment into alcohol. The fruit ferments are less stable than the vegetable ferments, and are best consumed within 2–3 months.

MAKING WHEY

Whey is the liquid that remains after milk has been curdled or strained. I make my whey by straining yogurt. Place yogurt in cheesecloth over a bowl and let the whey drip into the bowl. Let the bowl sit overnight in the refrigerator. Place the whey in a mason jar and keep it in the refrigerator for use in culturing foods, soaking grains, etc.

7 More Tips for a Raw Food Lifestyle

The more information you have on a subject, the better prepared you are, and the raw food lifestyle is no exception. In this chapter, we share additional helpful tips to set you up for success in your raw food lifestyle. We want to make sure that you are prepared to live your healthy raw food lifestyle in all aspects of your life. A healthy lifestyle isn't just about the food. It's also about the rest of your life and how it all comes together.

DO YOUR HOMEWORK

Reading labels and knowing where your food comes from and how it is grown are all vital to ensuring that you get the most out of your food. For example, organic foods, especially raw or non-processed foods, are substantially more nutritious. They contain higher levels of beta carotene, vitamins C, D, and E, are health promoting, contain cancer-fighting antioxidants, flavonoids that help ward off heart disease, essential fatty acids, essential minerals, and significantly lower amounts of saturated fats.

Organic vs. Non-Organic

Study after study after study shows that chemical-free organic produce is better for you than non-organic. Many of the chemicals used on the produce during their growing process are harmful, and some are even cancer-causing. Why is organic produce more expensive than non-organic produce? The answer is simple: the government in the United States does not subsidize organic farmers in the way it does non-organic farmers. When I changed my diet 25 years ago, there were only two places I could go to buy organic produce. Now, virtually *every* store has an organic section and a natural foods section. We are the ones who have to lead by example, using our voices and our purchasing power to guide our government and the large corporations it supports to wake up and give us what we want. Sometimes, the only way our government and large corporations can be made to pay attention is when we stop buying or demand they come up with healthier alternatives.

GMOs

When the first volume of *The Complete Book of Raw Food* was published, GMOs didn't seem quite as large an issue as they are today—or at least, we weren't quite as aware of them. But today, 70 percent of all food in the United States is genetically modified. GMOs (genetically modified organisms) are engineered using genetic information from bacteria and viruses in order to produce more deadly, targeted insecticides, as well as crops capable of surviving heavy doses of herbicides—which aren't healthy for humans *or* the environment.

More than 60 countries have banned GMOs or have laws requiring genetically modified products to be labeled as such. But the fact remains that GMOs (or their elements) are now present in more than 75 percent of conventional, processed food—another reason to eat organic whole foods over fast food, which stresses the importance of knowing where your food is coming from *and* how it was grown.

Of course, we have options available to us other than speaking with our shopping; supporting non-profit organizations like the Non-GMO Project (www.nongmoproject.org), which is committed to preserving and rebuilding the non-GMO food supply, can help to cut down on the number of GMOs in the marketplace. Educating consumers and providing verified, healthy choices is our responsibility, and the mission statement of organizations like the Non-GMO Project, who feel that everyone deserves an informed choice about whether or not to consume genetically modified organisms.

EATING OUT

One of the most common questions people ask about living the raw lifestyle is, "How (and where) do I eat out?" The easy answer is to go to a vegetarian, raw restaurant, if you are lucky to have them in your area. However, while steering the restaurant choice to raw restaurants works if most of the group is on a similar diet, it isn't always suitable for larger, more varied groups. If this is the case, or if you don't have a raw restaurant near you, today's restaurants are very accommodating, and are accustomed to people deviating from the menu. Now that people have awakened to food allergies, dietary restrictions, and gluten issues, most restaurants are much more open to menu variation and deviation.

If you can't make it to a raw restaurant, Japanese, Thai, and Mexican cuisine are all acceptable alternatives. Their ingredients tend to be healthier, and their menus tend to be more compatible with raw variation. However, you should still be courteous: look at the least amount of deviations needed to make a dish you'll enjoy. My advice is to go right to the salad section and make your selections and substitutions from there. Also look for any recipes that bill themselves as "build-it-yourself," as this will give you the best opportunity to get what you want with minimal hassle.

Another tricky situation for raw foodies is what to do when eating at someone's home. Years ago, Dr. Brian Clement, Director of Hippocrates Health Institute, spoke at one of my raw potlucks. He shared many sage words of wisdom but I liked what he said about eating as a guest in someone's home. After you have healed your body, if you get a cooked vegetable in your meal once in awhile as a guest in someone's home, don't beat yourself up about it. It is much more detrimental to your health and well-being to feel guilty as opposed to just eating a cooked vegetable once in awhile. Years ago, I would have beaten myself up relentlessly if I ate cooked food. But now, if I get a cooked vegetable once in a blue moon, it is what it is. With that being said, remember to be discerning about what cooked vegetables you eat, how they are prepared, and what they are prepared with. If you are a guest in someone else's home for a holiday dinner, regular dinner, or a potluck dinner, offer to bring a kale salad or a big salad to share with everyone. This way you know there will be something you can eat. Just think of the Girl Scout motto, "be prepared."

COMMUNITY AND COOPERATION

When we find ourselves facing "big-picture" challenges, our success or failure always comes back to community and cooperation, or isolation and solitude. The human spirit always comes through in the end, as the community comes together to help one another. Alex's Lemonade Stand Foundation, a fund started by little Alexandra Scott to help other kids battling cancer, is just one example. Fund raisers to help pay a family's medical expenses; an Amish community working together to raise a barn; the list goes on.

Starting Your Own Raw Potluck: A Communal Meal

Raw potlucks can fill in the gaps of our disjointed communities. If you have something that people want to participate in, they will come. So if you want to have your own raw potluck, try some of the recipes in this book and invite your friends and neighbors. I promise that you all will have a wonderful time (but don't forget to invite me).

A spread of delicious dishes from one of Lisa's raw potlucks.

If you want to start your own potluck in your community, start by making a list of all your friends and relatives who you would like to invite. I know that some of the people who came to my first potluck were just coming because they thought I was having a party, and really were not coming because it was going to be a raw potluck. So don't be afraid to invite people who do not typically follow a raw diet.

Here are some other ways to gather people for your potluck:

• When you send out invitations (whether via e-mail, paper, or verbally), ask people to invite their friends or anyone who they think might enjoy the raw potluck, as well.
• Go to your local health store and markets to ask if they will put a blurb on their website, newsletter, and/or bulletin board about your raw potlucks.
• If you are as lucky as I am to have several raw restaurants near you, ask the owners to let everyone know that you will be having a raw potluck.

Once you have invited your people, there are certain things that I have learned through the years:

• Make sure everyone e-mails or brings along a copy of their recipe, since some people may have food allergies and will need to know what each dish contains.
• I typically request that people bring their own dishes. I do provide disposable dishes, but if the potluckers bring their own dishes, it will save on expenses for the hostess, and will also lessen the amount of garbage that will end up in a landfill.
• It can be a lot of fun to have everyone share with the group why they decided to come to the potluck, where they are in their journey, or if they have a business that they want to network.

- After each potluck, I like to send out a newsletter with pictures of the dishes, recipes that were provided by the potluckers, upcoming scheduled events, etc.
- At some of my potlucks, we have had world-renowned speakers: some are local speakers and/or our own potluckers, and other times, it is just us sharing and caring. We have been blessed to have an amazing group of people who are all very talented and knowledgeable.

Oasis: An Exemplary Community

Oasis at Bird-in-Hand in Ronks, PA is one of those stories about a community coming together. Oasis is a newly formed collective of Lancaster County farmers, a county known for having some of the best soil in the world. The farmers in the community at Oasis use eco-friendly farming practices—no synthetic pesticides, herbicides or antibiotics or hormones. Their philosophy is to better understand the underlying elements of their work: soil microbes, the way they work together, and how their work can be enhanced through cooperation with the soil. The resulting plants and animals are more naturally resistant to enemy insects, illnesses and blight; the artificial and indiscriminate use of unhealthy chemical crutches is not needed. Their methods produce delicious, nutrient-dense crops that are resistant to pests, weeds and disease.

Eating nutrient-dense foods is one of the healthiest ways that anyone can eat. No principle is more likely to support healthy eating than the principle of nutrient density. Why is nutrient density so helpful? Because it gives you concentrated amounts of valuable nutrients, such as vitamins, minerals, fiber, essential fatty acid and phytonutrients, to name just a few. Many people are consuming processed foods, which are low in nutrients. The body cannot receive energy from enzymes or dead foods (GMOs), and for this reason the modern body is in a constant state of nutritional and energy deficiency.

I share Oasis's story because, if you don't have this type of cooperation in your community, you can be the one to bring people together. You don't have to be a farmer to start an "oasis" in your area.

And remember that community and cooperation doesn't have to be just about growing food! At Thanksgiving my local community came together—churches, businesses, and individuals—to help prepare Thanksgiving meals for those who could come and attend the meal. We put together over a hundred bags of food to be given out between Thanksgiving and Christmas. Get involved, and volunteer! Some folks donate their time at fire houses, hospitals, drive elderly or disabled. Some sing in local choirs or play in orchestras. Others rescue animals, or pick up trash along roads and streams. Whatever your talents are, use them.

CREATING THE PERFECT TASTING DISH

Many times when creating a dish, I look at what I'm in the mood for, what I have on hand, and what flavors I like, and try to combine the three to create something delicious. After you've been preparing your own dishes for a while, you'll begin to know innately (with a little help from trial and error) what goes well together, and what doesn't. For those of us who aren't quite there yet (or need a refresher on combining and balancing flavors in your recipe) here are a few helpful hints:

When looking for a balanced flavor in creating a recipe, the five flavors to keep in mind are: sweet, salty, sour, bitter, and spicy.

The following lists show different ingredients you can use in combination to create raw recipe flavors:

Sweet

Raw honey
Fruit (fresh and dried)
Dates
Figs
Raw sugar
Maple syrup
Coconut aminos

Salty

Celtic sea salt
Himalayan sea salt
Miso
Celery
Bragg's® liquid aminos
Wheat-free tamari
Nama shoyu
Sun-dried tomatoes
Olives

Sour

Lemon juice
Apple cider vinegar
Berries (cranberries, raspberries, etc.)
Fermented foods

Bitter

Dandelion greens
Mustard greens
Endive
Garlic
Onions
Turmeric
Cumin

Spicy

Cayenne pepper
Black pepper
Garlic
Ginger
Paprika
Horseradish
Wasabi

© NATALIE NORMAN

PRESENTATION

I always say that I want my food to taste good, be good for me *and* look good. And it's the presentation of the food that makes it look beautiful. Eating or drinking from beautiful dishes tastes so much better than eating off of paper plates. Take on a celebration of life and bring it into the presentation of your food. Start with beautiful dishes and organic whole foods. Try adding a sprig of mint or parsley as a garnish to a drink. When I make a smoothie with raw cacao nibs, after I pour the smoothie into my glass, I will sprinkle a few raw cacao nibs on top.

Side salads can become main dishes by combining them creatively, or by presenting them on a bed of lettuce. A bed of lettuce also adds a new sort of flair to a veggie burger, marinated mushrooms, fermented food, or even spiralized zucchini—dishes that look fine separately, but which, together with greens, look fantastic. Even something as simple as sprinkling cinnamon on your applesauce and placing an apple wedge on the side of the dish with a cinnamon stick can bring a dish to life. Very simple, certainly, but it adds pizzazz to your applesauce.

With just a few additional seconds when plating your dish, you can create an opportunity for a much more pleasant experience while eating. You have to create your happiness in life and if it just takes adding a dash of this or a splash of that to kick up your meal and create an air of happiness, aren't you worth it?

PART II | Recipes

8

Salads & Dressings

Halloween Salad

Antanas Vainius
Prep: 30 minutes   **Serves:** 3

4 ounces dry hiziki or arame
1 pound carrots, grated
½ bunch cilantro, coarsely chopped

2–3 teaspoons raw apple cider vinegar
Bragg's® Sesame-Ginger Vinaigrette
(or make your own)

Cover seaweed in warm water and vinegar, until rehydrated and plump, which should take about 15–20 minutes. Drain, combine with carrots and cilantro, and toss with Sesame-Ginger Vinaigrette to taste.

Optionally, add sprouted legumes (such as mung, peas, or aduki beans).

Julie's White Carrot Salad

Antanas Vainius
Prep: 10 minutes

2 teaspoons tarragon, crushed
1 lime, juiced
Bunch baby white carrots, sliced

⅔ cup medium daikon, grated
3 tablespoons olive oil
Full spectrum salt, to taste

Soak tarragon in lime juice for 5 minutes. Toss daikon and carrots, and pour tarragon mixture on carrots/daikon, add olive oil, salt, toss, and serve.

Serve on de-seeded tomatoes wedges.

Sweet and Savory Bean Salad

Naomi Hackathorn (Chili Smith Family Foods)
Prep: 25 minutes

Salad
1½ cups Christmas lima beans/chestnut beans, soaked and cooked
½ large red onion, diced
5–6 mini sweet peppers, diced
1 carrot, peeled and cut into bite-sized pieces
1 cup beet, peeled and cut into bite-sized pieces

2 stalks celery, diced
½–1 cup dried currants

Dressing
½ cups Organicville® organic sesame teriyaki dressing
½ cups Soy Vay® toasted sesame dressing
2 tablespoons Jimtown® fig and olive spread

Soak beans in water in a glass dish in a dehydrator to blossom. Combine with vegetables. Or, combine in slow cooker and/or crock pot with temperature set below 118°F. When beans are cooked, rinsed, and cooled, add ingredients into a bowl and mix all ingredients together. Shake dressing ingredients in a jar to mix and then pour over your salad. Enjoy!

Contributor's Note: Try to soak beans for 1–2 days, changing water each day. Rinse beans and cook on stovetop, covered in fresh water for approximately 1 hour or until beans are cooked. I don't add salt. Heirloom beans rarely need seasoning added.

Romano Flageolet Salad

Chili Smith Family Foods, adapted by Lisa Montgomery
Prep: 30 minutes   **Serves:** 3–4

1 pound cooked green flageolet beans,
    chilled
½ cup black olives, sliced
½ cup canned artichoke hearts, drained
⅓ cup freshly grated Romano cheese (for
    a raw version, use raw cheese, Daiya
    coconut cheese, or omit)
2 tablespoons pimiento, chopped

2 tablespoons capers
1 tablespoons fresh parsley, chopped
⅓ cup olive oil
⅓ cup white-wine vinegar
2 garlic cloves, finely minced
2 tablespoons fresh basil, chopped
Salt and freshly ground pepper, to taste

Place beans in slow cooker, making sure temperature is below 118°F. Once beans are mushy, drain water and set aside. In a medium mixing bowl, combine beans, olives, artichokes, pimentos, capers, and parsley. In a small bowl, blend cold-pressed olive oil, raw apple cider vinegar, garlic, basil, salt, and pepper. Pour over bean mixture. Chill and serve.

Contributor's Note: Optional: You can add in raw cheese or Daiya coconut cheese if you desire. You can also grind up raw pine nuts with a little water, lemon juice, and nutritional yeast (to substitute for cheese) if you like.

Zucchini Salad

Colin Brett (Kimberton Whole Foods, www.kimbertonwholefoods.com)
Prep: 25 minutes

6 baby zucchini, sliced into thin slivers
1 yellow bell pepper, diced
1 tomato, diced
10 fresh black olives, pitted and diced
1 bunch parsley, chopped
¼ cup basil, chopped
⅛ cup fresh mint, chopped

1 teaspoon thyme
1 teaspoon sage
⅛ teaspoon cayenne
2 cloves garlic
1 teaspoon sea salt
¼ lemon juice

Slice zucchini in thin slivers, dice peppers, dice tomato, dice olives, chop parsley, chop basil, chop mint, and mince garlic. Add all ingredients together. Add lemon juice, thyme, sage, and cayenne. Add sea salt and let sit for one hour.

Carrot Lime Salad

Colin Brett (Kimberton Whole Foods, www.kimbertonwholefoods.com)
Prep: 20 minutes

4 cups shredded carrot
½ lime juice
1 large bunch cilantro, chopped
¼ cup chopped basil

¼ cup pine nuts
¾ cup apricots, chopped
1 teaspoon sea salt

Mix all ingredients in a mixing bowl. Let sit for one hour and enjoy!

Avocado Mango Salad

Derek Batman
Prep: 15 minutes

2 ripe avocados, cubed
2 ripe mangoes, cubed
2–3 cups broccoli, cut into bite
  size pieces

½ cup red onion, chopped
¾ cup raisins
Himalayan salt and fresh ground pepper,
  to taste

Combine all ingredients. Chill and serve.

Kale Salad

Dr. Scott and Raechelle Walker
Prep: 15 minutes

16 ounces organic Tuscan kale, chopped
1 cup diced cucumber
1 cup diced red pepper
1 cup broccoli florets

1 teaspoon crushed garlic
½ cup Bragg's® liquid aminos
½ cup extra virgin olive oil

Toss ingredients together and enjoy!

Macro Beauty Salad

Janice Inella
Prep: 45 minutes

1 head curly kale, chopped fine
15 shitake mushrooms (no stems and sliced thin lengthwise)
1 stick burdock root (peeled and sliced into matchsticks)
1 cup arame seaweed (soak in pure water for 10 minutes, then strain)
1 large daikon radish (cut into small cubes)

1 carrot, shredded
4 tablespoons fresh grated ginger (squeeze juice out into the salad or just juice it)
4 tablespoons wheat-free tamari
4 tablespoons toasted or raw sesame oil
4 tablespoons brown rice vinegar

In a large bowl, add finely chopped kale, shredded carrot, and cubed daikon radish. Add marinade with the rest of ingredients, and give it a nice hand massage. Share with someone you love!

Stone Fruit Salad

Jenny Ross
Prep: 20–25 minutes   **Serves:** 2–4

Salad
2 cups baby arugula
4 cups mixed greens
2 cups mixed stone fruit (peaches and
    plums or cherries and nectarines),
    sliced thin
1 Hass avocado, diced
4 tablespoons walnut pieces

Dressing
⅓ cup peaches
1 cup extra virgin cold pressed olive oil
2 tablespoons raw honey, agave, or
    2 drops stevia
1 teaspoon sea salt

Begin by blending the dressing ingredients in a basic blender or with an immersion blender. Blend well until completely emulsified or well combined. Remove from the blender and store in the refrigerator until ready to use. This recipe will keep in the refrigerator for up to 10 days.

Prepare the salad by gently cleaning the leaves, and drying them out completely. In a medium-sized mixing bowl, toss together the mixed greens and arugula. Plate these greens, spreading evenly over each plate either creating side portions or entrée portions accordingly. Then, in a small mixing bowl toss together the stone fruit slices with 2 tablespoons of the dressing.

Arrange the stone fruit over the top of each salad evenly. Take the diced avocado and top the stone fruit with the diced avocado, and finally sprinkle with the walnut pieces. Enjoy this salad fresh as an easy starter dish, or as an entrée. If enjoying as an entrée, you may even elect to add a scoop of steamed quinoa to the top of each.

Contributor's Note: One whole peach is only 37 calories on average, making the peach a low calorie source of B vitamins, vitamin K (which is essential for healthy blood), and vitamin E (which promotes healthy hair, skin, and nails). Stone fruit includes peaches, nectarines, plums, and cherries, as well as special varieties of stone fruits like "dino-eggs," "sweet saturns," and more! The benefit of the stone fruit in this salad is that it creates a lovely sweet salad for the summer. Stone fruit are found in most grocery stores, but are especially nice from the farmer's market, or when picked fresh.

Good Faith Farm's Green Bean and Olive Salad

Karen Handman (Good Faith Farms)
Prep: 30 minutes   **Serves:** 4–6

Juice of 1 lemon
2 tablespoons brown rice vinegar
2 garlic cloves, chopped fine
1 teaspoon salt
2 pounds green beans, trimmed
½ small red pepper, chopped

15 cherry tomatoes, halved (Sungolds, Peacevine—any super sweet variety)
1 small red onion, finely chopped
½ cup raw-cured Kalamata olives, pitted and halved
½ cup fresh basil, snipped
⅓ cup olive oil
Sea salt and ground white pepper

Combine first four ingredients in small bowl. Trim ends of beans. Add the olive oil to marinade, whisking until dressing appears creamy. Combine green beans (keep whole), red peppers, cherry tomatoes, basil and red onion in serving bowl. Add pinch white pepper, and more salt if desired. Toss gently to mix well. Serve room temperature or chilled.

Contributor's Note: Substitute Good Faith Farm's Moroccan Spice Raw Sevillano olives for the Kalamatas, Moroccan spice brine for the brown rice vinegar, and ¼ cup fresh chopped parsley for the basil.

Crunchy Apple Almond Salad

Natalie Norman
Prep: 10 minutes

1 large carrot
1 large apple
2 celery stalks
1 handful fresh cilantro

Juice of half an orange (about 3 tablespoons)
¼ cup chopped raw almonds (or pecans)

Ideally, your almonds will have been soaked beforehand. A good habit to develop is to keep soaked nuts in your fridge so you have them handy to grab. They keep for about a week. To soak, place in bowl and cover with cold water, then let them sit overnight (about 8 hours), then rinse and strain.

Finely chop all ingredients, toss together in a large bowl, and serve.

Contributor's Note: Wow, these simple flavors play so well together—light, refreshing, crunchy, and delicious. This salad uses ingredients found year-round in any market, making it a go-to staple for quick and satisfying meals. It's filling and will give you long-lasting energy. Great to bring to work for lunch! And, notice there is no salt or oil in it!

Sweet Cranberry Kale Salad

Raw Can Roll Café (www.rawcanrollcafe.com)
Prep: 15 minutes

- 1 bunch kale, de-veined and chopped
- 4 ounces apple infused dried cranberries or plain dried cranberries
- ¼ chopped small apple (with or without peel)
- 2 ounces walnuts
- 2 tablespoons agave
- 1 teaspoon orange juice
- 1 teaspoon fresh ground ginger
- Himalayan pink salt

Combine ingredients together and toss, making sure it is thoroughly coated with the salt and orange juice.

Italian Sea Palm and Cucumber Salad

Larry Knowles (Rising Tide Sea Vegetables)
Prep: 35 minutes

½ ounce soaked sea palm
1 carrot, grated
1 tablespoon olive oil
1 tablespoon balsamic vinegar
½ green onion, sliced

½ cucumber, seeded and finely julienned
¼ teaspoons dried oregano, crushed
1 pinch celery seed, ground
1 clove garlic, finely minced

Soak sea palm in 1 cup of water for 15 minutes and drain. Blot sea palm dry with a clean towel. Cut sea palm into 1-inch pieces. Stir ingredients together, salt to taste, and enjoy.

Almond Sea Palm Waldorf Salad

Larry Knowles (Rising Tide Sea Vegetables)
Prep: 35 minutes

1 cup soaked sea palm
2 cups apples, diced
1 cup celery, chopped
1 cup carrots, grated

½ cup raisins
½ cup almonds, chopped
Unpasteurized mayonnaise (or olive oil/
     safflower oil, lemon juice, and salt)

Soak sea palm in 1 cup of water for 15 minutes and drain. Blot sea palm dry with a clean towel. Cut sea palm into 1-inch pieces. Stir ingredients together, add unpasteurized mayonnaise (or olive oil/safflower oil, lemon juice, and salt) to taste.

Spinach Quinoa Salad

Terry Ramsey
Prep: 20 minutes   **Serves:** 4–6

1 bag organic baby spinach
3 tablespoons extra virgin olive oil
2 limes
1 (15 ounce) can organic black beans,
    drained and rinsed
1 cup grape tomatoes, halved
1 shallot, finely diced

6 green onions, finely chopped
1 clove garlic, minced
1 cup cooked, cooled organic corn
1 cup cooked, cooled quinoa (white,
    red, or black)
Organic salt and pepper, to taste

Rinse 1 cup quinoa well in cold water in mesh strainer. Add 1½ cups vegetable broth to quinoa and soak in dehydrator until blossomed.

In a small bowl, whisk together the olive oil, lime juice, and salt and pepper to taste. Add the black beans, tomatoes, quinoa, shallot, green onions, garlic, and corn to a large bowl. Toss with lime vinaigrette. For a pretty presentation, line a serving dish with baby spinach leaves, and put your salad on top for additional nutrition.

Asparagus Salad

Joel Odhner
Prep: 20 minutes

1 pound asparagus, chopped
1 red pepper, diced
1 yellow pepper, diced
½ cup parsley, chopped
3 scallions, chopped

Zest of 1 orange
1 orange, juiced
1 lemon, juiced
2 tablespoons cold-pressed olive oil
Sea salt to taste

Toss all ingredients together and let stand for 1 hour. Lasts 2–3 days when refrigerated.

Beet & Carrot Salad

Cara Graver (The Cob Studio, www.thecobstudio.com)
Prep: 10 minutes

1 beet, scrubbed, unpeeled, and grated
2 carrots, scrubbed, unpeeled, and grated
Juice of one or more lemons

Combine shredded beet and carrots in a bowl and toss with juice of lemon.

Broccoli Miso Salad

Brenda Cobb (Founder of Living Foods Institute® and author of *The Living Foods Lifestyle*, www.livingfoodsinstitute.com)
Prep: 20 minutes

3 cups broccoli
1 cup carrots
2 cloves garlic
3 tablespoons raw tahini

3 tablespoons chickpea miso
3 tablespoons lemon juice
2 tablespoons water

First peel the broccoli stems to leave a thin outer skin and then chop the broccoli stems and florets into small pieces in a food processor. Don't chop the broccoli so much that it becomes mushy. Leave it in small bite-sized pieces. Remove from the food processor and put into a bowl.

Next chop the carrots in the food processor. Take out and put in the bowl with the broccoli. Don't chop the broccoli and carrots together at the same time as the broccoli will become mushy before the carrots are chopped fine enough.

Next put the garlic in the food processor and chop, then add the raw tahini, chickpea miso, lemon juice, and water into the food processor and blend all together. You do not have to clean out the food processor of the broccoli and carrots before you make the dressing. Just put it all in and whatever residue of broccoli and carrots are left in the processor will be blended up in the dressing.

Take the dressing out of the food processor and mix with the broccoli and carrots. Toss well until all is coated.

Serve on a bed of mixed baby greens and enjoy!

Colorful Corn Salad

Roger Haeska and Karymyn Malone (www.Howtogoraw.com, www.LightningSpeed Fitness.com, and www.KarmynMalone.com)

Prep: 20 minutes   **Serves:** 2

4 ears sweet corn, cut off cob
1 cup premium tomato, diced
½ cup diced orange bell pepper
½ cup fresh cilantro, chopped

1 scallion, finely chopped
1 tomatillo, diced
1 tablespoon jalapeño pepper, minced
Juice of one lemon or lime

Mix all ingredients in a large bowl and enjoy.

Curry Cabbage Lentil Salad

Brenda Cobb (Founder of Living Foods Institute® and author of *The Living Foods Lifestyle*, www.livingfoodsinstitute.com)

Prep: 25 minutes

4 cups purple or green cabbage, chopped
3 large cloves garlic
1 cup green onion
1 cup red bell pepper

1 cup sprouted lentils
1 heaping tablespoon curry powder
½ cup lemon juice
½ cup olive oil
1 teaspoon Himalayan salt

Chop the cabbage in the food processor and set aside. Chop the garlic, onions, and red pepper by hand so they won't get mushy. Combine with the cabbage and lentils in a large bowl. Add the curry powder, lemon juice, olive oil, and sea salt to the vegetables and toss.

Curry Carrot Salad

Joel Odhner

Prep: 20–30 minutes

Sauce
1 cup Brazil nuts
1 cup water
½ cup cold-pressed olive oil
1 tablespoon curry
1 tablespoon cumin

Salad
3 cups carrots, shredded
½ cup raisins
1 cup celery, diced
1 red onion, diced

Sauce
Place all the ingredients in a high-powered blender and blend until smooth.

Salad
Fold sauce into the remaining ingredients. Lasts 3–4 days, refrigerated (if you have not already eaten it up by then).

Contributor's Note: The flavors of cumin and curry add a unique flavor to an old-time favorite dish. Bring this salad to your next picnic for a new delight for all to enjoy.

The Essence of Spinach Salad

Joel Odhner

Prep: 30 minutes   **Soak:** 1–2 hours

4 cups spinach
½ teaspoon Celtic sea salt
1 medium avocado, diced
½ cup pine nuts, soaked 1–2 hours, then drained
¼ cup sun-dried tomato, soaked, drained, and finely chopped

¼ cup black olives, pitted and diced
2 tablespoons cold-pressed extra virgin olive oil
2 teaspoons lemon juice

Massage the spinach with sea salt until moist. Add all the remaining ingredients, mix well, and serve.

Contributor's Note: This is probably my all-time favorite spinach salad. Joel taught this in one of my very first raw cooking classes, and I have been making it ever since. Whenever I take it to a dinner, it always receives a great review. It is so simple, yet tasty: a true classic. After all these years, I still have not grown tired of it. Joel was one of my first raw teachers. He taught me so much, and I still love making many of the recipes he has shared with me through the years.

Fresh Fruit Salad with Macadamia Cream

Kimberton Whole Foods, www.kimbertonwholefoods.com
Prep: 15 minutes

Chopped fruit of your choice
One handful of raw macadamia nuts
Juice of half an orange (or a whole one juiciness)

2–4 large Medjool dates (or 4–8 smaller soaked ones)
Small piece of vanilla bean (optional)

Prepare your fruit salad using a wide range of fresh, juicy fruits of your choice. (A good mixture might be banana, orange, apple, strawberries, nectarines, and blueberries.) Next, make your topping by blending remaining ingredients together until a thick creamy mixture is created. Taste before using and adjust ingredients according to your preference. You may want to add a pinch of salt just to bring out the flavors a little more.

Serve the fruit salad topped with a good dose of the macadamia cream. The topping recipe will keep for about 2–3 days in the refrigerator.

Contributor's Note: Great for topping some breakfasts for something a bit more sustaining. Or why not throw a tablespoon or two of it into your fruit smoothie?

Italian Arugula Salad

Brenda Cobb (Founder of Living Foods Institute® and author of *The Living Foods Lifestyle*, www.livingfoodsinstitute.com)
Prep: 20 minutes

Salad
2 cucumbers, chopped and cubed
1 cup red bell pepper, seeded and chopped into cubes
4 cups fresh arugula
1 cup fresh cilantro leaves, chopped

Dressing
2 tablespoons fresh oregano, chopped
1 large clove garlic, minced
3 tablespoons basil, chopped
½ cup extra virgin olive oil
Pinch cayenne pepper
½ cup fresh lemon juice
1 teaspoon Himalayan sea salt

Salad
Combine all ingredients in a large bowl.

Dressing
Place all ingredients in a Vitamix® and blend until creamy. Add the dressing to the salad right before you are ready to serve.

Mexican Corn Salad

Joel Odhner
Prep: 20–30 minutes

2 cups fresh organic corn kernels
1 cup red pepper, chopped
¼ cup scallions, chopped
¼ cup fresh cilantro, finely chopped
2 tablespoons lemon juice

2 tablespoons cold-pressed extra virgin olive oil
½ teaspoon ground cumin
Sea salt to taste

Combine all the ingredients in a bowl, toss, and eat.

Pad Thai Salad

Kimberton Whole Foods, www.kimbertonwholefoods.com
Soak: Nuts, 8 hours
Prep: 25 minutes

2 zucchinis, sliced into strips with a vegetable peeler
2 large handfuls of bean sprouts, approximately 2 cups
¾ cup soaked nuts, chopped (use almonds, peanuts, or cashews)

1 red or yellow bell pepper, sliced into strips
4 green onions, diced
½ cup fresh chopped cilantro
Juice from one lime
1 tablespoon raw, cold-pressed olive oil
¼ teaspoon sea salt

Toss all ingredients together in a bowl until well coated. Add a dash more salt if desired and enjoy!

Rainbow Salad

Elaina Love (Author of *Elaina's Pure Joy Kitchen*, www.PureJoyLove.com)
Prep: 30 minutes   **Serves:** 8

Almond Mayonnaise
1 cup soaked almonds (½ cup before soaking)
¾ cup water
1 clove garlic
½ teaspoon Celtic sea salt or 1 tablespoon tamari
3 tablespoons lemon juice or 1½ tablespoons apple cider vinegar
½ teaspoon Italian seasoning
3 large dates or 3 tablespoons honey or maple syrup
Dash of cayenne pepper
1½–2 cups flax or olive oil

Salad
½ red cabbage, shredded
2 large carrots, shredded
3 broccoli stalks and 1½ heads, shredded
4 scallions, thinly sliced
1 cup raisins
¼ cup sliced almonds
1½ cups almond mayonnaise
½ teaspoon mustard powder
½ teaspoon ginger powder
½ teaspoon garlic powder
1–2 teaspoons Celtic sea salt or 4–6 tablespoons tamari

Almond Mayonnaise

Peel almonds for a whiter mayonnaise. Place all ingredients (except the oil) in a blender. Blend until creamy. Put your blender on a low speed, and drizzle the oil through the hole in the blender lid. Add oil until the mixture becomes thick.

Salad

Combine above ingredients with half the almond mayonnaise recipe.

Contributor's Note: Elaina said this is one of her most popular salads. I've made this recipe and loved it. Not only does it taste great but I love all the colors and textures.

Seaweed Salad

Cara Graver (The Cob Studio, www.thecobstudio.com)
Prep: 10 minutes, plus 15 minutes soaking time

¼ cup arame or hiziki sea vegetables
1 apple, with skin on, seeded, chopped

1 avocado, mashed
Juice of 1 lemon

Soak sea vegetables in water for at least 15 minutes. Pour off the water from the sea vegetables after they are finished hydrating. Combine sea vegetable, apple, and avocado in mixing bowl. Pour juice of one lemon over the salad and toss until the salad is thoroughly coated.

Sea Veggie Salad

Elaina Love (Author of *Elaina's Pure Joy Kitchen*, www.PureJoyLove.com)
Elaina is a raw food chef and teacher. She also certifies up-and-coming raw food chefs.
Prep: 25 minutes   **Yield:** 1 pint   **Serves:** 4

½ cup arame, dry
2 tablespoons flax oil
1–5 tablespoons lemon juice (1½ lemons)

3 scallions or ¼ red onion, shredded
¼–½ teaspoon Celtic sea salt

Cover the arame with purified water and let soak for 15 minutes.

Mix all ingredients together and let marinate an hour or more (overnight is best as the flavors have time to meld and the sea vegetable flavor mellows).

If you don't have time to marinade, omit or lessen the amount of onions.

Combine the ingredients in a mixing bowl. Place in a glass dish and dehydrate for 30 minutes to warm.

Contributor's Note: Ocean vegetables, like those in this recipe, greatly enhance the functioning of the immune system. They are also rich in minerals and help strengthen the thyroid.

Spicy Tropical Jicama Salsa & Salad

Kimberton Whole Foods, www.kimbertonwholefoods.com
Prep: 30 minutes

Salad
½ large pineapple, cut into small cubes
½ jicama, cut into small cubes
1 bunch cilantro, finely chopped
½ red onion, diced

Dressing
1 cup coconut milk (combine ⅔ cup coconut meat and 1 cup coconut water)

½ cup lime juice
4 tablespoons coconut nectar (or honey, maple syrup, agave)
½ teaspoon Himalayan pink salt
4–5 tablespoons coconut oil, warmed to liquid
½–1 teaspoon paprika
½–1 jalapeño (see note below)

Place all salad ingredients in a bowl and mix thoroughly. Place all dressing ingredients in a Vitamix® high-speed blender and blend until smooth. Pour dressing over salad and mix.

Salad will last 1–2 days in the refrigerator when dressed or 3–4 if dressing and salad are stored separately.

Contributor's Note: If you have a Vitamix® high-speed blender, you don't need to chop the jalapeño because the blender is powerful enough to chop up the pepper. If you are using a regular blender, you should chop the jalapeño before adding it to the blender, just in case it is not strong enough to blend the ingredients appropriately.

Sprout Salad

Barbara Shevkun (Rawfully Tempting)
Prep: 15 minutes   **Sprout:** Mung beans and lentils, 3 days

2 cups sprouted mung beans (¼ cup
   mung beans before sprouted)
1 cup sprouted lentils (¼ cup lentils
   before sprouting)
1 apple, sliced

½ to 1 cup finely chopped golden
   beets, peeled
½ cup raisins
2 tablespoons sauerkraut (such
   as Bubbies®)

Combine all ingredients. You can also add avocado, greens, mangoes, or any of
your favorite vegetables. Top with your favorite dressing. (I added a spoonful of
juice from the Bubbies® sauerkraut and it was delicious!)

Sweet Kale

**Sheryll Chavarria (Raw Can Roll Café and Pure Body Spa, Douglassville, PA,
www.rawcanrollcafe.com)**
Prep: 20 minutes   **Soak:** raisins, 1 hour   **Serves:** 4

3 bunches kale, removed from stem
   and chopped to desired size
½ cup orange juice
¼ cup sesame oil

2 apples, cored, cut into small pieces
1 cup raisins, soaked and drained
Pinch Celtic sea salt
1–2 tablespoons agave

Combine kale, orange juice, and sesame oil in a large bowl. Massage ingredients
together. To massage, you will need to pick up bunches of kale with both hands,
squeeze, and rub together relatively vigorously as if you were washing clothes by
hand. Kale is ready when it becomes softer in texture. Add remaining ingredients
together and serve.

Contributor's Note: If you have any kale salad left over, you can lay it out on dehydrator sheets and dehydrate at 105°F until crispy (4–6 hours), which turns it into
kale chips and makes a great snack.

Tammy's Fruit Salad

Tammy Jerome
Prep: 30 minutes

- 1 personal size seedless watermelon
- 1 cantaloupe
- 1 honeydew melon
- 1 pound red grapes

- 1 (16 ounce) container strawberries, sliced in quarters
- 1 (16 ounce) container blueberries
- 3 kiwis (fruit), to be used as garnish

Use a melon baller to cut the watermelon and cantaloupe. Combine all ingredients. Be sure to wash all fruit before handling and adding to your salad!

Thai Green Mango Salad

Sheryll Chavarria (Raw Can Roll Café and Pure Body Spa, Douglassville, PA, www.rawcanrollcafe.com)
Prep: 25 minutes

Salad
- 2 firm mangos (must not be ripe), shredded
- ¼ cup dry, shredded unsweetened coconut
- 2 cups bean sprouts
- 1 tablespoon coriander
- 3 scallions, chopped
- ⅓ cup fresh basil, chopped
- Handful peanuts, set aside

Dressing
- 3 tablespoons tamari
- 3–4 tablespoons lime or lemon juice, freshly squeezed
- 2 tablespoons orange juice
- 2 tablespoons agave, to taste (can add more)
- 1–2 tablespoons sesame oil
- Pinch cayenne pepper (optional)

Salad
In a large mixing bowl, toss all ingredients (except for the peanuts).

Dressing
In a separate small mixing bowl, whisk together all ingredients. Pour salad dressing over the salad and toss lightly. Garnish with peanuts.

Thai Tomato Salad

Kimberton Whole Foods, www.kimbertonwholefoods.com
Prep: 25 minutes

Salad
9 campari tomatoes, diced
4 pickling cucumbers (or 1 large English), chopped
1 red bell pepper, chopped
1 yellow pepper, chopped
½ red or yellow onion, diced
1 avocado, chopped
1 handful of freshly chopped cilantro

Dressing
¼ cup lime juice
2 tablespoons sesame oil
1½ tablespoons tamari (reduced sodium)
1 teaspoon miso
1 packet stevia
½ teaspoon red chili paste (1 teaspoon if you prefer more spice)

Salad
Combine all ingredients together in a bowl, set aside.

Dressing
Whisk all ingredients together and pour over salad. Serve immediately, or let marinate in refrigerator.

Watercress Salad

Joel Odhner
Prep: 15–20 minutes

2 bunches watercress
1 large Asian pear
¼ cup cold-pressed extra virgin olive oil

¼ cup maple syrup (optional)
Lemon pepper to taste

Toss all the ingredients and serve.

Contributor's Note: Watercress, like mustard greens, is a cruciferous vegetable and, like its cousins broccoli and cabbage, has been recognized as an important source of calcium, iron, and folic acid. It is one of the oldest known leafy greens eaten by humans. Perhaps the best incentive to add this delicious green to your culinary repertoire is the exciting research that came out of the University of Ulster (United Kingdom) about the anti-cancer properties of watercress. This study found that daily intake of watercress can significantly reduce an important cancer trigger; namely DNA damage to white blood cells. Eating watercress salad has also been shown to lower cholesterol and improve absorption of lutein and beta carotene, which are key minerals for eye health and the prevention of age-related conditions such as cataracts.

When eaten raw, watercress is prized for its peppery flavor. You can also mix watercress with fruit for a variety of flavor sensations.

If you are lucky enough to live near Alresford, Hampshire, in the United Kingdom, you can attend their annual Watercress Festival in the spring. There is also a newer watercress festival in Osceola, Wisconsin.

As a child, my neighbors grew watercress in their creek. Now that I know all of the amazing health benefits of this vegetable, I am planning on growing it in a tub in my backyard, since I do not have a stream running through my yard. There are several websites that provide detailed instructions on how to grow watercress in containers on your back lawn, your balcony, and/or patio.

Kale Cranberry Pine Nut Salad

Prep: 15 minutes

1 large bunch lacinato kale (equals about 26 stems)
1 teaspoon sea salt
½ lemon, juiced
⅔ cup dried cranberries

2 tablespoons Austria's Pumpkin seed oil
⅓ cup raw pine nuts
⅓ cup yellow raisins
1 green apple, cored and diced
1 avocado, peeled, pitted, and diced

Remove kale leaves from stem and shred leaves into bite-size pieces. Place shredded leaves in a large mixing bowl and combine with sea salt and lemon. Massage the salt and lemon juice into the kale until kale breaks down and is wilted. Add remaining ingredients to the kale. Toss and combine, and serve.

Pineapple Jicama Salad

Prep: 11 minutes

1 cup pineapple, chunks
1 cup jicama, peeled and cubed
1 cup cucumber, cut into chunks

½ cup raw honey
2 tablespoon fresh mint, finely minced

Combine the above ingredients in a mixing bowl. Serve and eat.

Seaweed & Shitake Salad

Prep: 20 minutes

2 cups dried seawood (hiziki or sea palm
  are my favorites)
1 cup shitake mushrooms, finely sliced
2 garlic cloves, minced
Pinch of sea salt

Pinch freshly ground black pepper
2 tablespoons cold-pressed olive oil
1 teaspoon wheat-free tamari
¼ teaspoon toasted sesame oil

Soak the seaweed in cold water until water is absorbed and sea vegetables have been rehydrated. Pour off water. In a separate bowl, whisk together remaining ingredients. Pour dressing over the sea vegetables. You can eat as is place in glass bowl and dehydrate at 105°F to heat the salad and/or meld the flavors. I add seaweed salad on top of a green salad. I also use it as part of filler in a wrap. You can eat it as is, or with a spoonful of the toasted sesame mayo on top.

Broccoli Salad

Prep: 15 minutes

4 cups broccoli florets
1 garlic clove, minced
1 teaspoon toasted sesame oil

1 teaspoon wheat-free tamari
Pinch of sea salt

Combine ingredients in a bowl and serve right away. Alternatively, you can place the broccoli salad in a glass bowl and place in dehydrator at 105°F until dish is warm and the flavors meld.

Sautéed Spinach

Prep: 15 minutes

6 cups baby spinach leaves
2 tablespoons Austria's Finest Pumpkin Seed Oil or cold-pressed olive oil
   (each oil gives it a different flavor)
1 tablespoon wheat-free tamari

Place greens in a large bowl and cover with oil and wheat-free tamari. You can also add a pinch of sea salt or pepper to taste. Add a dash of lemon or raw honey to taste. Make sure the greens are totally covered. You can eat them like this or place them in a glass dish and place in your dehydrator at 105 F° until the greens have been warmed and the flavors meld. If you wish to give this an Asian flavor, you could add a dash of toasted sesame oil. Be careful, because a little toasted sesame oil goes a long way.

European Meets Asian Salad or Kraut

Prep: 30 minutes

1 cabbage, shredded
2 cups mung beans
1 cup sliced cucumbers or zucchini
2 teaspoons cold-pressed olive oil
2 teaspoons toasted sesame oil

1 teaspoon sesame seeds
1 tablespoon raw honey
Sea salt to taste
3 to 4 tablespoons sea salt

Salad:
Combine ingredients in a large bowl and toss until vegetables are thoroughly coated. This is another salad that you can eat right away or you can place in a glass bowl in the dehydrator to marinate or meld the vegetables.

Kraut:
Combine ingredients in a large bowl and use fermentation directions found on page 27.

Asparagus & Mushroom Salad

Prep: 40 minutes

Salad
1–2 bunches asparagus, thinly sliced
   on a diagonal
1 clove garlic, minced
1–2 Gala apples, finely chopped
½ cup red onions, finely chopped
1 cup portabella mushrooms,
   finely sliced

2 tablespoons pine nuts
Sea salt to taste

Dressing
¼–½ cup cold-pressed olive oil
1–2 tablespoons lemon juice
Sea salt and ground pepper to taste

Salad

Cut off the ends of the asparagus and discard. Cut the asparagus diagonally into bite-sized pieces. Toss the asparagus, garlic, apples, onions, portabella mushrooms, pine nuts, and sea salt.

Dressing

Combine all the ingredients in a high-speed blender. Pour over the salad, toss, and serve. You can combine this salad with mixed greens as well.

Watermelon Salad with Basil

Prep: 15 minutes   **Serves:** 6

6 cups watermelon, cut	1 tablespoon lemon juice
2 cups fresh strawberries, quartered	½ teaspoon sea salt
2 green apples, cored and diced	¼ teaspoon ground black pepper
1 tablespoon cold-pressed extra virgin olive oil	¼ cup fresh basil, finely chopped

In a large bowl, combine the watermelon, strawberries, and apples. Set aside.

In a small bowl, whisk together the cold-pressed olive oil, lemon juice, salt, and pepper. Drizzle the mixture over the fruit. Gently toss to combine. Scatter the basil over the salad. Serve immediately at room temperature.

WORDS FROM LISA:

This is my own adaptation of J. M. Hirsch's (AP Food Editor) salad with meat. I obviously have removed the meat.

If you like, you could also add diced fresh cantaloupe to this salad. The original recipe called for cooked bacon for a nice crunch. To keep the crunch, you could add soaked, dehydrated, and finely chopped sesame seeds, pine nuts, or walnuts. Ground pumpkin seeds would also be really nice on this salad. I have even been known to finely chop macadamia nuts and sprinkle them over the top, as well. You can see how just changing the nut can make this salad come out differently, so do not get locked into thinking that you need to have specific ingredients on hand; just substitute something else. You could even try grating raw cacao over the top of this salad, as well. As you can tell, I can get carried away with all of the possibilities. It happens a lot; I am a foodie, after all.

Super Easy, Super Delicious Shredded Vegetable Salad

Wendy Landiak
Prep: 20 minutes

½ cup fresh coconut, shredded
1 cup fresh carrot, shredded
1 cup vegetables (your choice)
Pinch of paprika
1 tablespoon avocado oil
Pinch of cumin seed, ajwain seed, and
    fennel seed

1 tablespoon grated ginger
1 tablespoon fresh turmeric
1 red chili (optional)
Choice of seasoning (Himalayan sea salt,
    nama shoyu, Bragg's® aminos)

In a bowl, shred carrots and your choice of vegetables. Toss in coconut. In a separate bowl, mix spices, oil (optional), and seasonings. Add the spice mixture to the vegetables and enjoy!

Unfried Tomatoes

Prep: 15 minutes

Heirloom organic tomatoes, sliced
Almond meal
Sea salt

Cracked pepper
Pizza or Italian seasonings
Cold-pressed olive oil

Slice heirloom organic tomatoes and set aside. Pour your cold-pressed olive oil on a low flat dish with a rim. In a second dish, combine your almond meal, sea salt, cracked pepper, and pizza (or Italian) seasoning. Roll your sliced tomatoes in the oil, then roll and/or coat the tomatoes in the spiced almond mixture. Place coated tomato slices on your Teflex dehydrator tray and dehydrate at 105°F until desired consistency is reached.

California Dreamin'

Prep: 15 minutes

3 zucchini, spiralized
2 ears corn
1 cup figs, pitted and diced

½ cup cherry tomatoes, halved
Balsamic vinegar

Remove the kernels from the corn. Combine the corn with the zucchini, figs, and cherry tomatoes. Toss with balsamic vinegar to taste.

Thanksgiving Kale Salad

Prep: 10 minutes

2 bunches kale
1 tablespoon lemon juice
2 tablespoons cold-pressed olive oil or Austria's Finest, Naturally® pumpkin seed oil

Sea salt, to taste (enough to wilt the kale leaves)
¼ cup dried cranberries
¼ cup raw walnuts, soaked

Remove the kale leaves from their stems. Rip the leaves into bite size pieces or cut them chiffonade-style. Massage the lemon juice, oil, and sea salt into the kale to break it down. Make sure the kale is totally covered. Add walnuts and cranberries. Toss and eat.

Contributor's Note: If you haven't eaten all of your Thanksgiving Kale Salad and don't want to eat it the next day, you can put it in your dehydrator at 105°F and dehydrate until crisp. Now you have "Thanksgiving Kale Chips."

Fennel & Orange Salad

Prep: 20 minutes

1 fennel bulb, very thinly sliced
2 oranges, peeled and wedged
Spring mix greens
Vinaigrette
1 teaspoon finely grated lemon zest

1 teaspoon grated orange zest
4 tablespoons cold-pressed olive oil
Sea salt, to taste
Cracked pepper, to taste

Place fennel slices, orange wedges, and spring greens in a large bowl. In a Vita-mix® high-speed blender, combine lemon zest, orange zest, olive oil, and sea salt until well blended. Pour vinaigrette over the fennel, orange, and greens mixture. Toss and serve. Grind black pepper over salad to taste.

Fig & Pear Salad

Prep: 15 minutes

2 pears, cored and thinly sliced
8 figs, cubed and de-stemmed
1 tablespoon alcohol-free vanilla
1 teaspoon cinnamon

Shaved almond slices
Raw cacao nibs
Spring mix greens
Fig balsamic vinegar (optional)

Combine sliced pears, figs, alcohol-free vanilla, and cinnamon and set aside. Place spring mix greens on each plate, then place pear-fig mixture on each plate of greens. Sprinkle with shaved almond slices and raw cacao nibs. Drizzle fig balsamic vinegar over salad and serve.

Mung Bean Salad

Prep: 20 minutes

4 cups mung beans
3 scallions, cleaned and sliced on edge
⅛ cup red onion, chopped
½–1 cup shitake mushrooms (or your favorite), remove stems and slice
1 clove garlic, minced
¼ teaspoon fresh ginger, minced
2 raw nori sheets, broken into tiny pieces

½ teaspoon toasted sesame oil
1 teaspoon wheat free tamari
¼ cup sesame oil
2 carrots, peeled and sliced thinly on edge
1 tablespoon Austria's Finest, Naturally® pumpkin seed oil

Combine the above ingredients in a glass dish, making sure the vegetables are covered in the oils. You can either eat as is or place the glass dish in a Tribest® Sedona Dehydrator until the vegetables are warmed and softened.

WORDS FROM LISA:

Many folks can do raw foods in the summertime, when the temperatures are hot and the fresh summer vegetables are being harvested. But many also have a hard time staying raw when the temperatures dip. If you are someone who feels like they need the heat to stay warm, then try some of the unroasted dehydrated dishes (pages 116 and 129).

Simple Iceberg Wedge Salad

Prep: 7 minutes

Wedges of Iceberg lettuce
Red onion, peeled and very finely sliced
Fresh chives, finely sliced
Orange, juiced
Orange zest

Ground black pepper
Mint, to garnish or to taste (optional)
Pine nuts or almond slivers, to garnish
 or to taste (optional)

Place wedge of iceberg lettuce on each plate. Sprinkle red onions and chives on each lettuce wedge. Drizzle orange juice on each wedge. Garnish with orange zest and mint. Grind black pepper on each wedge. Another optional garnish is almond slivers or pine nuts.

Kale Fall Salad

Prep: 15 minutes

1 large bunch lacinato kale
   (equals about 26 leaves/stems)
1 teaspoon sea salt
½ lemon, juiced
3 tablespoons Austria's Finest,
   Naturally® pumpkin seed oil

½ cup raw olives, sliced
½ cup pecans and/or walnuts
½ cup cranberries

Remove kale leaves from stems and shred leaves into bite size pieces. Place shredded leaves in a large mixing bowl and combine with sea salt, lemon, and oil. Massage the salt, lemon juice, and oil into the kale until the kale breaks down and is wilted. Add remaining ingredients to the kale. Toss, combine, and serve.

WORDS FROM LISA:

If you don't have pumpkin seed oil you can substitute cold-pressed olive oil.

Asian Red Cabbage Salad

Prep: 30 minutes

Dressing
⅓ cup sesame oil
1 tablespoon toasted sesame oil
1 tablespoon wheat free tamari
1 teaspoon raw honey or raw agave
½–1 teaspoon ginger, peeled and minced finely
⅛–¼ cup lime juice
1 teaspoon dulse flakes
1 teaspoon kelp powder
Sea salt, to taste

Salad
½ head red cabbage or 5 cups, thinly sliced/shredded
2 medium carrots, peeled and shredded
1 cup baby spinach, shredded
6 scallions, sliced thinly on angle
½ cup fresh cilantro, chopped finely
1 tablespoon raw hemp seeds
1 tablespoon raw sesame seeds, hulled

Combine the dressing ingredients in a large bowl and whisk together until well blended. Add shredded cabbage, carrots, scallions, spinach, and cilantro. Toss until vegetables are coated with the liquid seasoning mixture. Top with sesame seeds and hemp seeds.

Caesar Salad

Prep: 30 minutes

Salad
3 heads romaine lettuce (break leaves into bite size pieces)
½–1 cup pine nuts
Sliced olives, pitted (optional)

Dressing
1 pinch Kosher salt or sea salt

1 garlic clove, minced
1 tablespoon dulse, minced finely
1 teaspoon kelp powder
2 tablespoons lemon juice
¼–½ teaspoon mustard powder
½ cup cold-pressed olive oil
1–2 tablespoons nutritional yeast
Cracked black pepper, to taste

Combine dressing ingredients in a high-speed blender or whisk together in a bowl until well combined and set aside.

Place romaine leaves in a bowl. Pour as little or as much dressing on the salad as you like. Toss and garnish with pine nuts and optional olives. You can leave the dressing in a pitcher and let your guests pour as little or as much dressing as they would like. If you are packing the salad for lunch, keep the dressing in a separate sealed container and toss it right before you eat so the greens don't wilt.

Carrots & Almond Salad

Prep: 20 minutes

6 carrots, peeled and sliced on angle
    approximately 1 inch long
¼ cup raw almonds, soaked, dried, and
    coarsely chopped
1 tablespoon maple syrup or raw honey
1 tablespoon Austria's Finest, Naturally®
    pumpkin seed oil

1 teaspoon lemon juice
1 small shallot, finely chopped
1 tablespoon fresh rosemary, chopped
Sea salt, to taste
Cracked black pepper, to taste

Combine ingredients in a glass dish, making sure the carrots, almonds, and rosemary are well covered with the herbs and liquids. Add a little more oil and maple syrup if carrots, almond, and rosemary needs a little more liquid to cover. Salt and pepper to taste. Place glass dish with carrot and almond mixture in a Tribest® Sedona Dehydrator until warmed and softened through, or to desired doneness. You can also eat as is, without dehydrating.

WORDS FROM LISA:

Since I created this dish in early winter, my mind would tend to want to warm everything up. But this dish is great just as is. In the summertime you wouldn't want to place it in the dehydrator—you'll want to eat it clean, fresh, and raw. Prepare the dish the way you would like it. If you don't like rosemary, pick a different herb that you would like, such as oregano, sage, or tarragon.

Zebra Cucumber & Tomato Salad

Prep: 15 minutes

3 small cucumbers, zebra striped
Heirloom tomatoes, zebra striped,
    cut in bite-sized pieces
¼ cup scallions, sliced finely on
    an angle

½ cup mixture of fresh herbs (such
    as dill, mint, and chives), chopped
Black cracked pepper, to taste
Sea salt, to taste
Balsamic vinegar, to taste

To zebra stripe a cucumber, run a peeler down the side of the cucumber and make stripes. You can save the peelings and add as a garnish to the dish. Cut zebra striped cucumbers in half and finely slice. Combine cucumbers, tomatoes, scallions, and fresh herbs together in a serving bowl or plate individually. Drizzle with balsamic vinegar, season to taste with black cracked pepper and sea salt.

Summer Salad

Prep: 15 minutes

Scallions, sliced
1 cup mushrooms, sliced
½ cup red pepper, chopped
1 cup cherry tomatoes, halved
1 tablespoon basil
1 tablespoon oregano

1 clove garlic, minced
1 teaspoon lemon juice
¼ cup pumpkin seed oil or
    cold-pressed olive oil
Salt, to taste
Cracked pepper, to taste

Combine scallions, mushrooms, red pepper, and tomatoes in a bowl and set aside. In another bowl, combine sea salt, cracked pepper, basil, oregano, garlic, lemon juice, and oil, and whisk together. You can marinate the salad with the dressing, serve on the side and use the amount you desire, or plate the salad on a bed of greens and drizzle dressing on top of the entire salad. This is a clean, fresh salad.

Artichoke Fig Salad

Prep: 15 minutes

1 cup artichoke hearts, chopped
1 cup figs, remove stems and chopped
1 cup baby bella mushrooms, sliced
1 cup olives, pitted and sliced
½ teaspoon mustard powder

1 tablespoon parsley, minced
Pinch sea salt
¼ teaspoon lemon juice
¼ cup balsamic vinegar, or fig balsamic
    vinegar or blueberry vinegar

Combine ingredients in a bowl and serve over a bed of greens or eat as is.

WORDS FROM LISA:

I love the extra flavor the flavored fig and blueberry vinegars give to a dish. I prefer those over the regular balsamic, but just in case you don't have them, you can use regular balsamic vinegar. Better yet, combine blueberries, figs, and some cold-pressed olive oil to make your own dressing!

Chickpea Radish Salad

Prep: 15 minutes

1 cup chick peas, sprouted
1 bunch radishes, thinly sliced
¼ cup red onion, chopped
½ cup black olives, pitted and quartered
¼ cup scallions, sliced
1 cup fresh flat-leaf parsley leaves,
    hand shredded

1 tablespoon capers, drained
½–1 teaspoon lemon juice
¼–½ cup cold-pressed olive oil
Cracked black pepper, to taste
Sea salt, to taste

Toss ingredients together and serve. Can be served on a bed of greens, as a crunchy filling in a collard wrap with pâté filler, or eat as is.

The 3 A's Salad (Arugula, Artichoke, Asparagus Salad)

Prep: 20 minutes

½ pound mung bean noodles, soaked
½ cup artichoke hearts, chopped
½ cup asparagus, cut on angle, bite size pieces

1 bunch arugula, shredded
Scallions, sliced
¼ cup fresh chives, chopped

Soak mung beans in a glass dish in water in dehydrator or on kitchen counter until softened. Once the mung bean noodles are softened, drain. Combine mung bean noodles, scallions, chives, artichoke hearts, asparagus, and arugula in a large glass dish and set aside.

3 A's Dressing

Prep: 10 minutes

¼ cup cold-pressed olive oil
2 tablespoons orange juice

1 tablespoon orange zest
1 tablespoon almond butter

Combine ingredients in a Vitamix® high-speed blender. Add sea salt and black cracked pepper to taste or as desired. Pour dressing over noodles or serve separately and let each guest pour as little or as much dressing as they like. Optionally, sprinkle with pine nuts.

Rainbow Chard Salad

Prep: 15 minutes

2 bunches rainbow colored Swiss chard,
  remove stems, shred, or chiffonade
2 tablespoons pumpkin seed oil
1 teaspoon sea salt

1 tablespoon lemon juice
¼ cup black olives
¼ cup hemp seeds
¼ cup red pepper, chopped

In a bowl, combine the rainbow Swiss chard, pumpkin seed oil, lemon juice, and sea salt. Using your hands, massage the Swiss chard with the seed oil, lemon juice, and sea salt until it breaks down and becomes wilted. Set aside.

Combine black olives, hemp seeds, and red pepper with the wilted Swiss chard, toss, and serve. I like the rainbow Swiss chard because it makes your salad look so colorful.

Wilted Spinach Salad

Prep: 15 minutes

Large bag or container of baby spinach
2 tablespoons Austria's Finest,
  Naturally® pumpkin seed oil
1 tablespoon lemon juice
1 teaspoon sea salt
1 teaspoon wheat free tamari

¼ cup sun-dried tomatoes, chopped or
  cut into small pieces
¼ cup olives, chopped into small pieces
½ cup shitake mushrooms, remove
  stems and sliced
Pearl onions, peeled and chopped

In a large bowl, combine baby spinach, pumpkin seed oil, lemon juice, sea salt, and tamari until the spinach is thoroughly coated and wilted. Combine sun-dried tomatoes, olives, mushrooms, and onions with wilted spinach; toss, serve, and eat.

Watermelon Radish Salad

Prep: 15 minutes

1 pound watermelon meat, cubed
1 bunch watermelon radishes,
  sliced thinly
⅛ cup lime juice

¼ cup fresh mint leaves, shredded
¼ cup sliced almonds
1–2 tablespoon raw cacao nibs

Combine cubed watermelon and radishes in a bowl. Toss with lime juice, shredded mint leaves, raw cacao nibs, and sliced almonds.

Rosemary & Chive Scallions

Prep: 10 minutes

1 pound scallions, root end removed,
  cut on angle into 1-inch slices
¼ cup fresh chives, chopped
¼ cup fresh rosemary, chopped

¼ cup Austria's Finest, Naturally®
  pumpkin seed oil
1 teaspoon orange juice
Sea salt, to taste

Combine the ingredients together and toss. This is another dish that can be dehydrated at 105°F so that the flavors meld, and so that the scallions and herbs soften.

WORDS FROM LISA:

This dish can be eaten as a side salad or as part of a green salad. You can start with the greens, add a little sauerkraut, several spoonfuls of rosemary, chives, scallions, sliced avocado, and tomatoes, or you can combine and build your salad with whatever you like.

My Favorite Fruit Salad

Prep: 30 minutes

2 Gala apples, cored and cubed
Figs, quartered and stems removed
2 peaches, cubed and pit removed
4 cups watermelon, cubed, seed
   removed
2 bananas, sliced
2 pears, cored and cubed

½ cup blueberries
½ cup strawberries, quartered
½ cup raspberries
2 cups pineapple
½ seedless grapes, halved
Orange juice, freshly squeezed

Combine fruit salad ingredients in large bowl and cover with freshly squeezed orange juice. The orange juice not only adds flavor, but helps to keep the fruit from turning brown before it is served.

Asparagus Artichoke Salad

Prep: 15 minutes

1 bunch asparagus (or 10 spears)
5 artichoke hearts, quartered
1 tablespoon lemon juice
1 tablespoon fresh chives, chopped
1 tablespoon fresh dill, chopped

1–2 cloves garlic, minced
2 tablespoons cold-pressed olive oil
1–2 tablespoons pumpkin seed oil
Sea salt, to taste
Cracked black pepper, to taste

Combine ingredients in a bowl and toss. Remove the hard end of the asparagus spears and cut in one inch pieces on an angle. This dish can also be placed in a glass dish and warmed in a dehydrator.

Snap Pea Pine Nut Salad

Prep: 20 minutes

1 cup sugar snap peas, trimmed and
   strings removed
4 cups spring mix
¼ cup fresh basil, chopped
¼ cup fresh mint, shredded

⅛ cup fresh rosemary, chopped
¼ cup pine nuts
1 tablespoon cold-pressed olive oil
1 tablespoon lemon juice
¼ cup raspberries

Combine ingredients in large bowl and toss.

Cauliflower Kale Salad

Prep: 20 minutes

1 cup cauliflower, chopped into crumbly,
   couscous sized pieces
¼ cup red onion, chopped
1–2 cloves garlic, minced
1½ teaspoons dried thyme
1½ teaspoons ground cumin

1 tablespoon lemon juice
1 tablespoon cold-pressed olive oil
4 cups kale, chiffonade
Sea salt, to taste
Cracked black pepper, to taste

Combine kale, lemon juice, sea salt, and cold-pressed olive oil. Massage ingredients
together until kale starts to wilt. Add to the kale salad the cauliflower, red onion,
garlic, and seasonings, and toss.

Baby Bok Choy Broccoli Salad

Prep: 25 minutes

4 cups baby bok choy, chopped and
   shredded
½ cup kelp noodles, drained
1 cup broccoli flowerets
6–8 shitake mushrooms, sliced thinly
4 scallions, sliced

1 teaspoon ginger, finely grated
1 tablespoon yellow miso
1 tablespoon wheat free tamari
½ cup sesame oil
1 tablespoon toasted sesame oil

In a large bowl, combine the bok choy, kelp noodles, broccoli, shitake mushrooms, and scallions. In a Vitamix® high-speed blender, combine the ginger, yellow miso, wheat free tamari, sesame oil, and toasted sesame oil. Pour the dressing over the vegetable mixture, toss, and serve. If you want the flavors to meld and marinate, set in a dehydrator at 105°F until flavors meld and marinate.

Apple & Fig Salad

Prep: 15 minutes

4 granny smith apples, cored and sliced
   thinly
5 figs, coarsely chopped
1 cup raw walnuts, soaked, drained,
   dried, and roughly chopped
½ teaspoon ground cinnamon

¼ teaspoon ground ginger
⅛ teaspoon ground cloves
1 teaspoon raw honey, maple syrup,
   or agave
1 cup orange juice

Combine apples, figs, and walnuts in a bowl and set aside. In a bowl, whisk together the cinnamon, ginger, cloves, raw honey, and orange juice. Pour over apple, fig, and walnut mixture. Coat well. Eat as is, or you can warm it in a glass dish in a dehydrator at 105°F.

   Sprinkle with additional cinnamon to garnish.

Cabbage Salad & Dressing

Prep: 15 minutes

Salad
4 cups green cabbage, shredded
1 cup red cabbage, shredded
Carrots, peeled and shredded
3 tablespoons fresh dill, chopped
1 cup red pepper, chopped
6 scallions, chopped

Dressing
1 teaspoon sea salt
1 tablespoon pineapple juice
1 tablespoon wheat free tamari
1–2 cloves garlic
½ cup pine nuts or cashews
½ cup cold-pressed olive oil
Water, if necessary

Salad
Toss cabbage salad ingredients together in a bowl and set aside.

Dressing
Combine the cabbage salad dressing in a Vitamix® high-speed blender until well blended. Add water a little at a time for a thinner dressing. Pour dressing over cabbage salad and serve, or allow your guests to pour their own dressing over the salad.

Walnut Rice Salad & Dressing

Prep: 30 minutes

Salad
1 cup Wilderness Family Naturals wild rice, blossomed and drained
¼ cup raw walnuts, soaked, drained, and chopped or broken in half
¼ cup dried blueberries, cherries, or cranberries
1 cup cherry tomatoes, quartered (or for a different taste replace tomatoes with figs)
¼ cup black olives, pitted
Dates, pitted and minced

Dressing
2 tablespoons lemon juice
1 tablespoon agave, raw honey or maple syrup
¼ cup cold-pressed olive oil
2 tablespoons wheat free tamari
Cracked pepper and sea salt to taste (optional)

Salad

Combine walnut rice salad ingredients in a bowl and set aside.

Dressing

Combine salad dressing ingredients in a Vitamix® high-speed blender or whisk together in a bowl. Pour over Walnut Rice Salad and toss. You can also place in glass bowl and warm in a dehydrator at 105°F to meld the flavors and to warm the salad.

WORDS FROM LISA:

To blossom Wilderness Family Naturals rice, place rice covered in water in a glass dish in your dehydrator. The warmth of the dehydrator speeds up the blossoming of the rice. This rice grows naturally in the northwest part of the U.S. and Canada, and is not processed rice. Please note that the blossoming of the rice could take a couple of days. You'll know when it is ready when the rice looks like it has been cooked.

Napa Cabbage Salad with Creamy Jalapeño Pepper Dressing

Natalie Norman

Prep: 25 minutes

1 cup raw cashews

1 head Napa cabbage, core removed and thinly sliced

3 stalks celery, diced

¾ cup water, or as needed

3 tablespoons nutritional yeast

2 small green jalapeño peppers, seeded

1 Medjool date, pit removed

2 tablespoons lemon juice

3 tablespoons apple cider vinegar

Ground black pepper, to taste

1 teaspoon pink salt, or to taste

In a large bowl, toss together sliced cabbage and celery. Set aside. In your Vita-mix® or other blender, add all other ingredients and blend until perfectly creamy. Taste and adjust salt and lemon juice as desired. Toss repeatedly with cabbage/celery and refrigerate for about 30 minutes in order to allow the flavors to marry. Enjoy!

Contributor's Note: Napa cabbage is like that friend who goes along with any plans you make and just adopts the characteristics of her surroundings. While that's not necessarily the strongest trait in a person, it's a great trait in cabbage! It means that you can consume large amounts of raw cabbage in delicious sauces that are so good you won't be able to stop eating it by the bowlful. This is also a great recipe to bring to a potluck or other event where food is being served socially.

Coconut-Hemp Seed Dressing

Antanas Vainius
Prep: 5 minutes **Soak:** 15–30 minutes

½ cup hemp seeds
2 teaspoons lime juice
1 cup coconut milk or water
1 medium garlic clove
½ inch ginger, grated

½ yellow onion, minced
1 inch tamarind or 1 teaspoon paste
2 tablespoons nama shoyu
½ teaspoon lemongrass

Soak hempseeds in lime juice, coconut/water for at least 15 minutes. Add all other ingredients, and blend until creamy.

Asian "No Oil" Blender Dressing

Ken Immer
Prep: 15 minutes   **Yield:** approximately 1 cup

¼ cup apple cider vinegar (Bragg's®)
3 tablespoons tamari
3 limes, juiced
½ teaspoon umeboshi plum paste
½ garlic clove

½ tablespoon ginger, freshly grated
2½ ounces Graw Foods grawnola nuggets, sweet and sour flavor (or your favorite granola)

Combine all ingredients in a high-speed blender and blend until creamy and thick. If you prefer a thinner dressing, you can add 1–2 tablespoon of water.

Mayonnaise and Dip/Dressing Base

Natalie Norman
Prep: 7 minutes

½ cup raw cashews
1 tablespoon apple cider vinegar

1 tablespoon extra virgin olive oil
1 pinch salt, or to taste

Blend in your Vitamix® or other blender. Depending on the speed and power of your machine, you might need to drizzle in tiny bits of water to help thin the mayonnaise to achieve the right consistency. You can store this for up to a week in the refrigerator.

Contributor's Note: This super simple mayonnaise recipe can be used on its own or modified to form the basis of salad dressings and dips including garlic aioli, ranch, or herb dip. Some delicious modifications include:

- Garlic Aioli: Blend with one small clove of garlic and a squeeze of lemon juice. Adjust salt if desired.
- Ranch Dressing: Blend with one small clove of garlic, a few tablespoons of water (watch for consistency), and a squeeze of lemon juice, then *lightly* pulse in a small handful of chopped fresh parsley, chives, dill (optional), and black pepper.
- Herb Dip: Lightly pulse in your favorite chopped herbs with a dash of garlic powder and onion powder.

Creamy Lemon, Dill & Garlic Salad Dressing/Dip

Kimberton Whole Foods, www.kimbertonwholefoods.com
Prep: 15 minutes   **Serves:** 4

½ cup raw cashews, soaked and drained
Juice from half a lemon
1½ tablespoons dill weed (or to taste)
1 clove garlic (or 2 cloves for more
    garlic flavor)

2 tablespoons olive oil
1 tablespoon flax or hemp oil
½ teaspoon sea salt (or to taste)
¼ cup water

Toss all ingredients into a food processor and process until smooth and creamy.
Toss with your favorite salad or serve as a dip with your favorite raw crackers or
veggies.

    Your taste buds will tingle with this delicious dressing that is full of flavor. It is
tangy and creamy and can be used as either a dressing for salads or as a dip for
crudités.

Creamy Green Garlic & Dill Dressing

Barbara Shevkun (Rawfully Tempting)
Prep: 15 minutes

½ cup cashews
6 tablespoons olive oil
1–2 large cloves garlic, minced
2 tablespoons fresh dill, chopped
½ cup water (add more if needed)

2 tablespoons horseradish, grated
    (optional)
2 teaspoons raw honey or liquid
    sweetener
⅛ teaspoon Himalayan sea salt

Blend all ingredients until creamy. Drizzle over salad or serve as a dip for
vegetables.

Creamy Peppercorn Ranch Dressing

Kimberton Whole Foods, www.kimbertonwholefoods.com
Prep: 15 minutes   **Yield:** 2¼ cups

⅓ cup water
⅓ cup lemon juice
⅔ cup hemp seed
5 cloves garlic

2 teaspoons whole black peppercorns
1 teaspoon Himalayan salt
1 cup cold-pressed olive oil

Place all ingredients (except olive oil) in a high-powered blender. Blend from low to high speed until smooth. With the blender running on low, pour in the olive oil to emulsify. Gradually turn up the power until ingredients are combined. The result should be very thick, creamy, and delicious. Add as a topping to any variety of fantastic fresh veggies!

Bok Choy with Ginger Peach Dressing

Tiffany Robbins
Prep: 10 minutes

4 cups bok choy

Ginger Peach Shrub
2-3 peaches
A thumb's length of ginger (or more, if desired)
¼ cup sweetener (honey, agave, or maple syrup)
Apple cider vinegar

Dressing
½ cup ginger peach shrub
¼ cup extra virgin olive oil
1 tablespoon light miso

Peel peaches. Blend peaches, ginger, and sweetener. Strain and measure the mixture. Add an equal amount of apple cider vinegar to the mixture. Stir and let sit overnight, stirring occasionally. Blend all dressing ingredients to emulsify. Chop bok choy and marinate with ginger peach dressing.

Contributor's Note: Ginger Peach Shrub can also be enjoyed by adding a few table-spoons to a bottle of sparkling water. Just pour off a few inches of the sparkling water from the bottle and reserve. Add ginger peach shrub and stir with a long wooden skewer. Add reserved sparkling water. Cap and refrigerate to chill or serve over ice.

Asian Slaw

Kimberton Whole Foods, www.kimbertonwholefoods.com
Prep: 25 minutes

¼ cup raw peanuts
1 chunk ginger (about 2 tablespoons),
 freshly grated
¼ cup sesame seeds
2 tablespoons olive oil
1 tablespoon sesame oil
1 tablespoon peanut oil
5 tablespoons nama shoyu

4 tablespoons raw apple cider vinegar
4 tablespoons raw honey
½ head of green cabbage, thinly sliced
¼ (or more) head of red (purple) cabbage,
 thinly sliced
2 carrots, julienned
1 yellow pepper, thinly sliced lengthwise

To make the dressing, first process the peanuts, ginger, and sesame seeds and set aside in a bowl. Add the liquid ingredients (olive oil, sesame oil, peanut oil, nama shoyu, apple cider vinegar, and raw honey) and stir.

For the salad, toss all sliced ingredients (cabbages, carrots, and yellow pepper) into a huge bowl and pour on the sauce and mix well.

For a lighter salad, use less dressing or more cabbage.

Contributor's Note: You can use another sweetener, such as agave, if honey doesn't sit well with you. You can also use all olive oil instead of the varied oils suggested here.

Date Dill Slaw

Brenda Cobb (Founder of Living Foods Institute® and author of *The Living Foods Lifestyle*, www.livingfoodsinstitute.com)
Prep: 30 minutes

2 cups purple or green cabbage, chopped
½ cup carrots, chopped
½ cup yellow, orange or red pepper, chopped
½ cup green onions with tops, chopped

½ cup olive oil
½ cup lemon juice
2 teaspoons Celtic or Himalayan sea salt
2 tablespoons dried dill or
    6 tablespoons fresh dill
6 Medjool dates, pitted

Using a food processor, chop the cabbage into chunky pieces and put in a bowl. Do the same for the carrots and put in the bowl. Chop the pepper and green onions by hand and put in the bowl. Put the olive oil, lemon juice, sea salt, dill, and dates into another bowl. Mash up the dates so the dressing becomes creamy, but leave some of the dates in small chunks. Add the vegetables and toss.

Cabbage Salad Kraut

Prep: 25 minutes

4 cups green cabbage, shredded
1 cup red cabbage, shredded
1 cup red pepper, chopped
3 carrots, peeled and shredded

1 tablespoon fresh dill, chopped
1–2 tablespoons kosher salt or sea salt
Caraway seeds to taste (optional)

Combine vegetables in a large bowl or run through a Tribest® Slowstar juicer using the mincing blade. If you are doing this by hand, pound the vegetables with a can, a mallet, or whatever you have available to release the juices. Once the juices are released, add one tablespoon of salt and work it in. Taste to see if it is salty enough. Add a little more salt at a time. Remember, sauerkraut is supposed to be salty, but not *too* salty. The salt and the juices are what help the salad to ferment.

Once you have combined the salt, and the juices are released from the cabbage kraut, tightly pack in to a canning jar, making sure to leave 1 inch of air space at the top and be sure that the mixture is coated in liquid. Screw on the lid loosely and set on the counter to ferment. This should take approximately 5 days. In the heat of the summer it could ferment within a couple of days; in the winter time it will take a little longer.

Herb Dressing

Prep: 15 minutes

½ cup fresh dill, chopped
½ cup chives, chopped
1 scallion, chopped
½ cup cold-pressed olive oil

½ teaspoon orange zest
1 tablespoon orange juice
Sea salt, to taste
Cracked black pepper, to taste

Combine ingredients in a Vitamix® high-speed blender. Pulse, so you still keep the texture of the herbs and scallions. You can replace the fresh herbs with your favorite herbs.

Caesar Dressing

Brenda Cobb (Founder of Living Foods Institute® and author of *The Living Foods Lifestyle*, www.livingfoodsinstitute.com)
Prep: 10 minutes

3 large cloves garlic
⅔ cup lemon juice
⅔ cup olive oil

3 tablespoons dulse seaweed flakes
1 teaspoon Himalayan sea salt

Mince the garlic very fine and combine with the lemon juice, olive oil, dulse, and sea salt. Place dressing mixture in a glass jar, cover, and shake well.

Wait until right before you are ready to serve this and toss with romaine salad greens, completely coating all the leaves.

Serve and feast.

Creamy Cucumber Dressing

Karen Ranzi (Author of *Creating Healthy Children*)
Prep: 15 minutes

2 tablespoons pine nuts
1½ cups cucumbers, peeled and chopped
2 stalks celery

2 pitted dates, soaked for ½ hour if not soft
½ lemon, juiced
½ cup fresh dill, chopped

Blend all the ingredients in a high-speed blender. Great as dressing on a leafy green salad.

Creamy Sweet Balsamic

Sheryll Chavarria (Raw Can Roll Café and Pure Body Spa, Douglassville, PA, www.rawcanrollcafe.com)
Prep: 10 minutes

¼–½ cup olive oil
¾ cup water
1 cup balsamic vinegar
3 or 4 cloves garlic

1 tablespoon sea salt
4 tablespoons agave
2 handfuls basil
1 avocado

Place all ingredients together in a Vitamix® and blend until creamy.

Creamy Tahini Salad Dressing

Sheryll Chavarria (Raw Can Roll Café and Pure Body Spa, Douglassville, PA, www.rawcanrollcafe.com)
Prep: 7 minutes

1 cup tahini
½ cup apple cider vinegar
3 cloves garlic
1 tablespoon ginger
2 tablespoons agave or raw honey

¼ cup tamari
¼ cup fresh orange juice
1 tablespoon psyllium
¾ cup water

Combine ingredients together in a Vitamix® High Speed Blender until blended well. Use as a dressing on greens, as a dipping sauce for your sushi or nori rolls, or as a dipping sauce for crudités.

Ginger Salad Dressing

Laura Sipes Wright (YouTube: StarFlower99654)
Prep: 30 minutes
Soak: while you are working prepping second set of ingredients (about 30 minutes)

First Set of Ingredients:
¼ cup raw ketchup
2 tablespoons fresh tomato, diced
1 date, pitted and diced
2 tablespoons sun-dried tomato
¼ cup soaking water

Second Set of Ingredients:
¼ cup ginger root, grated
¼ cup celery, minced

1 cup onion, minced
1 clove garlic, minced
1 teaspoon sea salt
½ teaspoon ground black pepper
1 cup cold-pressed olive oil
⅔ cup apple cider vinegar
2 tablespoons + 2 teaspoons nama
    shoyu or wheat-free tamari
2 tablespoons + 2 teaspoons raw honey
2 tablespoons + 2 teaspoons lemon juice

First Set of Ingredients:
Soak all ingredients for 30 minutes. Once ketchup soaking ingredients have finished soaking, blend together in a high-speed blender and set aside.

Second Set of Ingredients:

Combine all ingredients with the soaked ingredients and blend on high speed. Add the soaking water, if necessary, to reach the desired thickness.

Contributor's Note: You can also use this dressing on an avocado salad.

Traditional Ranch Dressing

Sheryll Chavarria (Raw Can Roll Café and Pure Body Spa, Douglassville, PA, www.rawcanrollcafe.com)

2 cups cashews, soaked
Water (as needed)
1 teaspoon lemon juice
½ tablespoon onion powder
½ tablespoon garlic powder
¼ cup dill
¼ cup parsley
Sea salt to taste

Blend all the ingredients (except dill and parsley) together in a high-speed blender. Then add the herbs for a very light blend (you do not want the dressing to turn green; you just want flecks of green).

9

Soups

Eagle Skyfire's Soup

Eagle Skyfire

Prep: 30–40 minutes   **Yield:** approximately 8 cups

5 pounds potatoes
8 ounces sharp cheese, cut into thick
    slices (white cheddar or Hoffman)
8 ounces cream cheese, cut into chunks
3 tablespoons onion powder

3 tablespoons garlic powder
½ cup milk
Salt, to taste
Black pepper, to taste (enough to
    give the soup a nice "snap")

Peel and cut the potatoes into coarse chunks. Put the potatoes into a pot and fill the pot with water until it just covers the potatoes. Boil the potatoes for approximately 40 to 50 minutes. A knife should easily go through them when cooked thoroughly.

Separate the potato water but do not throw it out. Put potatoes back into the pot. Put cheeses onto the steaming potatoes and mash until cheese and potato are smooth. It is important that the cheese and potatoes are mashed *before* adding the liquids or else the soup will turn out lumpy. Add enough potato water and milk to make the consistency that of a smooth but thick chowder. Stir in onion powder and garlic powder. Stir in salt and black pepper to taste.

Note: Potatoes will reabsorb liquid; hence this soup will thicken when it is stored. Add just enough milk (which might only be a splash) and stir to restore the soup to its original smooth texture.

Contributor's Note: This recipe is from my father's people. It is a traditional Native recipe that has been carried down for many generations. Potatoes are one of our favorite foods and we have many varieties, including one that is very tasty and purple in color. Here I give the cheeses that are easiest to find in this country, and which taste the closest to the ones that are used back home. This potato soup is different from others that I've had in that it is very smooth and has the consistency of thick chowder with no lumps. This soup is commonly made during the winter, when hearty food helps a person to keep warm during a cold night in the Andes Mountains. This is definitely a comfort food that makes you feel cozy and content.

I asked Eagle Skyfire to share a traditional Native recipe. Remember that whether it's a traditional Native recipe or your personal family traditional recipe, you can always convert your favorite dishes to match your eating lifestyle and needs. We hope this very traditional recipe will inspire you to look at your family's traditional recipes and see how you can make them healthier for your holiday and family gatherings.

To make Eagle Skyfire's recipe raw, cook the potatoes in the potato water, keeping the temperature below 118°F. For the cheese, you can substitute raw cheese if you are not allergic to dairy.

Snowcap Chowder

Chili Smith Family Foods, adapted by Lisa Montgomery
Prep: 35 minutes   **Serves:** 6–8

10 ounces snowcap beans
2 tablespoons butter
2 tablespoons onion, minced
3 tablespoons flour
½ teaspoon paprika
2½ cups coconut milk

2 cups water (combined with 1 tablespoon curry powder)
3 medium potatoes, peeled and diced
2 carrots, sliced
1 medium onion, coarsely chopped
⅓ pounds mushrooms, sliced (optional)
Salt and pepper, to taste

Rinse and pick over beans. Place beans in a slow cooker and cover with 2 inches of water. Place slow cooker's temperature setting on low, so temperature is 118°For lower, ensuring the dish remains raw. Once beans are tender and mushy you can either drain off the water or add potatoes, carrots, onions, mushrooms, and seasonings. Cook on low (below 118°F) until desired doneness.

South of the Border Gazpacho

Karmyn Malone (www.karmynmalone.com)
Prep: 20 minutes   **Serves:** 2

4 cups Campari or other fine tomatoes, halved or quartered
1 cup red bell pepper, sliced
2 medium celery stalks

8 sun-dried tomatoes, halved, soaked, and drained
2 tablespoon raw honey or raw agave
2 handfuls fresh cilantro
½ jalapeño pepper (more or less to taste)

Add all the ingredients to a high-speed blender in the order listed.

Pour gazpacho into 2 serving bowls. Garnish with chopped, peeled cucumber and some fresh chopped cilantro.

Contributor's Note: If using a Vitamix® blender, I recommend using the slowest 2 speeds. Otherwise, you will end up with a marinara sauce instead of gazpacho.

Make sure to push down the ingredients in the blender with the tamper. This recipe works best in a high-powered blender like the Vitamix®. If using a regular blender, use a celery stalk to push the ingredients down.

Sweet Corn Chowder

Brenda Hinton (Rawsome Creations, www.rawsomecreations.com)
Prep: 20 minutes

6 cups of sweet corn divided into equal portions (about six ears of fresh corn or two 16-ounce bags frozen sweet corn)
1 cup almond milk, see page 162
2 tablespoons lime juice
2 teaspoons white miso
1 teaspoon fresh garlic, (1 garlic clove)

1 tablespoon Red Star Nutritional yeast
1 teaspoon cumin
1 teaspoon salt
⅛ teaspoon jalapeño chili powder
¼ cup minced red onion
Chili flakes and freshly ground pepper, to garnish

In a Vitamix® High Speed Blender, place 3 cups of the corn, along with the almond milk, lime juice, white miso, garlic, nutritional yeast, cumin, salt, and jalapeño powder. Blend until mixture is smooth. Transfer mixture to a mixing bowl and gently fold in the remaining three cups of corn and the minced onion. Garnish with chili flakes and freshly ground pepper. Serve chilled or at room temperature. May be stored in an airtight glass container the in the refrigerator for up to one week, or frozen for up to two months.

If there is any corn soup left it can be used to make corn tortillas using Brenda's "More Than a Wrap Mold." Brenda's "More Than a Wrap" mold is a tool that can help you form perfectly shaped tortillas and is available at Rawsome Creations. Yields 5 cups.

Summer Awakening

Arnold Kaufman
Prep: 7 minutes

> 2 cucumbers, quartered
> 2 tomatoes, quartered
> 2 oranges, quartered

Blend the ingredients together and enjoy.

WORDS FROM LISA:

Get ready to charge with the power of the light brigade! Arnold feels there is a charge of light, peace, and sun when the colors of three different fruits are blended together.

Arnold's Soup

Arnold Kaufman
Prep: 5 minutes

4 ingredients (examples include apples, avocados, lemon juice, and greens)

Combine four ingredients in a Vitamix® high-speed blender. Arnold is leaving it up to you to decide which four ingredients you would like in your soup. This example shows which four we picked.

Smokey Backyard Tomato Soup with Hot Red Pepper Sauce

Barbara Shevkun (Rawfully Tempting)
Prep: 30 minutes

Soup
3 cups mixed garden tomatoes, roughly chopped
¼ cup sundried tomatoes, soaked
¾ cup soak water (from sundried tomatoes)
¼ cup cashews
½ small clove garlic, minced
1 red bell pepper, roughly chopped
¼ cup red onion, chopped
¼ teaspoon onion powder
⅛ teaspoon garlic powder
1 tablespoon fresh basil, chopped
1 tablespoon cilantro leaves, chopped
1/16 teaspoon smoked paprika
1 pinch cayenne
⅛ teaspoon sea salt (eliminate if sundried tomatoes are salty)

Hot Red Pepper Sauce
2 tablespoons leftover soup (from sides of blender)
3 tablespoons olive oil
½ red bell pepper
1 red chili pepper, chopped

To Serve
Sliced avocado, for garnish
Red onion, for garnish
Fresh basil or cilantro, for garnish
Pepper, to taste

Soup

Blend garden tomatoes, sundried tomatoes, and half of the soak water. Add more soak water as needed.

Add remaining ingredients and blend until creamy. Taste for seasoning and adjust as needed.

Pour into bowl, leaving about 2 tablespoons of soup in blender.

Hot Red Pepper Sauce

Scrape remains of soup into blender and add remaining ingredients. Add more oil (or water) if needed to blend.

To Serve

Pour soup into individual bowls.

Drizzle a small amount of Hot Red Pepper Sauce over soup and garnish with sliced avocado, red onion, and fresh basil or cilantro. Add fresh cracked pepper and serve.

Vegetable Soup

Brenda Cobb (Founder of Living Foods Institute® and author of *The Living Foods Lifestyle*, www.livingfoodsinstitute.com)

Prep: 20 minutes

Soup Base
1 red, yellow, or orange bell pepper
9 very ripe Roma tomatoes
3 stalks celery
⅔ cup water
1 teaspoon Celtic sea salt
2 teaspoon dried oregano

Pinch cayenne pepper

Vegetables
2 Roma tomatoes, chopped
½ cup celery, chopped
½ cup red pepper, chopped
½ zucchini or yellow squash

Soup Base

Blend all the ingredients in a Vitamix® blender until creamy. Remove and put in a bowl.

Vegetables

Chop the vegetables into very small bite-size pieces. Combine the chopped vegetables with the soup and enjoy.

Tomato Squash Soup

Prep: 20 minutes

4 cups, tomatoes, chopped
4 cups butternut squash, peeled and
    seeded
1 cup, sun-dried tomatoes
1 teaspoon lemon juice
1⅓ tablespoons sea salt
3 cloves garlic

1 teaspoon coriander
1 teaspoon curry
1 cup water
½ teaspoon garlic powder
½ cup red onion, chopped
Cracked pepper to taste

Blend ingredients together in a Vitamix® High Speed Blender and warm on a low heat in a Crock-Pot® or in a pot on low, or use hot water, and the Vitamix® process will warm the soup.

Cream of Tomato Soup

Arnold Kaufman
Prep: 7 minutes

3 tomatoes
3 sun-dried tomatoes, soaked
1 stalk celery

1 date, pitted
1 cup water

Place all ingredients in a Vitamix® high-speed blender until the mixture becomes creamy. Blend a little longer if you wish your soup to be warm.

Pho Base

Brooke Preston
Prep: 30 minutes **Serves:** 8

1½ cups coconut aminos
1 cup Brazil nuts
1 cup cashews
⅔ cup honey
6 cloves garlic
1 teaspoon black pepper
⅓ cup rice vinegar
½ cup toasted sesame oil
¾ cup olive oil

4 cups Thai coconut meat (with coconut water, as needed)
½ teaspoon cinnamon
½ teaspoon ground cloves
1 bunch cilantro
½ teaspoon cardamom
½ teaspoon ground dried ginger
½ teaspoon fennel
¾ cup lime juice

Blend ingredients in a high-speed blender until completely smooth. Pho can be stored for up to 5 days in an airtight container in the fridge.

To serve, use 1 cup of pho for each serving. Add 1 cup of hot water for each cup of pho when ready to serve. Serve with spiralized zucchini noodles, cilantro, mild green chilies, mint, Thai coconut, basil, red chili pepper flakes, sprouts (any sprouts or dandelion greens), and ¼ lime wedge.

Sunset Runner Bean Soup

Chili Smith Family Foods, adapted by Lisa Montgomery
Prep: 45 minutes **Serves:** 6–8

2–3 cups sunset runner beans
2 tablespoons extra virgin olive oil
1 medium onion, chopped
½ cup celery, chopped
2 cloves garlic, peeled and crushed
1 leek, cleaned and chopped
3 carrots, peeled and chopped
2 turnips, peeled and chopped
1 cup mushrooms, sliced (optional)
2 zucchini, sliced

3 medium potatoes, peeled and chopped
3–4 cups water
1–2 tablespoons curry powder
1 tablespoon dried basil
2 tablespoons dried parsley or 3 tablespoons fresh parsley, chopped
Pinch of sage
2 cups chopped cabbage
½ cup dried pasta
Salt and pepper, to taste

Rinse and pick over beans. Combine water and curry powder to create your own vegetarian broth. Combine the ingredients (except the broth) in a slow cooker with the temperature set below 118°F. Start checking doneness at 45 minutes. Drain cooked beans when desired doneness is reached. Add broth with enough water to cover the beans by an inch or so. Add salt and pepper to taste.

Runner Cannellini Bean Soup

Chili Smith Family Foods, adapted by Lisa Montgomery
Prep: 25 minutes

2 cups (1 pound) runner cannellini beans
4 cups (1 quart) all natural chicken broth
   (for a raw version, substitute water,
    1 tablespoon curry powder, or poultry
    seasoning)
1 medium size red onion
2 stalks celery, thinly sliced
8 strips cooked smokehouse bacon,
   diced (remove for a raw/vegetarian
   option)

1 tablespoon Dash original seasoning
1 tablespoon hickory smoke flavor
   (optional)
Salt and pepper, to taste
Low sodium chicken broth powder,
   to taste (optional)

Place beans in a large pot with 8 cups cold water and cover. Let beans soak overnight (at least 8 hours) or use quick soak method. After soaking, always drain and rinse the beans. Discard the soaking water.

Cover beans with 8 cups fresh water and 4 cups water with poultry seasoning/curry powder. Place in slow cooker with temperature set on low (less than 118°F). Heat beans until desired doneness. Add the celery, onions, and seasonings. Options: You can also add sun-dried tomatoes and chopped fresh tomatoes as well.

Pineapple Soup

Joel Odhner
Prep: 20 minutes

1 pineapple, cubed with skin removed
1–2 cucumbers
1 jalapeño (optional)
¼ cup lime juice

Pinch sea salt
¼ cup cold-pressed olive oil
⅛ cup onion, chopped

Blend together the ingredients in a high-speed blender and serve.

Contributor's Note: I love this soup. The pineapple and cucumber make it so cool and refreshing.

Apple and Butternut Squash Raw Soup

Kimberton Whole Foods, www.kimbertonwholefoods.com
Prep: 25 minutes   **Soak:** Pumpkin seeds, 4 hours

2 apples, cored and cut
3½ ounces peeled butternut squash
½ orange, peeled
2 tablespoons lemon juice
½ red onion

1 cup almond milk
3 tablespoons pumpkin seeds, soaked
1 tablespoon sundried tarragon
2 tablespoons chopped parsley
Salt and pepper, to taste

Blend all ingredients (except the parsley) until you have obtained a smooth and creamy soup. (You may need to add up to a glass of fresh water to obtain the desired consistency.) Serve with sprinkled parsley and season with salt and pepper to taste.

Apple Butternut Squash Soup

Cara Graver (The Cob Studio, www.thecobstudio.com)
Prep: 20 minutes

3 cups butternut squash, cubed
   (unpeeled)
1 large apple unpeeled and cored
2 ribs celery
1 tablespoon cold-pressed olive oil
1 small onion

½ clove garlic
Small piece ginger, to your liking
Fresh thyme and/or other fresh or dried
   herbs to taste
Salt to taste
1¼ cups water

Place all ingredients in a Vitamix® High Speed Blender. You can add the squash seeds for extra nutrition. Blend until smooth, start with low speed and then move to high, and then warm.

Pineapple Green Soup
(*or* Is It a Soup or Smoothie?)

Prep: 10 minutes

2 handfuls greens
1 cup cucumber
1 green apple, cored and sliced

2 cups pineapple chunks
1 cup water

Combine the above ingredients in a Vitamix® High Speed Blender. This soup is a cool refreshing soup. I created this recipe in the wintertime, so don't be afraid of eating a cool refreshing soup in the wintertime.

Intuitive Tomato Rice Cabbage Soup (Two Versions)

Prep: 15 minutes

1 quart cold-packed raw tomatoes
½ red onion, finely chopped
1–2 cups shredded cabbage, bite-size
1 cup frozen heirloom organic cherry
  tomatoes

½ cup sun-dried tomatoes
1 cup nature's wilderness rice
1 teaspoon sea salt
3 cranks of freshly ground pepper
½ teaspoon garlic granules

Combine all of the ingredients in a Crock-Pot® on low, making sure that the temperature is less than 118°F.

Another time I added:

2 stalks celery, finely chopped
1 medium red onion, finely chopped

½ cup red onion, finely chopped
Substitution of quinoa for the rice
  (optional)

Mango Tomato Soup

Dr. Douglas Graham
Prep: 5 minutes   **Yield:** one full blender

2–3 ripe mangoes
4 medium red tomatoes

Cut the side "cheeks" off the mango and use a large spoon to scoop out the flesh into a blender bowl. Squeeze the remaining flesh from the pit into the blender and blend with the chopped tomatoes until smooth.

This soup can be served warm by running a Vitamix® blender for 2–3 minutes. Add a squeeze of lemon, lime, or some fresh chopped herbs. Enjoy!

Contributor's Note: This is a tomato soup like you've never tasted before. With just two ingredients you can experience the satisfaction of sweet and savory flavors in this easy, low-fat dish.

Dr. Douglas Graham, author of *The 80/10/10 Diet*, happily offers you this simply delicious recipe! To learn more about improving your health with the 80/10/10 diet, visit FoodnSport.com. Also, check out our new "Simply Delicious" eBook series, created by Doug Graham himself with culinary assistance from Chef Katy Craine!

If you enjoyed this recipe, give us your feedback by connecting with us through FoodnSport's Facebook page and YouTube channel.

Creamy Asparagus Soup

Janice Inella
Prep: 30 minutes

1 bunch asparagus (cut tips off) and chop stems for blender
1 avocado (save half for garnish)
2 tablespoons fresh dill, chopped and set aside for garnish
1 cup pure water
1 strip or stick kombu seaweed

1 teaspoon fresh lemon juice
2 cups almond milk
1 small red onion
1 garlic clove
1 tablespoon coconut aminos
2 stalks celery
½ teaspoon sea salt

In a high-speed blender, add all ingredients except asparagus tips, kombu, avocado, and some dill for garnish. Blend until smooth. In a bowl, add asparagus tips and soaked kombu, then pour in the soup and add avocado. Garnish with fresh dill.

This is a wonderful spring soup!

Contributor's Note: To make almond milk, blend together 2 cups almonds and 5–6 cups pure water for 20 seconds, then strain through a nut milk bag.

Red Soup

Marina Grubic
Prep: 15 minutes

17 ounces ripe pears
7 Swiss chard leaves

3 ounces beet
A couple of lemon balm leaves

De-stem the Swiss chard. Remove the seeds and stalks from the pears, peel the beet, and chop both the pears and beets. Blend all together, adding just enough water to blend. Serve in a pudding bowl and decorate with a lemon balm leaf.

Coconut Curry Soup

Ultimate Superfood
Prep: 2 hour   **Serves:** 6

Soup
6 cups coconut milk (homemade or bought)
2 tablespoons ginger, minced
1 teaspoon chopped garlic
2 tablespoons lemon juice
½ cup Ojio™ sacha inchi oil
1 tablespoon Ojio™ palm sugar
1 teaspoon dates
1 teaspoon Ojio™ Himalayan salt
2 tablespoons Ojio™ coconut aminos

1 tablespoon curry powder
1 teaspoon Ojio™ turmeric extract
1 jalapeño pepper, diced

Toppings
1 avocado, cubed
⅓ cup tomato, diced
⅓ cup cucumber, diced
½ cup cilantro leaves
1 cup shitake mushrooms, marinated

To make coconut milk, use 4 fresh coconuts. Scoop or cut away coconut meat and add to blender together with coconut water. Blend on high until liquefied. Make the shitake marinade by marinating the shitake mushrooms in a mixture of equal parts Ojio™ coconut aminos and Ojio™ yacon syrup, about 1 tablespoon each.

Add soup base ingredients to blender and puree until smooth. Adjust flavor to taste, with additional Ojio™ Himalayan salt or Ojio™ palm sugar and continue to blend until smooth. Pour soup into six bowls; add toppings and serve.

Contributor's Note: Featuring the healing power of coconut milk and omega-3 rich sacha inchi oil, this soup is a refreshingly lighter twist on traditional curry soups, yet it is packed with nutritional value. Cilantro, tomato, cucumber, and avocado toppings make for a cool, satisfying palette experience.

Cream of Broccoli Soup

Ultimate Superfood
Prep: 30 minutes   **Serves:** 4–6

3 cups water
1 cup Ojio™ hemp seeds
1 teaspoon Ojio™ agave nectar
2 cups broccoli, florets only
1 avocado, pitted
1 garlic clove, peeled
1 tablespoon Ojio™ sacha inchi oil

1 teaspoon Ojio™ holy basil extract
1 teaspoon onion, minced
1 teaspoon Ojio™ Himalayan salt
3 teaspoons nutritional yeast
⅛ teaspoon cumin
⅛ teaspoon black pepper

Blend water, hemp seeds,s and agave until smooth. Add the rest of the ingredients and blend until creamy. Warm on the stovetop or the dehydrator before serving.

Contributor's Note: This warm soup offers a heap of nutritious iron and omega in a flavorful combination of rich superfoods and tasty spices. Cream of broccoli soup is perfect on a cold winter's day or when a warm healthy comfort food would hit the spot.

Red Pepper Split Pea Soup

Prep: 30 minutes

2¼ cups dried split peas

2 quarts water

5 pearl onions, peeled and roughly chopped

2 tablespoons lemon juice

1 teaspoon curry

1 tablespoon cumin

1 teaspoon salt, or to taste

2 red peppers, cleaned and blended in Vitamix® high-speed blender, pour into soup mixture

1 ¼ red onion, chopped

Carrots, peeled and sliced finely

3 celery stalks, cleaned and chopped

Garlic cloves, minced

1 (13.55 ounce) can coconut milk

Cracked pepper, to taste

Soak split peas in water overnight. Next morning, place soaked split peas in slow cooker at temperature on low and/or below 118°F and combine with remaining ingredients. Three hours into the slow cooking time, add the coconut milk. You can make your own coconut milk by blending together the juice and meat of a young Thai Coconut in your Vitamix® high-speed blender.

WORDS FROM LISA:

To make this soup a noodle soup, add mung bean noodles, kelp noodles, or spiralize zucchini to make noodles. You can kick up the seasonings if you need more of an impact.

Almond Creamy Soup Base for 100 Soups

Rhio (author of *Hooked on Raw*)
Prep: 20 minutes   **Sprout:** almonds, 24 hours

1½ cups raw almonds, sprouted
2 cups filtered water
2 lemons, juiced
1 clove garlic

1 tablespoon flaxseed oil
½ teaspoon ground cumin
½ teaspoon Celtic sea salt
Dash Nama Shoyu (optional)

Place all the ingredients in a high-speed blender and blend very well.

Contributor's Note: This is a fantastic soup base that can be used to create numerous wonderful soups.

Creamy Cucumber Soup

Kimberton Whole Foods, www.kimbertonwholefoods.com
Prep: 25 minutes

26 ounces cucumber juice
Meat from one mature coconut
5 marigold flowers
1 seeded cherry bomb pepper
1 tablespoon miso (optional)

½ English cucumber
1½ cups soaked wakame
3 chive flowers (or use chives)
Handful cilantro flowers (or other flower)

Blend the cucumber juice with the meat from one mature coconut. Take the blended mixture and use a nut milk bag to make "cucumber milk". Blend the cucumber milk with the marigolds, cherry bomb pepper, and miso (if desired). Use a spiral slicer to spiralize half of an English cucumber. Pour the cucumber milk into a medium bowl. Add 1 ½ cup of wakame and half of the cucumber spaghetti to the soup base. Garnish with chive flowers and cilantro flowers.
    Note: To make 26 ounces of cucumber juice, juice five regular cucumbers.

Creamy Mushroom Soup with Parsley Garnish

Sheryll Chavarria (Raw Can Roll Café and Pure Body Spa, Douglassville, PA, www.rawcanrollcafe.com)
Prep: 20 minutes

2 cups almond milk
½ cup celery
2 cups mushrooms
1 tablespoon tahini

1 teaspoon cold-pressed olive oil (optional)
¼ cup parsley or scallions, finely chopped (for garnish)
1 tablespoon white miso (or to taste)

Place all the ingredients into a high-speed blender and blend until lightly creamy, being careful not to over-blend. Serve in bowls and garnish with parsley or finely chopped scallions.

Cucumber-Pineapple Gazpacho

Joel Odhner
Prep: 30 minutes

4 cups cucumber, chopped and peeled
4 cups pineapple, chopped
1 small jalapeño pepper, seeded and diced
1 green onion, chopped
1 tablespoon lime juice

2 teaspoons sea salt
Handful cilantro leaves
2 tablespoons cold-pressed virgin olive oil

Place all the ingredients in a food processor or high-speed blender and blend. Chill and enjoy.

Curried Creamy Mushroom Soup

Tribest (Home of the Green Star Juicer and Sedona Dehydrator)
Prep: 30 minutes

1 cup Sun Jewels Organics curried
   cashews
1 cup mushrooms, sliced
1 teaspoon pepper
Water

1 teaspoon poultry spice blend
1 teaspoon sea salt
Pinch curry powder
Raw butter or cold-pressed olive oil
Fresh parsley for garnish

Place cashews, mushrooms, and pepper into Soyabella's stainless-steel chamber. Add enough water to reach the 0.8-liter mark. Follow the instructions for making creamy/pureed soup from the Soyabella directions sheet. Mix in the poultry spice, sea salt, curry powder, and pat of raw butter or cold-pressed olive oil. Garnish with minced parsley.

WORDS FROM LISA:

This recipe is from the folks at Tribest and is designed to be made in their Soyabella. Besides making soup in my Soyabella, I also use it to make almond milk.

    Tribest's original recipe calls for a pat of butter, which I have replaced with cold-pressed olive oil because I am allergic to dairy, and dairy is not generally part of the raw lifestyle.

Healing Soup

Kimberton Whole Foods, www.kimbertonwholefoods.com
Prep: 20 minutes

Water of one young Thai coconut
  (or if unavailable, water)
1 English cucumber
2 celery ribs
½ avocado
2 large or 4 small chard leaves
3 green onions
Juice from 1 lime

Small handful of dulse seaweed
  (optional)
Pinch of cayenne pepper
½ bell pepper
Small handful of cilantro, mint, rosemary,
  or any favorite combo of fresh herbs
Tomato, avocado, bell pepper, green
  onion, seaweed, and herbs, for garnish

Blend coconut water, ½ English cucumber, 2 ribs celery, ½ avocado, chard leaves, 1 green onion, lime juice, seaweed, and pinch of cayenne in a powerful blender until smooth. Then add the ½ bell pepper, ½ English cucumber, 2 green onions, and the handfuls of fresh herbs. Pulse a few times until the herbs are roughly chopped. Garnish with tomato, avocado, bell pepper, green onion, torn dulse seaweed, and fresh herbs.

Lemon-Zucchini Bisque

Rhio (author of *Hooked on Raw*)

Almond Creamy Soup Base (page 110)
2 small zucchinis, grated
½ cup shallot or onion, finely minced
1 ear corn, cut off the cob

¼ cup shallot, finely minced
¼ red bell pepper, finely chopped
2 mushrooms, finely chopped

Place all the ingredients in a high-speed blender and blend very well.

Sexy Gazpacho

Karmyn Malone (www.karmynmalone.com)
Prep: 20 minutes   **Serves:** 2 sexy people

4 cups grape or red cherry tomatoes
  (or Campari or other premium
  tomatoes), halved or quartered
½ cup red bell pepper
8 sun-dried tomato halves, soaked
  and drained

2 tablespoons raw honey or raw
  agave nectar
2 handfuls fresh basil
Thai red pepper (½ pepper or
  more to taste)

Add all the ingredients to a high-speed blender in the order listed.

Pour gazpacho into 2 serving bowls. Garnish with chopped, peeled cucumber and some fresh basil.

Contributor's Note: If using a Vitamix® blender, I recommend using the slowest 2 speeds. Otherwise, you will end up with a "Sexy Marinara Sauce" instead of Sexy Gazpacho.

Make sure to push down the ingredients in the blender with the tamper. This recipe works best in a high-powered blender like the Vitamix®. If using a regular blender, use a celery stalk to push the ingredients down.

10

Snacks & Sides

Unroasted Carrots & Raisins

Prep: 15 minutes

1 pound carrots, cleaned and sliced into bite size pieces
½ cup raisins

1 tablespoon cinnamon
Raw agave, enough to cover carrots

Combine sliced carrots, raisins, and cinnamon in a glass dish. Cover with agave, making sure the entire mixture is coated. Place in a Tribest® Sedona Dehydrator until warmed and the carrots are softened.

Crunchy Zucchini

Antanas Vainius
Prep: 10–15 minutes   **Serves:** 3

2 medium zucchini, sliced into ⅛-inch cubes
½ cup Jerusalem artichokes, peeled and sliced into ⅛-inch cubes
3 tablespoons favorite fresh pesto (sunflower/pumpkin seed, basil/cilantro/parsley, use your imagination!)

¼ cup sun-dried tomatoes, finely chopped
1½ tablespoons apple cider vinegar
½ teaspoon lime juice
⅓ cup sprouted and dehydrated buckwheat groats

Combine pesto, lime juice, and vinegar, add tomatoes, and marinate for 3–5 minutes. Toss zucchini and Jerusalem artichoke cubes with pesto dressing. Mix in buckwheat just before serving, toss, and serve.
Serve on slices of raw (smoked) goat Gouda.

Banana Wrap

Arnold Kaufman
Prep: 2 minutes

> 1 banana, peeled
> 1 lettuce leaf

Wrap banana in lettuce leaf and eat.

Pear Stacks

Arnold Kaufman
Prep: 7 minutes

> 2 ripe pears, cored and sliced
> 5–6 raspberries
> 3 dates, pitted and soaked

Combine the raspberries and dates in a food processor, pulsing just a few times. Slice each pear into 4 or 5 slices. Spread the raspberry date cream in between each layer of pear and stack.

Nori Rolls with Sunflower Seed Filling

Brenda Cobb (Founder of Living Foods Institute® and author of *The Living Foods Lifestyle,* **www.livingfoodsinstitute.com)**

Prep: 30 minutes

Filling
2 cups sunflower seeds
2 cloves garlic
⅔ cup fresh lemon juice
1 cup chopped green onions
¼ cup raw tahini
1 tablespoon powdered kelp seaweed
2 tablespoons dulse seaweed flakes
Pinch cayenne pepper

Nori Roll Assembly
Nori seaweed sheets (sun-dried raw
   sheets, not the toasted sheets)
Mixed baby greens
Red pepper strips, julienned
Carrot strips, julienned
Cucumber strips, julienned
Avocado, sliced
Sunflower or broccoli sprouts

Filling
Soak the sunflower seeds in filtered water for 4 hours and drain. In food processor chop the garlic into minced pieces and then add the sunflower seeds, lemon juice, green onions, raw tahini, kelp, dulse, and cayenne pepper. Process until smooth. You can put this in the fridge until you are ready to make the nori rolls. It will keep up to 3 days.

Nori Roll Assembly
Assemble nori rolls as close to serving time as possible because they tend to get soggy if they sit too long. Slice the avocado right before you are ready to make the rolls.

Place a nori sheet on your cutting board. Place a layer of mixed baby greens on the sheet, then spread 2 to 3 tablespoons of the sunflower seed filling on the greens. If you put the filling on top of the greens rather than next to the nori wrapper it will keep the wrapper from getting soggy.

Arrange the julienne vegetable strips on top of the filling and top with slices of avocado, then cover with sprouts. Carefully roll up the nori wrapper and seal using a little water on your fingertips. Slice into bite-sized pieces, rolls about 1-inch thick, and serve with wasabi and nama shoyu raw soy sauce.

Trail Mix Chews

Janice Inella

Prep: 2 hours (Oplus dehydration time)

2 cups sunflower seeds (soak for 1 hour,
 then rinse and drain well)

2 cups pumpkin seeds (soak for 1 hour,
 then rinse and drain well)

½ cup golden flax seeds (grind fresh)

1 cup pure water

1 cup cranberries (soaked in pure water
 for 1 hour)

1 cup non-GMO frozen organic corn
 (or fresh and local when in season)

1 cup dry coconut

4 pink lady apples (core and chop
 small for the Cuisinart®)

½ cup raw honey

4 tablespoons vanilla extract

4 tablespoons fresh ginger juice

4 tablespoons pumpkin seed oil

1 teaspoon sea salt

In a large bowl, add ground flax seeds and water, let sit for 20 minutes. In another large bowl, add the rest of your ingredients and hand mix, and then add the flax seeds and water. Hand mix well.

In a Cuisinart®, use the S-blade to cream all of the ingredients in small batches and blend until smooth, or chunky if you like. Spread 12 ounces each on three dehydrator trays. Set heat at 115°F, dry for 12 hours then flip and peel off sheet. Dry for another 12 hours. Break into large pieces and store in cool dry place.

This is a great travel snack or handout for all parties. Fabulous!

Blueberry Muffins

Rhio (author of *Hooked on Raw*)
Prep: 30 minutes   **Soak:** barley, 24 hours; Brazil nuts, 8 hours or overnight;
Hunza raisins, 1 hour   **Dehydrate:** 24 hours at 100°F

2 cups soaked and/or sprouted barley
1½ cups Brazil nuts, soaked and drained
¼ cup golden flax seed, ground
2 fresh dates (or 4 dried, soaked 1 hour)
2 cups Hunza raisins, soaked and
  strained (this will swell so you will
  have more than 2 cups)

2–4 tablespoon raw honey
1 tablespoon extra-virgin olive oil
2 teaspoons cinnamon
½ vanilla bean, ground (approximately
  ½ teaspoon)
¾–1 cup blueberries

Place the first 3 ingredients into a food processor with the "S" blade and blend as finely as possible. You might have to do this in batches depending on the size of your food processor. Transfer mixture to a large mixing bowl.

Place dates, 2 cups of the raisins, honey, olive oil, cinnamon, and vanilla bean into the food processor, and blend very well using the "S" blade. Add mixture to the bowl. Also, add in ½ cup of soaked raisins and mix everything very well by hand.

Place the blueberries into the food processor utilizing the "S" blade. Pulse-chop to break up the blueberries a little bit, and then add blueberries to the ingredients in the bowl and mix well.

Form into round, flat muffins approximately ½-inch high and 2–2½-inches in diameter.

Place on Teflex-lined trays and dehydrate at 100°F for 24 hours or until resembling muffin consistency. Halfway through, turn the muffins over on the mesh screen (removing Teflex sheet) and finish dehydrating.

Contributor's Note: When soaking the barley, be sure to change the water twice during the 24 hours. If you want to sprout the barley as well, allow it to sprout for a few days after soaking and be sure to rinse twice each day.

Pickles (Bubbie's Raw Pickles)

Prep: 10 minutes   **Dehydrate:** Overnight

Bubbie's pickles (dill chips or spears)
Nutritional Yeast Flakes
Assorted dried seasonings

I just took the dill chips as well as the spears (sliced), rolled them in the Nutritional Yeast Flakes, and dehydrated them until reaching the desired consistency. If you want assorted flavors, you can roll in sea salt, Italian seasoning, cajun seasoning, or pizza seasoning. Whatever works for you!

   I threw the left-over Nutritional Yeast Flakes out for my chickens, and they loved it. They looked so cute with yellow Nutritional Yeast Flakes on their beaks. I know, only faces that a mother could love.

WORDS FROM LISA:

You can also make your own pickles using the Perfect Pickler (perfectpickler.com). I did this last summer, using heirloom-organic cucumbers that I grew in my own raised-bed garden. It is so cool growing the cucumbers, pickling them, and then eating them, especially in the winter time.

Nacho Cheese Tomato Sliders

Natalie Norman
Prep: 10 minutes

Tomatoes
Cheese
Minced cilantro

Green onion, chopped
Sprouts

Here's a quick and satisfying way to use my Easy Mac Nut Nacho Cheese recipe (page 277). Simply slice ripe juicy tomatoes, and then top with some of the cheese, minced cilantro, chopped green onion, and sprouts of your liking. Enjoy!

Creamy Camu Avocado Yogurt

Ultimate Superfood
Prep: 30 minutes   **Serves:** 4

Yogurt
½ cup fresh orange juice
1 mango, chopped
1 avocado, diced
½ teaspoon Ojio™ camu camu powder
1 orange, halved and hollowed

Toppings
2 strawberries, sliced
2 tablespoons blueberries
2 mangos, chopped
2 tablespoons Ojio™ organic coconut shreds

Refrigerate the mango and avocado for an hour prior to recipe preparation. Prepare toppings in advance by chopping into bite-sized pieces; refrigerate during yogurt preparation. Prepare yogurt by placing the orange juice, chopped mango, diced avocado, and Ojio™ camu camu powder into the blender and mix on high speed until the yogurt is creamy and smooth. Divide the yogurt mixture into two orange peel shells. Add toppings and finish with a sprinkle of coconut shreds.

Contributor's Note: This creamy tropical "yogurt" highlights avocado, orange, and plenty of fresh mango with the organic blending powder of the camu camu fruit, nature's highest concentration of natural vitamin C to add the finishing touch to this delicious yogurt.

Pickles

Annmarie Cantrell
Prep: 30 minutes

4 pounds pickling cucumbers
1 bunch dill
3–4 (or more) large garlic cloves
2–3 tablespoons pickling spice (allspice,

mustard seed, cloves, bay leaf,
black pepper, juniper berry)
3–4 tablespoons sea salt
1–2 grape leaves

Add pickling cucumbers to jar. Add garlic, dill, and spice. Add grape or horseradish leaves.

Make brine with 3 tablespoons salt to 1 quart water, dissolving the salt well. Add water and make sure that vegetables are submerged completely. Ferment for 10 days in a cool place (warmer temperatures seem to make the pickles lose their crunch) and serve.

Contributor's Note: Pickles ferment best and stay crunchy with the addition of grape leaves, oak leaves, horseradish leaves, or black tea—it is the tannins that help the cucumbers stay crisp. It is best to use pickling cucumbers for this recipe.

Moroccan Carrots

Annmarie Cantrell
Prep: 25 minutes

1 pound carrots, sliced in rounds or
    on a diagonal
½ teaspoon red pepper flakes (or more
    to taste)
1 cinnamon stick

1 teaspoon coriander seeds
1 teaspoon cumin seeds
1 garlic clove
3 tablespoons salt
Water

Place carrots in clean jars. Add garlic and spices. Thoroughly mix salt in water and pour over carrots. Ferment for 2–3 weeks.

Antipasto Platter

Annmarie Cantrell
Prep: 30 minutes

1 cup cauliflower florets
1 cup carrots, sliced
1 cup red bell pepper (or mix yellow,
  orange, and red), sliced
1–2 bay leaves

1 teaspoon coriander seed
½ teaspoon black peppercorn
½ teaspoon dried thyme
4 tablespoons sea salt
1½ quarts water

Layer vegetables in a fermenting crock along with the spices and herbs. Dissolve salt in the water and pour over the vegetables to fully submerge them. Let it ferment for 2 weeks.

Cheesy Popcorn Cauliflower

Prep: 7 minutes

1 cup cauliflower, cut into pieces
¼ cup cold-pressed olive oil

1 tablespoon nutritional yeast
Pinch sea salt, to taste

Place cauliflower pieces in a flat bottomed glass dish. Combine the rest of the ingredients in a Vitamix® high-speed blender. Pour liquid mixture over cauliflower and place in Tribest® Sedona Dehydrator until desired warmth is reached (though it tastes good cold, too).

Crunchy Munchy Trail Mix

Prep: 15 minutes

1 cup pistachios, shelled, soaked, and dried
1 cup raisins
1 cup raw almonds, soaked and dried
1 cup raw walnuts, soaked and dried
1 cup dried cherries

1 cup dried banana slices
1 cup dried pineapple
1 cup dried apple slices
1 cup raw cacao nibs
1 tablespoon kosher salt
1 tablespoon cinnamon

Combine ingredients. You can either buy the dried fruits or dehydrate them yourself in your dehydrator.

WORDS FROM LISA:

I call this trail mix the Crunchy Munchy Trail Mix beause when you get the crunchy munchies this will satisfy your needs.

Nuts About Granola

Sheryll Chavarria (Raw Can Roll Café and Pure Body Spa, Douglassville, PA, www.rawcanrollcafe.com)
Soak: 24 hours **Prep:** 20 minutes **Dehydrate:** 24 hours at 115°F

3 cups walnuts or pecans
8 cups steel cut oats (soaked overnight) or buckwheat groats (soaked for 4 hours)

5 cup banana purée
2½ cups agave
¼ cup vanilla extract
Pinch Celtic sea salt

Put nuts into food processor until coarsely processed. Mix all ingredients together and spread mixture out onto Teflex sheets on top of Dehydrator trays. Dehydrate for 24 hours or more at 115°F.

Serve with a nut milk and fresh-cut fruit. You can also try topping it with blueberries, which make a nice color contrast.

Tropical Applesauce

Prep: 15 minutes

2 apples, cored and peeled
1 banana
1 mango, cored and peeled

Water, to thin
1 tablespoon shredded, dried coconut

Combine all the ingredients in a food processor to desired consistency and serve. If you wish to thin the applesauce, add water to desired consistency. Stir in dried coconut by hand.

WORDS FROM LISA:

You can also add cinnamon and/or raisins to taste. If you want to increase the amount that you wish to make, just increase the quantity, keeping the same proportions (for example, 2 to 2 or 3 to 3).

Seasoned Austria's Finest Pumpkin Seeds

Prep: 10 minutes   **Dehydrate:** 24 hours   **Yield:** 2 cups or 8 servings

2 cups Austria's Finest Naturally®
    Pumpkin Seeds
2 tablespoons wheat-free tamari

1 teaspoon onion powder
1 teaspoon garlic powder

Combine all the ingredients and mix well. Place on a Teflex-lined dehydrator tray and dehydrate at 105°F for 24 hours or until crisp. Store in an air-tight container in the refrigerator.

   I would recommend doubling or tripling this recipe if you want to make sure that you have enough for the quinoa recipe above. The reason is they are a great snack, and I tend to eat them a lot. This is also a great recipe just to have in ball jars on your counter or in a Ziploc bag/Tupperware container in your car so you always have a healthy snack handy.

Spur of the Moment Trail Mix

Prep: 5 minutes **Soak:** seeds, 4 hours; almonds, 8 hours

1 cup soaked and dehydrated Austria's
  Finest Naturally® Pumpkin Seeds
1 cup raw almonds

1 cup raw walnuts
1 cup raw sesame seeds
Sea salt and garlic powder, to taste

Toss the nuts, seeds, and spices together and store in a sealed container.

WORDS FROM LISA:

One day, I needed to make a quick trail mix. I always have on hand jars of raw nuts that I have soaked, dehydrated, and stored in sealed canning jars, so I was able to easily create this tasty treat. You can add any spices you like to this mixture, including dried coconut shavings, raisins, or any other assorted dried fruits.

Nori Snacks

Prep: 15 minutes

1 cup raw soaked nuts
Your choice of vegetables (carrots, red peppers, onions, garlic, or celery work well)
Spices to taste

Combine ingredients in a food processor and/or Vitamix® High Speed Blender and blend until smooth. You'll note that I haven't been specific about what needs to be in your pâté. The reality is that if you are in an emergency situation, you will have to use what you have and you won't be able to go out to the market.

After making a nut pâté, spread paste over a nori sheet. Roll up the nori sheet, and dehydrate it at 105°F until desired dryness. You can leave it in long rolls or cut it in bite-size pieces.

Banana Pear Sunny Fruit Leather

Cara Graver (The Cob Studio, www.thecobstudio.com)
Prep: 7 minutes

2 ripe bananas, peeled
1 ripe bosc pear, cored and seeded
¼ cup sunflower seeds, soaked

Purée the ingredients in a Vitamix® High Speed Blender. Spread on Teflex sheet and dehydrate overnight.

Unbaked Sweet Potatoes

Prep: 15 minutes

2 sweet potatoes, peeled and grated
1 carrot, peeled and shredded
1 apple, cored and shredded
1 tablespoon alcohol free vanilla

Raisins (optional)
Shredded coconut (optional)
Cinnamon, to taste
Agave, to taste

Place shredded sweet potatoes, apple, and carrots in a glass casserole dish. Sprinkle with cinnamon to taste, add vanilla, and cover with agave. Make sure the sweet potatoes are totally covered with the cinnamon, vanilla, and agave mixture. Dehydrate at 105°F until warm and the flavors meld.

> ### WORDS FROM LISA:
>
> This is my version of baked sweet potatoes. The longest portion of making this dish is peeling and grating the sweet potatoes.

Unroasted Sweet Potatoes

Prep: 20 minutes

2 sweet potatoes, peeled and grated
1 apple, peeled and grated
¼ cup fresh parsley, chopped
¼ cup fresh rosemary, chopped

1 teaspoon fresh thyme, chopped
1 garlic clove, minced
¼ cup cold-pressed olive oil
Sea salt and cracked pepper, to taste

Combine the above ingredients together in a glass dish, making sure that the mixture is thoroughly combined. Place glass dish in the Tribest® Sedona Dehydrator at 105°F until warmed and/or unroasted. It should take a good 4 hours; although, because the sweet potatoes are shredded, the process is a little faster.

Unroasted Red Pepper & Asparagus

Prep: 15 minutes

1 bunch asparagus
1 red pepper, cleaned and diced
¼–½ cup Austria's Finest, Naturally®
    pumpkin seed oil

Sea salt and cracked black pepper,
    to taste

Cut asparagus on an angle into bite size pieces. Be sure to remove hard tips and discard. Place cleaned and sliced asparagus and red pepper in a glass dish. Toss and cover with pumpkin seed oil. Season with sea salt and black pepper to taste. Place dish in a Tribest® Sedona Dehydrator until warm or unroasted. This should take about 4 to 6 hours.

Mild Kimchee

Betti-Lou Kramer
Prep: 30 minutes

1 large cabbage, thinly sliced (save some
   of the whole leaves)
3 red peppers
2 large carrots
2 stalks celery
1 medium daikon radish

4 red radishes
3 cloves garlic
1–2 tablespoons grated ginger
3 tablespoons Himalayan salt
Spring water, as needed

Wash and sterilize large crock or glass container (dark is better than clear) with lid. Place cabbage in a large bowl and sprinkle with salt. Using a wood tamper (or wooden spoon), work salt into the cabbage for 3–5 minutes or until the cabbage starts giving off some liquid, set aside.

Quarter and slice pepper. Slice carrots, celery, daikon, and regular radishes until all are similarly sized. Press garlic and chop well, add to mixture.

Combine vegetables with cabbage, and add 1–2 tablespoons of ginger (depending on how spicy you want it). Press garlic and chop well, then add to mixture. The mixture should be giving off enough liquid to fully cover cabbage and vegetables; if not, add enough water to cover. Mix thoroughly.

Place mixture into crock or glass container and press down well with tamper. Cover with whole cabbage leaves and weight it down with a glass bowl. Cover and let sit at room temperature for several days (up to a week). After desired flavor is obtained, store in refrigerator.

Heirloom Tomato Stacks with Feta and Drizzled in Basil Glaze

Brooke Preston
Prep: 45 minutes   **Serves:** 4

Stacks
4 large heirloom tomatoes, preferably
    of different colors
½ cup basil leaves, thinly sliced
    into ribbons

"Feta" Cheese
1 cup cashews (soaked for 2–4 hours,
    rinsed and drained)
1 cup macadamia nuts (soaked for
    2–4 hours, rinsed and drained)
⅛ teaspoon vegan probiotic powder
1 cup purified water

2 teaspoons chickpea miso
⅛ sweet yellow onion
2 tablespoons onion powder
¼ cup lemon juice
Pinch of white pepper
Pinch of sea salt (optional)

Basil Glaze
1 bunch fresh basil
⅓ cup cold pressed extra virgin olive oil
3 teaspoons lemon juice
Dash salt
Dash fresh ground pepper

"Feta" Cheese
To prepare the "feta," place soaked, rinsed, and drained nuts into a high-speed blender. Blend together with all other "feta" ingredients until completely smooth, adding pure water if necessary. Once the mixture is smooth, wrap in several layers of cheesecloth, and tie with a rubber band. Hang from a hook or knob in your kitchen, in a place where there is little activity but good airflow. Check for your desired tartness once a day for 2–3 days. Once you have the flavor that you want, store in the fridge in an airtight container. The culturing will slow considerably once it is refrigerated, but should be enjoyed within the first 5 days.

Basil Glaze
Place all basil glaze ingredients into a food processor and pulse until thoroughly combined. Assemble tomato stacks by slicing off the top and bottom of each tomato. Set aside. Slice all tomatoes into 3 thick slices crosswise.

Using slices from each tomato, arrange the stacks as follows: 1 slice tomato, cover with "feta," drizzle with basil glaze, and sprinkle with basil ribbons. Repeat for 3 layers, using slices from different tomatoes to give color to each stack. Top with ribbons of fresh basil, fresh ground pepper, and a dash salt if desired.

Contributor's Note: This recipe is so simple, so delicious, and so beautiful! It's a favorite at The Green Boheme (www.thegreenboheme.com) during tomato harvest!

Spicy Baked October Beans

Chili Smith Family Foods, adapted by Lisa Montgomery
Prep: 30 minutes

6 cups October beans, cooked, cooled, and drained
5 garlic cloves, minced
1 sweet red onion, finely diced
4 tablespoons Dijon mustard
6 ounces tomato ketchup

6–7 chipotle chilies
2 large tomatoes
2 sun-dried tomatoes
3 large apples, chopped and cored
Salt and pepper, to taste

Soak raw beans in water in a slow cooker at 118°F. Combine drained beans, onion, garlic, mustard, 2 large tomatoes, 2 sun-dried tomatoes, and 3 large apples, chopped and cored. Add seasonings. Cook on low (less than 118°F) in your slow cooker until desired doneness. Remember to cook below 118°F to keep this dish raw!

Black-Eyed Slaw

Dr. Scott and Raechelle Walker
Prep: 10 minutes

1–2 cups black-eyed peas (soaked, sprouted, or canned)
1 cob corn kernels (removed from cob)
1 teaspoon garlic, chopped
1–2 tomatoes diced
1–2 jalapeño peppers

1 avocado, chunked
¼ cup red onion
1 cup shredded cabbage and carrots
Sea salt, to taste
Cilantro, to taste

Combine all ingredients in one large bowl, toss, and serve.

Massaged Kale Slaw

Ken Immer
Prep: 30 minutes   **Serves:** 4–6

¼ cup tamari
⅛ cup umeboshi vinegar
⅛ cup water
⅛ oz arame seaweed, dry
¼ cup apple cider vinegar (Bragg's®)
1 lemon, juiced

¼ cup fresh basil, sliced thin
⅛ cup red onion, thinly sliced
¼ cup red pepper, thinly sliced
1 teaspoon extra virgin olive oil
2 bunches green kale
Freshly ground black pepper, to taste

Combine tamari, umeboshi vinegar, and water. Submerge arame seaweed to hydrate. Allow it to stand for at least 30 minutes or overnight, during which time the arame will soften. Combine cider vinegar, lemon juice, basil, olive oil, and pepper in a separate large bowl. Add onion and red pepper; allow to soften. Meanwhile, chop kale finely (¼-inch wide or less). Add to onion and pepper mixture and toss to coat. Drain seaweed, reserving liquid. Add seaweed to kale, and 1–3 teaspoons of the arame soak liquid, to taste. Massage slaw by squeezing and pressing between hands and/or bottom of bowl until softened and bright green. The dish can be enjoyed immediately, or covered and refrigerated overnight.

Roasted Garlic Hummus

Joe Barr
Prep: 20 minutes

1 pound fresh chickpeas, soaked, rinsed, and sprouted (canned if fresh is not available)
6 cloves roasted garlic
5 tablespoons lemon juice

¼ cup water
¼ cup tahini paste
⅓ cup extra virgin olive oil
Sea salt, to taste
Fresh ground black pepper, to taste

In a food processor, blend together chickpeas, garlic, and water, scraping the bowl occasionally. Blend until smooth. Add in lemon juice and tahini paste and blend again. While food processor is running, slowly add in the olive oil until incorporated. Season with salt and pepper to taste, and serve with vegetable crudités or pita chips.

Cauliflower Spanish Rice

Karen Ranzi (Author of *Creating Healthy Children***)**
Prep: 25 minutes

1 head cauliflower, chopped in the food
    processor to a rice texture
1 cup fresh cilantro, chopped
1 jalapeño pepper, seeded and chopped
    (optional)
1 small red onion, chopped
1 cup sun-dried tomatoes, soaked
    and drained

Juice of one lime
1 tablespoon ground cumin
1 teaspoon chili powder
1 avocado, peeled, pitted, and chopped
1 large red pepper, seeded, and finely
    chopped
3 medium to large tomatoes,
    finely chopped

Place cauliflower rice in a large bowl. Pulse-chop jalapeño, cilantro, and onion in food processor into fine pieces and add to cauliflower. Process avocado, sun-dried tomatoes, lime juice, cumin, and chili powder and add to cauliflower. Add finely chopped red pepper and tomato to complete the Cauliflower Spanish Rice.

Contributor's Note: Most of the recipes in my new book, *Raw Food Fun for Families*, have only a few to several ingredients and are oil-free. Families have been asking me for this book and it's finally completed! This recipe is satisfying for those who like a heavier feeling when transitioning to the raw food lifestyle.

Good Faith Farm's Raw Olive Tapenade

Karen Handman (Good Faith Farms)
Prep: 25 minutes

1½ cups raw Sevillano olives
3 tablespoons capers
½ teaspoon fresh rosemary
½ teaspoon fresh oregano

1 teaspoon fresh Italian parsley
1 teaspoon lemon zest
¼ cup olive oil

Puree first six ingredients in food processor. Add oil and pulse a few times until oil is mixed evenly.

Guacamole with a Kick!

Lany Wenke
Prep: 11 minutes

1 avocado
¼ cup diced onions
1 teaspoon garlic

¼ cup diced tomatoes
Salt, to taste
Pepper, to taste

Peel the avocado and mash up into a dip-like consistency. Add garlic and salt and pepper, mix throughout. Add the onions and tomatoes and mix. Enjoy!

Thanksgiving Stuffing

Raw Can Roll Café (www.rawcanrollcafe.com)
Prep: 20 minutes

Base
2 cups soaked sunflower seeds
1 cup soaked walnuts
2 tablespoons lemon juice
2 tablespoons psyllium husk powder
  (or other thickener)
1 tablespoon Himalayan pink or
  Celtic sea salt
3 tablespoons onion
2 teaspoons fresh dill
2 teaspoons fresh sage

2 teaspoons nutmeg
2 teaspoons poultry seasoning

Garnish
3 scallions, chopped fine
3 shredded carrots
2 cups dried cranberries
½ bunch celery, chopped small
½ cup chopped parsley
1 chopped apple (chopped into
  small pieces)

Chop all base ingredients in food processor. Hand mix garnish ingredients with base and serve. Can be dehydrated for about 3–4 hours; however, it is not necessary.

Mango Chutney

Wendy Landiak
Prep: 20 minutes

3 cups mango
1 tablespoon vinegar
1 tablespoon lime juice and zest
1 tablespoon freshly grated ginger
1 tablespoon freshly grated turmeric

1 bunch cilantro, chopped
1 Indian chili, chopped
½ cup red bell pepper
A couple pinches of Himalayan sea salt

Blend ingredients in a Vitamix® blender. If you desire more sweetness, use ½ cup dates/raisins purée or a ¼ cup maple syrup.

Chutney

Wendy Landiak
Prep: 15 minutes

1 cup raisins
2 tablespoons raw vinegar (Bragg's®)
2 tablespoons fresh cilantro

1 tablespoon fresh ginger
½ cup coconut
2 teaspoons garam masala spices

Blend ingredients in a Vitamix® blender. Add salt as desired. You can also add hot pepper if you wish. If mixture is too thick, add water to thin.

Caraway Kraut

Annmarie Cantrell
Prep: 30 minutes

5 pounds green cabbage
3 tablespoons Celtic sea salt
1 tablespoon caraway seeds

Chop vegetables by hand or put through the grater setting of the food processor. The more finely the vegetables are chopped, the more surface area will be present for the bacteria to infiltrate. (The vegetables will also ferment more quickly when chopped more thinly.) Place vegetables in a large bowl. Sprinkle salt over and begin to massage salt into the vegetables. You can either use your hands or a pounder to do this. As you pound, you are breaking up the cell wall and allowing the liquid to be released. This liquid will serve as your brine.

Pack vegetables into a clean jar and push them down so that there are no air bubbles. Be sure that the liquid rises above the vegetables and covers them. If the brine does not cover, add water with a pinch more salt. Let vegetables sit on the counter (out of direct sunlight) for anywhere from 5 days to 3 weeks; taste it as time goes on and see how you like it. When it suits your taste, transfer to the refrigerator. Consume within 8–12 months.

Unfried Mushrooms

Prep: 15 minutes

Button mushrooms, cleaned and
   de-stemmed
Almond meal
Cold-pressed olive oil

Sea salt
Cracked pepper
Assorted dried spices and herbs
   (optional)

Clean your mushrooms, remove the stems, and set them aside. In a saucer, pour cold-pressed olive oil. In a third flat dish (with a lip), add your almond meal, sea salt, cracked pepper, and any other dried herbs that you would like to use in your coating. Roll each mushroom one at a time in the cold-pressed olive oil, and then roll in the almond meal/herb mixture to coat them. Place coated mushrooms on your dehydrator tray and dehydrate until desired warmth and softness is reached.

WORDS FROM LISA:

This is another one of those dishes that I tend to eat before they're even finished. I am not giving quantities as to how much almond meal and spices you will need, because it all depends on how many mushrooms you are coating, how thick you are coating them, and how spicy you like your mushrooms. If you prefer your mushrooms sweet, an alternative would be to roll them in honey instead of oil.

Brussels Sprouts Kimchi

Prep: 30 minutes

1 pound Brussels sprouts, quartered
½ cup carrots, peeled and shredded
¼ cup red onion, chopped
1 clove garlic, minced
1½ teaspoons coriander seeds, crushed

1 teaspoon fennel seeds, crushed
½ pound red cabbage, shredded bite
   size pieces
2–3 tablespoons sea salt

Combine all of the ingredients except the spices and the sea salt in a large bowl. With a wooden mallet or potato masher, pound the ingredients until the juices flow. If you have a Tribest® Slowstar Juicer, run the vegetables through the juicer using the mincing blade. Once the juices are flowing, add the coriander seeds and fennel seeds. Add one tablespoon of salt at a time, mixing in thoroughly. Once the salt is thoroughly mixed in, taste to check and see how salty the mixture is. Remember: fermented foods always tend to taste a little salty.

   If you use the Tribest® Slowstar Juicer mincing feature, you may get more juice than you need; pour off excess juice. Pack the entire mixture into a glass canning jar, making sure the vegetables are covered in the liquid. Leave a 1-inch space at the top. Set on your kitchen counter and the mixture should ferment in 3 to 5 days. Keep an eye on it; if the liquid starts to build up, pour it off.

Raw Sauerkraut

2 pounds green cabbage
2 pounds red cabbage

1 pound carrots
3 tablespoons sea salt

Cut cabbages and carrots small enough to feed through a juicer using the mincing feature. Once fed through the juicer, place in a bowl and add salt. Take the minced vegetables that you have worked the salt into and pack into canning jars. Press the seasoned vegetables into the jar firmly until you are one inch below the top of the jar. I usually stop at the rings on the jar, making sure the vegetables are covered with the juices. Screw the lid and ring on the jar and set on your counter to ferment.

Creamed Baked Corn

2 cups corn kernels
2 eggs
3 tablespoons butter

4 tablespoons flour
1 cup milk
Salt and pepper, to taste

Run the corn through a juicer using the mincing feature. Combine the ingredients in a bowl and stir together well. Pour into a glass dish and bake in your oven at 350°F for one hour.

Lisa's Unbaked Cream Corn

4 ears corn, remove kernels from cob
2–4 tablespoons raw almond milk
    (depends on how juicy the corn is
    that you are using)

1 tablespoon agave or raw honey
Salt and pepper, to taste

Stir ingredients together well and pour into a glass dish. Place dish in your Tribest® Sedona Dehydrator at 118°F. If you want the Unbaked Corn to have a similar consistency to baked creamed corn, you will need to leave the dish in the dehydrator for 8 to 12 hours. Stir occasionally to make sure all the flavors are blending well.

Olive Tapenade

1 cup pitted olives
1 tablespoon cold-pressed olive oil

½ teaspoon lemon juice
1 teaspoon raw honey

Run the olives through a juicer using the mincing feature. Combine all of the ingredients in a bowl until well blended. Store in a glass canning jar (with lid on) in your refrigerator.

Beet Kvass

Melissa Miles (Permanent Future Institute)
Prep: 20 minutes

2 large organic beets, peeled and
    coarsely chopped
¼ cup whey, substitute with additional
    1½ teaspoon of salt (optional)
2 teaspoons Celtic® Sea Salt,
    kosher salt, or Himalayan salt

Non-chlorinated water
¼ cup beet kvass (helps inoculate the
    brine with lactic acid producing
    bacteria, adds color and flavor)

Place beets, whey, and salt in a 1 quart jar with lid. Add non-chlorinated water to fill the jar, leaving one inch of head space. Stir and cover jar with lid. Keep the jar at room temperature (out of direct sunlight) for three days (contents should be slightly fizzy). Place in refrigerator and use as needed.

Once most of the kvass has been drunk, refill the container with water, keep at room temperature another three days then refrigerate. The same beets can be used to make kvass twice. Kvass liquid can be used in place of whey in this recipe the next time you make kvass.

Fermented Italian Green Beans

Scott Zukay
Prep: 20 minutes   **Ferment:** 2–3 weeks

1 pound fresh, raw green beans
1 clove garlic
½ teaspoon dried oregano
½ teaspoon dried basil

1 teaspoon Celtic sea salt
4 ounces Zukay Kvass, preferably Veggie
    Medley
Well or spring water (non-chlorinated)

Take the ends off the green beans. Depending on what you prefer, either keep the green beans whole or cut them in half. Dice the garlic clove.

In a quart mason jar, combine all the ingredients and fill until all the beans are below the surface of the water. Make sure you leave at least a 1-inch space between the lid and the top of the water, as the mixture will expand. Close fairly tightly.

Keep the jar inside a casserole dish (in case it leaks), and leave it in a warm place (70–80°F) for 2–3 weeks. It should become fizzy—if it's not fizzy after 5 days, throw it out. You can open it to check, but this is not necessary. After 3 weeks, eat and refrigerate!

Contributor's Note: These are delightful crudités! Enjoy by yourself, or with friends who may not understand your diet—this should be loved by all!

Mashed Taters

Joel Odhner

1 head cauliflower, chopped
1 cup raw cashews
½ cup cold-pressed olive oil

1–2 cloves garlic
Salt and pepper to taste

Place all the ingredients in food processor and blend until smooth.

Contributor's Note: I must confess that one of the standard American dishes I actually do miss is my Mom's homemade mashed potatoes. In fact, once we found that I was allergic to dairy, she made her mashed potatoes with potato water, and they were still just as good. Since my Mom has passed, and I am seeking a healthier alternative to mashed potatoes (a major comfort food for me), Joel's "Mashed Taters" help to fill the potato void.

Mellow Kim Chi

Sally Bowdle (Sally B Gluten Free, www.sallybglutenfree.com)
Prep: 25 minutes
Ferment: Approximately one week (in winter, could take as long as two weeks)

1 pound Napa cabbage	Ginger root, grated
Bok choy, 1 head	Chili peppers, finely chopped (optional)
Daikon or red radishes	Onions, leeks, or scallions, to taste
2 carrots	Sea salt, to taste
Garlic cloves (optional)	

Make a brine by combining ¼ cup sea salt and a quart of water.

Chop cabbage and bok choy, shred daikon (or radishes) and carrots, and submerge in the brine. Let soak a few hours or overnight, until soft and salty (make another batch of brine if there isn't enough to cover).

Prepare the spices by slicing the garlic and onions (or leeks or scallions) and grating the ginger. Mix with chilies.

Drain the brine from the veggies and set aside. Make sure the veggies are salty enough; rinse if too salty or add a few teaspoons if more salt is needed.

Mix the veggies with the spices and pack into a jar or fermentation vessel. Pack down until the brine rises. Weigh down with another jar or a plastic bag filled with brine. Or just check it by tasting. Also be sure to press it down daily with clean fingers.

Let it sit (covered with a cloth) for about a week, tasting the progress every few days. Move it to the refrigerator when desired taste is reached.

Mock Chicken Salad
(or Mock Tuna Salad)

**Sheryll Chavarria (Raw Can Roll Café and Pure Body Spa, Douglassville, PA,
www.rawcanrollcafe.com)**
Prep: 25 minutes

Mock Chicken Salad
3 cups almond pulp
8 stalks celery, chopped
3 scallions, chopped
¼–½ cup fresh dill, chopped
2 tablespoons dulse flakes
    (for Mock Tuna Salad only)

Dressing
¼ cup cashews, soaked
2 cloves garlic, pressed
1–2 tablespoons lemon juice
¾ tablespoon Celtic or
    Himalayan Sea Salt
½ cup water

Almond Pulp
Almond pulp is made from 3 cups of soaked almonds. Put almonds in Vitamix®
High Speed Blender with 8 cups of water. Blend well. Strain mixture through a
seed-nut bag. This liquid is your fresh homemade almond milk and the pulp can be
used for your Mock Chicken or Tuna Salad. To make this recipe as Mock Tuna, just
add two tablespoons of dulse flakes.
    Combine all Mock Chicken ingredients together in a large bowl.

Dressing
Combine dressing ingredients together in a Vitamix® High Speed Blender until
very creamy. Mix the dressing in to the Mock Chicken (and/or Tuna) Salad a little at
a time. You may not need to use the entire dressing for the salad. You can save the
excess dressing and use it on your greens.

Pesto Spinach Portobello

Brenda Cobb (Founder of Living Foods Institute® and author of *The Living Foods Lifestyle***, www.livingfoodsinstitute.com)**

Prep: 30 minutes   **Soak:** walnuts and sunflower seeds, overnight

1 cup walnuts, soaked and drained
1 cup sunflower seeds, soaked and drained
24 small Portobello mushroom caps
½ cup plus 1 tablespoon nama shoyu raw soy sauce
½ cup fresh lemon juice
2 tablespoons fresh ginger, chopped
½ cup water

2 tablespoons garlic
2 teaspoons fresh jalapeño pepper, seeded
4 cups spinach, packed very tightly
½ cup parsley, packed very tightly
½ cup fresh basil
¼ teaspoon psyllium
1 teaspoon Himalayan sea salt
1 red bell pepper, seeded

Soak the walnuts and sunflower seeds in 5 cups of filtered, alkaline water overnight and drain.

Remove the stems from the mushrooms. Combine the ½ cup of nama shoyu, lemon juice, ginger, salt, and water to create a marinade. Marinate the mushrooms overnight. Take the mushrooms out of the marinade and pat dry.

Chop the garlic, jalapeño pepper, spinach, parsley, basil, and 1 tablespoon of nama shoyu in the food processor until well-blended. Add the walnuts, sunflower seeds, and psyllium to the mixture, and continue to blend until creamy and thick.

Fill the mushroom caps with the spinach pesto and decorate with minced red pepper.

Real "Pickled" Eggs (aka Lacto-Fermented Eggs)

Melissa Miles (Permanent Future Institute)
Prep: 30 minutes

1 dozen fresh eggs, hard-boiled, peeled, and cooled
5–6 cloves of garlic
3 teaspoons pickling spices
½ cup fresh dill

Kosher salt, sea salt (non-iodized salt)
Non-chlorinated water
¼ beet kvass (helps inoculate the brine with lactic acid—produces bacteria, adds color and flavor)

Sprinkle some pickling spices and salt in the bottom of a half-gallon jar with lid, and then add a garlic clove and a few sprigs of dill. Add a layer of hard-boiled, peeled eggs. Repeat the process until all the ingredients have been added. Pour beet kvass over the eggs. Add water as needed so that the eggs and brine fill the jar (leave one inch of head space). Loosely seal the jar and place on kitchen counter out of direct sunlight for three days. Ferment until the flavor suits your taste, then place in refrigerator (or cool basement) to slow the fermentation process.

Add a splash of white vinegar to the egg water to aid boiling—do so only if eggs are very fresh (optional).

Tabouli

Sheryll Chavarria (Raw Can Roll Café and Pure Body Spa, Douglassville, PA, www.rawcanrollcafe.com)
Prep: 15 minutes

3 cups fresh parsley, chopped fine
½ cup lemon juice
½ cup cauliflower (food processed or chopped very fine)

1 cup cucumber, chopped into small pieces
1 cup tomato, chopped small
½ tablespoon sea salt

Combine ingredients together in a mixing bowl and serve.

Truly Raw Coleslaw (and Mayonnaise)

Kimberton Whole Foods, www.kimbertonwholefoods.com
Prep: 25 minutes

Mayonnaise
1 cup water
1 cup macadamia nuts
1 cup pine nuts
1½ cups cashew nuts
½ teaspoon crystal salt
1 tablespoon apple cider vinegar
2 tablespoons lemon juice

Slaw
4 large carrots, chopped
1 small onion, chopped
1 small cabbage, chopped or shredded

Mayonnaise

Combine all ingredients in a Vitamix® high-speed blender or food processor until thoroughly blended and set aside.

Slaw

Chop the carrots, onion, and cabbage into fairly small pieces and place in a food processor. Pulse until all ingredients are well combined and become the perfect slaw shape and size. Pour them into a large bowl and set aside for mixing. Rinse the food processor then add the mayonnaise ingredients. Be sure to mix very well adding more water if needed or desired. When fully blended, pour three quarters of the mayonnaise on top of the slaw and mix with a large spoon until the salad mixture is thoroughly coated. If you like more coverage, add more mayonnaise.

This mayonnaise recipe also makes a great dressing, dip, or filling for nori rolls and wraps whether they be collard leaves or flax wraps.

The refrigerator life span of mayonnaise is 5–7 days. The coleslaw mixture with mayonnaise is good for three or four days in the refrigerator (don't worry, you'll eat it by then).

Cauliflower Spanish Rice

Karen Ranzi (Author of *Creating Healthy Children*)
Prep: 30 minutes

1 head cauliflower, chopped in food
    processor to a rice texture
1 jalapeño pepper, seeded and chopped
    (optional)
1 cup fresh cilantro, chopped
1 small red onion, chopped
1 avocado, peeled, pitted and chopped
1 cup sun-dried tomatoes, soaked
    and drained

1 juice of one lime
1 tablespoon ground cumin
1 teaspoon chili powder
1 large red pepper, seeded and
    finely chopped
3 medium to large tomatoes, finely
    chopped

Place cauliflower rice in a large bowl. Pulse-chop jalapeño, cilantro, and onion in food processor into fine pieces and add to cauliflower. Process avocado, sun-dried tomatoes, lime juice, cumin, and chili powder, and add to cauliflower. Add finely chopped red pepper and tomatoes to complete the Cauliflower Spanish Rice. ¡Olé!

11

Smoothies, Shakes, & Juices

Autumn Green Smoothie

Antanas Vainius
Prep: 15 minutes   **Serves:** 1

½ cup goat raw kefir (ideally raw and homemade)
1 tablespoon bee pollen (local is ideal)
1 cup rejuvelac
1–2 teaspoons favorite green powder
2–5 ounces fresh or semi-thawed frozen mango

½ cup favorite herbal infusion (chamomile, red clover, oat straw, etc.)
½ acorn squash, cooked
1 handful of buckwheat greens
2 teaspoons flax oil

Soak bee pollen in goat kefir for 5–10 minutes or longer. Add green powder, mango, and rejuvelac to bee pollen/kefir and blend. Add infusion, acorn squash, and buckwheat and blend.

Add flax oil, quick pulse, and enjoy!

Contributor's Note: This is definitely an unusual concoction, but eminently delicious. The individual ingredients take quite a bit more time to prepare/procure. The higher quality you can find (or make), the more heavenly the result, but the actual prep time is about 15 minutes. This recipe is easiest prepared in a bullet-type personal blender.

The Enchanted Strawberry Forest Smoothie

Dave Biddison (Kimberton Whole Foods, www.kimbertonwholefoods.com)
Prep: 7 minutes

1 apple, chopped
1 cup frozen white grapes (or ½ cup white grape juice)
1 packed cup green kale

1 packed cup baby spinach
1 cup frozen strawberries
1 cup filtered water

Combine the above ingredients in a Vitamix® high-speed powered blender until well blended. Enjoy!

Go Nuts Smoothie

Lany Wenke
Prep: 20 minutes

Handful raw almonds
Handful raw cashews
2 handfuls spinach
1 banana

¼ cup strawberries
¼ cup blueberries
⅔ cup coconut water
Ice cubes

Mix it all together in a blender until smooth and enjoy!

Contributor's Note: The Go Nuts Smoothie is a little creation I made one morning, and I haven't turned back since. With its mixture of fruit, vegetables, and protein, it gives me a boost of energy to start the day and keeps me going for hours.

Cinnamon Roll Milkshake

Natalie Norman
Prep: 7 minutes

5 frozen bananas in chunks
10 Medjool dates, pits removed (or 15–20 average-sized dates)

1 tablespoon ground cinnamon powder
1 teaspoon fresh lemon juice

Blend all ingredients in your Vitamix® or other high-speed blender; you'll need to go slowly at first and possibly use your tamper or scrape down the container (only scrape down when machine is turned off) because there's no water in this to smooth it out right away. You're essentially working with a frozen ice cream texture. Store finished product in airtight containers. (I prefer glass jars with plastic lids.)

Contributor's Note: Have you ever eaten a big, goopy cinnamon roll, and you get to the center of it to find that it's doughy and wet, super-sugary, and cinnamony? Every bite of this milkshake tastes exactly like that. So, if you're experiencing a serious sweet tooth craving and love sticky cinnamon rolls, this recipe is for you! Plus it's made super fast and with simple ingredients, so you get nearly instant gratification. Best of all, unlike cinnamon rolls, this milkshake will leave you energized, lean, and glowing with radiant health!

Goji Very Berry Smoothie

Natural Zing
Prep: 7–10 minutes

2 cups ice
¼ cup raw, organic goji berries
1 organic banana
½ cup fresh or frozen organic berries (blueberries, raspberries, strawberries, blackberries, etc.)

1 tablespoon raw, organic acai berry powder or raw, organic maqui berry powder
Raw, organic honey or stevia, to taste (optional)

Blend all ingredients in your blender and enjoy!

Contributor's Note: When people ask us how they can start eating healthier, goji berries are one of the first foods we recommend. Most kids approve of them as well, and we all know getting kids to eat healthy can sometimes be a challenge. If you enjoy goji berries, you'll love this smoothie recipe! Simply blend the following ingredients together in your Vitamix® blender.

Candy Cane Smoothie

Raw Can Roll Café (www.rawcanrollcafe.com)
Prep: 7 minutes   **Yield:** 24 ounces

12 ounces almond milk
1 teaspoon Madagascar vanilla
1 cup frozen bananas
1 tablespoon fresh mint

2 tablespoons cacao nibs
2 tablespoons agave (or 10 drops of liquid stevia)
1 cup ice (or more as needed)

Put all ingredients (except for the cacao nibs) into a blender and blend well until smooth. Add cacao nibs and blend for about 6–10 seconds. Pure yum!

Contributor's Note: Optional: Blend in 1 teaspoon of fresh beet for a pink color.

Green Goodness Smoothie

Strawberry Fields Naturally
Prep: 7 minutes   **Yield:** 12 ounces

3 large kale leaves or handful spinach
1 cup banana
½ cup mango

½ cup pineapple
1 cup ice

Blend in Vitamix® for 20 seconds or until desired consistency is reached.

Contributor's Note: For larger yields:
- 16 ounces of smoothie requires 4 large kale leaves or handful spinach, 1⅓ cup banana, ⅔ cup mango, ⅔ cup pineapple, and 1 cup ice.
- 20 ounces of smoothie requires 5 large kale leaves or handful spinach, 2 cups banana, ¾ cup mango, ¾ cup pineapple, and ¾ cup ice.

Start Me Up Energy Boost Rx Smoothie

Strawberry Fields Naturally
Prep: 7 minutes   **Yield:** 16 ounces

8 ounces apple juice
1 Sambazon® acai packet
2 ounces mango

2 ounces strawberry
2 ounces pineapple

Blend in Vitamix® for 20 seconds or until desired consistency is reached.

Contributor's Note: For larger yields: 20 ounces of smoothie requires 10 ounces apple juice, 1 frozen Sambazon® acai packet, 2½ ounces mango, 2½ ounces strawberry, and 2½ ounces pineapple.

Blueberry Smoothie

Richard Golden (BleepCancer.org)
Prep: 10 minutes   **Yield:** 32 ounces

16 ounces water
½ avocado
1 large kale leaf, cleaned and de-veined
1 loose cup spinach

Pinch pure stevia
1 teaspoon vanilla or almond extract
¾ cup frozen blueberries

Blend the ingredients, in order, until thoroughly mixed with no lumps. You should come out with something the consistency and thickness of a milkshake. This recipe makes two servings. Enjoy!

Contributor's Note: You can substitute the frozen blueberries with your favorite fruits for a range of flavors. Here are some suggestions:

¾ cup frozen strawberries
½ large apple, cored
1 frozen banana, cut in 1-inch chips prior to freezing

½ cup frozen peach, deseeded
¼ cup frozen mango
½ pear, cored

Peach Melba Smoothie

Prep: 10 minutes

3 peaches, pitted
1 tablespoon raw honey
3 bananas, peeled

1 tray ice cubes
1 young Thai coconut (meat and liquid) or raw almond milk

Combine ingredients in Vitamix® high-speed blender until well blended. Drink up!

Vitamin C Smoothie

Prep: 10 minutes

2–3 oranges, peeled
1 young Thai coconut, meat and liquid

3 bananas
1 tray ice cubes

Combine the above ingredients in a Vitamix® High-Speed blender and blend until smooth. If you want your smoothie to have a lighter consistency, just add more water.

Brazilian Smoothie

Prep: 10 minutes

2 bananas
¼ cup blueberries
1 orange, peeled
2 cups cashew/Brazil nut milk (page 164)

1–2 tablespoon raw cacao nibs
1 tablespoon raw honey
1 tray ice cubes

Combine the above ingredients in a Vitamix® high-speed blender until well blended. Drink up!

Almond Milk Smoothie

Kimberton Whole Foods, www.kimbertonwholefoods.com)
Prep: almond milk, 10–15 minutes: smoothie, 7 minutes
Soak: almonds, 8 hours or overnight

Almond Milk

2 cups, raw almonds, strained
2–3 cups spring water
Vanilla, non-alcoholic; I use 2 teaspoons
    or more as I love vanilla
12 Medjool dates, pitted
6 cups water, pure

Smoothie

1 tray ice cubes
3 bananas, peeled
4–6 ounces blueberries
Almond milk, enough to cover all of the
    above in your blender
1 tablespoon raw honey
Raw cacao powder, to taste

Almond Milk

Let almonds soak overnight in water (for better digestion). In the morning rinse and drain the almonds. Then put them in your blender or jar. Add 2–3 cups of clean (spring) water along with the vanilla, dates, and a pinch of salt. Blend well. Pour the almond milk in the nut bag or through cheesecloth. It's easiest if you have a large bowl underneath to catch the filtered milk. Now holding the bag with one hand, squeeze out the additional milk with your other hand.

    Tip: If you dehydrate the almond pulp, you can use it to make raw cakes and cookies. Many save it in the fridge for about 2 days (shake before drinking), although I prefer to drink it fresh. You can buy nut bags at most health stores and online. You can also use nylons, cheesecloth, or a paint strainer.

Smoothie

Place all of the smoothie ingredients in a Vitamix® blender, pouring in the almond milk last. (I pour in enough to cover all of the ingredients and depending on how thirsty I am I may keep adding a bit more.) Blend all of the ingredients until desired consistency is reached. If you like your smoothie to have texture, then don't blend it very long. If you want your blend to be very smooth then blend the mixture a bit longer.

Contributor's Note: The wonderful thing about smoothies is that you can make a batch for the day and store them in ball jars and drink them the rest of the day.

    Also you can add all sorts of goodies to your smoothies like maca, goji berries, nutritional powders, protein powders . . . basically you can get carried away with what you add.

Berry Green Smoothie

Dave Biddison (Kimberton Whole Foods, www.kimbertonwholefoods.com)
Yield: 32 ounces or 2 16-ounce cups.

2 cups filtered water
2 cups frozen raspberries
2 whole apples, washed and chopped
  coarsely (seeds and all)

1½ cups fresh spinach, washed and
  packed
1 heaping teaspoon minced ginger

Blend on number 3 and then number 6 speeds using your Vitamix® blender.

Carrot-Banana-Ginger Smoothie

Dave Biddison (Kimberton Whole Foods, www.kimbertonwholefoods.com)
Yield: 32 ounces or 2 16-ounce cups

1½ cups filtered water
2 whole apples, washed and chopped
  coarsely (seeds and all)
1 banana
1 cup fresh carrots (grated carrots are
  easier to measure)

½ cup orange juice
½ lemon, juiced
1 teaspoon ginger, pureed

Blend on number 3 and then number 6 speeds in a Vitamix® blender.

Cayenne-Honey-Kale Smoothie

Dave Biddison (Kimberton Whole Foods, www.kimbertonwholefoods.com)
Yield: 32 ounces or 2 16-ounce cups

2 cups filtered water
2 whole apples, washed and chopped
   coarsely (seeds and all)
2 cups fresh kale, washed and packed

1 lemon, juiced
2 tablespoons raw honey
1 teaspoon ginger, pureed
¼ teaspoon ground cayenne

Blend on number 3 and then number 6 speeds in a Vitamix® blender.

Cranberry Smoothie

Dave Biddison (Kimberton Whole Foods, www.kimbertonwholefoods.com)
Yield: 32 ounces or 2 16 ounce cups

1½ cups filtered water
1 cup fresh-organic cranberries, well-
   washed (or frozen will do)
1 whole apple, washed and chopped
   coarsely (seeds and all)
½ orange, well-washed (rind, seeds,
   and all)

½ cup fresh orange juice
½ cup fresh carrot (grated carrots are
   easier to measure)
1 teaspoon ground cinnamon

Blend on number 3 speed in a Vitamix® blender.

Ginger-Mint Green Smoothie

Dave Biddison (Kimberton Whole Foods, www.kimbertonwholefoods.com)
Yield: 32 ounces or 2 16-ounce cups

2 cups filtered water
2 whole apples, washed and chopped
    coarsely (seeds and all)
2 cups fresh spinach, washed
    and packed

½ lemon, juiced
1 teaspoon ginger, pureed
10 leaves fresh mint (approximately)

Blend on number 3 speed in a Vitamix® blender.

Kimberton's Ginger-Mint Green Smoothie

Dave Biddison (Kimberton Whole Foods, www.kimbertonwholefoods.com)
Yield: 32 ounces or 2 16-ounce cups

2 cups fresh green spinach, washed
    and packed
2 whole apples, washed and chopped
    coarsely (seeds and all)

1 teaspoon pureed ginger
10 leaves fresh mint
½ lemon, juiced
2 cups filtered water

Combine the ingredients together in a high-speed blender.

Contributor's Note: Kimberton Whole Foods has four locations of health markets in southeastern Pennsylvania. Besides the markets, they also have a healthy restaurant. Kimberton Whole Foods is one of my "home away from home" places. They have such warmth, kind of like **Cheers**, where everyone knows your name. I hope that you have a place like this near you. If you don't, you may want to start one in your neighborhood.

Pumpkin Smoothie

Sheryll Chavarria (Raw Can Roll Café and Pure Body Spa, Douglassville, PA, www.rawcanrollcafe.com)

8 ounces almond milk
1 cup pumpkin, chopped

½ banana, frozen
1 teaspoon pumpkin spice (or to taste)

Combine all of the ingredients together in a high-speed blender. If the smoothie is too watery, blend in ice cubes.

Contributor's Note: Green smoothies are so nutritious (about sixty percent fruit with about forty percent green vegetables). They taste like fruit, but have all the nutrition found in dark leafy greens. When you are first starting, you may want to use fewer greens and let your taste buds develop a taste for them (especially when getting children to drink green smoothies). You can also use blueberries to disguise the color. When blended well, all of the valuable nutrients become easy for the body to digest. As opposed to juices, green smoothies are a complete food because they still have fiber.

Raspberry-Banana Yogurt Smoothie

Dave Biddison (Kimberton Whole Foods, www.kimbertonwholefoods.com)
Yield: 32 ounces or 2 16-ounce cups

2 cups frozen raspberries
1½ bananas
1 cup Seven Stars Plain Yogurt (please
note that this is not raw)

1 cup filtered water
1 tablespoon maple syrup

Blend on number 3 and then number 6 speeds on your Vitamix® blender.

Tammy's Breakfast Smoothie

Tammy Jerome
Prep: 5 minutes

6 large strawberries
2 medium bananas
1 handful of red grapes
1 handful of blueberries
1 8-ounce glass ice cubes

½ to 1 cup water (depending on desired consistency—less water for a thicker smoothie or more water for a thinner smoothie)

Combine ingredients in a Vitamix® high-speed blender until blended.

Note: This recipe makes enough smoothies for about 2 glasses. I sometimes also put it into small plastic containers and freeze them for a healthy ice cream snack. Yummy!

Coconut or Almond Milk

Dave Scully
Prep: 10 minutes   **Yield:** 1½ cups

6 tablespoons cacao powder
½ cup chia seeds
1 tablespoon goji berries
1 tablespoon (or to taste) agave, honey, or grade B maple syrup

⅛ teaspoon cayenne or cinnamon and nutmeg (spicy or nice)
Sprinkle of cacao nibs on top

Mix all the ingredients together and put in the fridge for at least 20 minutes. Save cacao nibs to sprinkle on top, though you can also sprinkle goji berries on top.

Contributor's Note: Although maple syrup is commonly used by raw foodists as a sweetener, for a *truly* raw version, it is safer to stick with raw honey or stevia.

Very Delicious Almond Milk

Tiffany Robbins
Prep: 15 minutes   **Yield:** 2½ cups

1 cup raw almonds
2 cups coconut water (or stinging
   nettle tea)
4 dates

½ vanilla pod (or splash of pure
   vanilla extract)
Pinch Celtic or Himalayan sea salt

Soak almonds for 8 hours (before going to bed is a good idea) in enough water to cover almonds. Dates ideally should be soaked for a couple of hours, but this is not necessary if using a high-speed blender. Drain almonds and discard soaking liquid. Blend drained almonds with coconut water, dates, vanilla, and salt. Strain through a nut milk bag or two layers of cheesecloth (use the technique of milking a cow). Catch liquid in a clean bowl. Do not discard pulp, this process can be repeated for additional milk.

It is common for the curd (solids) to separate from the whey (liquid) upon settling. If this should happen, shake vigorously. Almond milk should be stored refrigerated in a sealed container for 3–4 days.

Hemp Milk

Prep: 10 minutes

1 cup hemp seeds
5 dates, pitted

1 tablespoon vanilla
3 cups water

Combine the above ingredients in a Vitamix® high-speed blender until well blended. I use hemp milk in my smoothies.

Apple Milk

Prep: 15 minutes

2 apples, remove cores
2 cups raw almonds, soaked
1 teaspoon cinnamon

12 Medjool dates, pitted
6 cups water
1 tablespoon vanilla

Combine the above ingredients in a Vitamix® high-speed blender until well blended. Pour the blended milk through a milk bag over a bowl and milk the bag. The milk will come out through the bag into the bowl, while the pulp will be caught in the bag. The pulp can be turned into crackers. Store milk in a glass canning jar with a screw top.

Cashew / Brazil Nut Milk

Prep: 15 minutes

1 cup raw cashews
1 cup raw Brazil nuts
6 cups water

1 tablespoon vanilla
12 Medjool dates, pitted

Combine the above ingredients in a Vitamix® high-speed blender until well blended. Pour the blended milk through a milk bag over a bowl and milk the bag. The milk will come out through the bag into the bowl. The pulp will be caught in the bag. Store milk in glass canning jar with screw top.

Raw Almond Milk

Prep: 10 minutes

2 cups raw almonds
12 Medjool dates, pitted and softened

2 tablespoons vanilla extract
6 cups water

Combine the above ingredients in a Vitamix® high-speed blender until well blended. Pour the milk through a milk bag over a large bowl, milking the pulp while holding the bag to release the rest of the milk. I freeze my pulp and use it to make crackers.

Almond Milk

Tribest (Home of the Green Star Juicer and Sedona Dehydrator)
Prep: 15 minutes   **Soak:** almonds, 6–8 hours

1 cup almonds, soaked and drained
2 cups water

1 tablespoon maple syrup
1 teaspoon vanilla

Blend the above ingredients together until smooth and creamy. Strain liquid in a milk bag or fine strainer using a large bowl. Store in a sealed glass jar. Serve cold in glass.

> **WORDS FROM LISA:**
>
> This recipe is from the folks at Tribest and is designed to be made in their Soyabella.

Maple-Almond Milk

Make in Tribest Soyabella milk maker
Prep: 25 minutes   **Soak:** almonds, 4–6 hours

1 cup almonds, soaked/rinsed (2.5 ounces)

0.8 liter or approximately 3 cups (27 fluid ounces) filtered water (fill to the lower line in Soyabella chamber)

2–5 tablespoons maple syrup (grade B is best)

1 teaspoon alcohol-free vanilla

1–2 pinches sea salt

Fill the chamber with 0.8 liter (approximately 3 cups or 27 fluid ounces) of filtered water (to the lower line).

Fill the milk screen with soaked almonds and attach to the heat unit, turning counter-clockwise. Make sure it is secure.

Follow instructions for making raw nut milk.

Pour the unflavored almond milk in a glass container. Combine almond milk with maple syrup, vanilla, and sea salt.

Chill before serving.

Green Morning Drink

Derek Batman
Prep: 10 minutes

2 cups spinach

1½ cups grapes

2 carrots

½ cucumber

½ inch piece ginger

1 stalk celery

2 dates

Handful ice

½–1 cup water

Combine all ingredients in blender or Vitamix®. Start with ½ cup water and add more to desired thickness. Blend until smooth.

Baja Pineapple Drink

Elysa Markowitz
Prep: 10 minutes   **Serves:** 2

½ cup pineapple, skinned and cut across
    height-wise into rectangular pieces
1 lime, juiced

½ cup cilantro
3 greenleaf lettuce leaves

Remove the skin from the pineapple. Cut pineapple across, not lengthwise, and into rectangular pieces. Slice half a lime and juice the lime with its rind. Juice pineapple, cilantro, lettuce leaves, and the other half of the lime together. Serve in a fancy glass, running lime around the rim of the glass. Garnish with lime and cilantro.

Contributor's Note: The cilantro and green lettuce in this recipe cut the sweetness of the pineapple. The mix also has a delightful taste. The ingredients also help prevent the sugar highs or lows some people experience from drinking plain pineapple juice.

Tribest has graciously allowed us to share some of Elysa Markowitz's recipes from their book *Living with Green Star: A Gourmet Collection of Living Food Recipes.*

Berry Red Juice

Elysa Markowitz
Prep: 10 minutes   **Serves:** 2

¼ watermelon
½ cantaloupe
6–12 strawberries

Juice the strawberries with the melon, including the rind and watermelon seeds.

Contributor's Note: This cooling juice is great for cleaning blood and skin, and is a gentle nerve food, complete with a natural painkiller. This is a refreshing summer drink as melons are 92% water.

Blushing Green Power Drink

Elysa Markowitz
Prep: 10 minutes   **Serves:** 2

4–6 carrots
2 romaine lettuce leaves
1 beet

2 celery stalks
¼ cup cilantro

Cut carrots and beets to a size to fit into the machine and feed into the machine, alternating with the romaine, celery, and cilantro.

Contributor's Note: Combining carrots with beets makes this juice a dynamite blood cleanser and liver tonic. The greens make this a perfect blend for the heart and lungs. It is an all-around body building drink blushing with beet juice and powered by greens.

C Boost Drink

Elysa Markowitz
Prep: 10 minutes **Serves:** 2

3 apples
3 celery stalks
1 red bell pepper

Cut apples and bell pepper to fit into a juicer, and juice only two of the celery stalks with the rest of the ingredients. Serve in a fancy glass, with a celery stick as a stirrer.

Contributor's Note: This recipe gets its name from the high vitamin C content in both apples and red bell peppers.

Coffee Quitter's Juice

Elysa Markowitz
Prep: 10 minutes **Serves:** 4

1 pear
2 apples

4 oranges
1 grapefruit

Peel and cut the oranges and grapefruit. Cut the apples and pear to fit into the machine. Juice all the ingredients and serve.

Contributor's Note: One of Elysa's students went to her class and was so excited that he had been able to give up coffee. She asked him how, and he told her that after making this juice, he felt so good that he did not need to drink coffee. If you are ready to kick the habit, here is his recipe.

Digester's Delight

Elysa Markowitz
Prep: 15 minutes   **Serves:** 4

1 pineapple, skinned
3–4 oranges, peeled

3 celery stalks (juice one stalk to start with)
2 apples

Peel and cut pineapple in rings and then slices. Put through the juicer with the peeled oranges and apple; alternating with one of the celery stalks. Serve with a celery stick as a stirrer.

Contributor's Note: The celery is the surprise ingredient in this delightful drink. It can make this a salty drink, so go lightly with it at first, adding more to taste.

How Do You Spell Relief Juice

Elysa Markowitz
Prep: 10 minutes   **Serves:** 2

1 apple
6 carrots
2 slices purple cabbage

Cut the apple, carrot, and cabbage in the appropriate size to feed into the juicer and alternate putting the different ingredients into the juicer. Juice all ingredients.

Contributor's Note: Relief is spelled j–u–i–c–e. This juice's rich digestive aids from both the apple and cabbage give new meaning to the word relief.

Fat Meltdown Juice

Elysa Markowitz
Prep: 10 minutes   **Serves:** 2

2 apples
2 pears
1 slice fresh ginger

Cut apples and pears to fit into the machine. Juice all ingredients alternating with sliced apples, pears, and ginger.

Contributor's Note: This juice helps reduce fat from the places we tend to store cellulite, in our arms and lower body. Plus, the ginger warms and stimulates the blood to circulate while we are slimming down.

Tomato Pepper Celery Juice

Natalie Norman
Prep: 10–15 minutes

5 red bell peppers, seeded (or equivalent of other sweet peppers)
5 large tomatoes

2 heads celery
1 large apple

Juice, strain, enjoy!

Get Yer MoJo Back Juice

Raw Can Roll Café (www.rawcanrollcafe.com)
Prep: 15 minutes

3 ounces juiced collard, kale, or
  Swiss chard
3 ounces juiced apple or pomegranate
3 ounces juiced celery

3 ounces juiced cucumber
1 teaspoon lemon juice
1 teaspoon fresh ginger

Run the above ingredients through your juicer and drink up!

Strawberry Fields Juice

Strawberry Fields Naturally
Prep: 7 minutes   **Yield:** 12 ounces

1 apple, cut into quarters and
  de-stemmed
8 ounces apple juice

3 mint leaves
½ cup strawberries

Juice apples, and then blend juice, strawberries, and mint leaves in blender.

Contributor's Note: For larger yields:
- 16 ounces of juice requires 10 ounces of apple juice, 4–5 mint leaves, and ⅔ cup of strawberries.
- 20 ounces of juice requires 12 ounces of apple juice, 5 mint leaves, and 1 cup of strawberries.

Wake Up Juice 2.0

Will Eddy
Prep: 7 minutes

2 small tomatoes
5 sticks celery
½ lemon, juiced

1 cup ice
2 cups greens

Put all ingredients in your Vitamix® machine and blend on high about 1 minute. The trick is to blend it on high until *all* the ice is melted. This will create a liquid base for the juice. This is the juice I drink for energy on my long, long Vitamix® demonstrator days.

Tomato/Pineapple Juice

Prep: 5 minutes

1 cup tomato
1 cup pineapple

Place equal parts tomato and pineapple in your Vitamix® High-Speed Blender or juice in your Tribest® Slowstar Juicer.

WORDS FROM LISA:

I know this is a unique combo; it comes from the inspiration of "whatever is in the refrigerator." Be creative; you never know what will work!

Carrot Ginger Juice

Brenda Hinton (Rawsome Creations, www.rawsomecreations.com)
Prep: 7 minutes

½ medium lemon peeled
4 large celery stalks
1 medium apple, cored and peeled

2 large carrots
Thumb-sized knob of ginger
½ cup water (optional)

Roughly chop the lemon, celery, apple, and carrots into medium pieces (approximately 1 inch). Place all ingredients in Vitamix® High Speed Blender in the order they are listed. Blend smooth (about 1 minute cycle). The plunger may be needed to get things started. Strain blended mixture through a nut milk bag, easily milking the pulp and catching the juice in a bowl or pitcher. Serve immediately. Save the pulp for use in other recipes, such as Carrot Ginger Crackers on page 191. Pulp can be refrigerated for three days or frozen for up to one month. Yields about 16 ounces of juice, approximately 1 cup pulp.

Down on the Bayou

Sheryll Chavarria (Raw Can Roll Café and Pure Body Spa, Douglassville, PA, www.rawcanrollcafe.com)

10 ounces coconut milk (can add coconut
  meat, as well)
1½ cups frozen pineapple

¼ banana (for texture)
½ cup ice (optional)
Agave to taste

Combine ingredients together in a high-speed blender. Blend well and enjoy.

Good Vibrations

Raw Can Roll Café (www.rawcanrollcafe.com)
Yield: 24-ounce drink

2 leaves kale (remove leaves from stem)
½ apple
1 stalk celery
12 ounces water

Handful cucumber (optional)
½ banana (optional)
1 thin slice lemon with rind (optional, to help slow down oxidation)

Place ingredients in a high-speed blender and blend well.

Green Giant Juice

Brenda Hinton (Rawsome Creations, www.rawsomecreations.com)
Prep: 15 minutes

½ cup water
1 medium lemon, peeled
2 large celery stalks
½ medium apple, cored and peeled
¼ cup parsley, packed measure (4–5 sprigs)

1 cup spinach, packed measure (1 large handful)
Thumb-sized knob of ginger
1 cup kale leaves, packed measure (3 large-sized leaves)

Rough chop the lemon, celery, and apple into medium pieces (approximately 1 inch). Place all ingredients in a Vitamix® High Speed Blender in the order they are listed. Blend smooth (about 1 minute cycle). The plunger may be needed to get things started. Strain blended mixture through a nut milk bag, easily milking the pulp and catching the juice in a bowl or pitcher. Serve immediately. Save the pulp for use in other recipes, like the Spinach Wraps on page 229. Yields 16 ounces of juice, approximately 1 cup pulp.

Additions:
Add 1 roughly chopped cucumber for another level of flavor and nutrition.

Honey Lemonade with Coconut Water

Adagio (aged 6, daughter of Jinjee, www.TheGardenDiet.com)
Prep: 10 minutes

Water of 1 coconut
½ pitcher Honey Lemonade

Honey Lemonade
3 lemons, juiced
2 tablespoons raw honey
½ blender of water (3 cups)

Honey Lemonade
Blend lemons and honey on high for 30 seconds. Top off blender with water and pour into pitcher.

Combine all ingredients and serve.

Afternoon Satyr Tea

Antanas Vainius
Prep: less than 1 minute

1–2 cups nettles and mugwort (or favorite earthy infusion)
1–2 tablespoons low-temperature goat whey mineral powder

½ cup raw goat milk
A few drops of Stevia

Mix, serve, and enjoy!

Sage Oxymel

Sue Hess (Farm at Coventry)
Prep: 15 minutes

2 cups raw apple cider vinegar
2 cups raw local honey

2–3 cups fresh garden sage leaves, shredded (or 1 cup dried garden sage leaf)

Combine honey and vinegar and warm until well blended. When the mixture is steaming, take off the heat, add the sage leaf, and cover with a lid. Allow to steep overnight. Strain into a sterilized bottle, label, and refrigerate.

Contributor's Note: Oxymel is a simple mixture of honey and vinegar, simmered to a thin syrup. Herbs and spices can be added for culinary or medicinal purposes during the heating process and allowed to steep then strained out before serving. The addition of sage leaf, rose petals, and bee balm leaves and flowers all make a very nice oxymel. Sage is particularly good for a sore throat but tastes delicious any time!

Peach Shrub

Sue Hess (Farm at Coventry)
Prep: 20 minutes

6 ripe peaches, seeded
2 cups raw apple cider vinegar
2 cups raw local honey (or organic sugar)

Slice and seed 6 very ripe peaches over a two-quart stainless steel saucepan to catch all the juices. Chop large pieces into small ones. The skins and pit can also be added for additional flavor. Pour 2 cups of raw apple cider vinegar over prepared peaches. Bring the mixture to a very low simmer, mashing fruit to extract juices. Add an equal measure of raw local honey or organic sugar and heat through until all is dissolved and combined.

Put a lid on the pan, take off the heat, and allow to steep overnight. Strain solids out of the fruity syrup and decant into a sterilized glass bottle or jar. Label, date, and refrigerate. The taste mellows very nicely over time. Add 1-2 tablespoons of finished shrub to cracked ice and sparkling water in the summer, or hot tea water in the winter months.

Contributor's Note: A "shrub" is made by combining vinegar and honey (or sugar) with the addition of fruit. Shrubs were primarily used as a preservation method in colonial times. Berries, strawberries, peaches, and elderberries all make exceptionally good shrubs. Herbs and spices can be added to enhance flavors.

Elderberry Elixir

Sue Hess (Farm at Coventry)
Prep: 25 minutes

4 cups freshly picked black elderberries, small branches and stems removed
4¼ cups water
1 tablespoon fresh grated ginger root (or ½ teaspoon ground ginger)

½ teaspoon ground cloves
½ teaspoon cinnamon
Brandy

In a medium sauce pan, combine 4 cups freshly picked black elderberries, small branches and stems removed. Cover them with an equal amount of water. Cover the saucepan with a lid and bring to a low simmer until the water begins to steam and the berries begin to pop and release their juices. Stir often, until the berries have collapsed and juices are flowing. A potato masher helps to encourage the process along. Simply press down on the berries as they simmer to release more juice.

Put the lid back on and allow to cool slightly, so that the contents can be handled in the next phase. Pour the warm contents of the saucepan into a clean wide mouth glass jar using a wide funnel. Cover the berry/juice mixture two-thirds of the way full with a good quality brandy (I prefer E&J) and add enough honey to cover the mixture completely. Put the lid on tight and shake gently to combine all ingredients. Store for 4 weeks and strain before serving.

Contributor's Note: Begin elderberry preparations by heating the fresh berries first to release the juice. By doing so, you can capture fresh elderberries at the peak of vitality and then preserve it in a variety of ways. It is also possible to strain the finished preparations in as little as 2 weeks.

Rose Petal Syrup

Sue Hess (Farm at Coventry)
Prep: 20 minutes

> 2 cups organic sugar
> 1 cup water
> 1 cup fragrant rose petals

Bring water and sugar to a low boil in a stainless steel saucepan, dissolving sugar completely. Add finely chopped flowers to the hot syrup and keep at a low boil for 5 minutes. Take off of the heat, put a lid on the pot, and allow to steep overnight. The next day, strain the flowers out of the syrup and put syrup in a sterilized jar and refrigerate.

Contributor's Note: Stir a spoonful of herbal syrup into your favorite beverage—it's good in lemonade or hot tea. Or drizzle it over waffles, French toast, scones, fruit salad, cake, or ice cream. The possibilities are endless. Experiment and delight your friends. Nothing hits the spot better on a hot summer night than sparkling water over crushed ice with a splash of any homemade herbal syrup!

Tiffany's Beauty Elixir

Tiffany Robbins
Prep: 5 minutes

> 2 cups coconut water
> 1 inch aloe vera gel
> 1 tablespoon acai powder

> 3 capsules pearl powder
> Squeeze of lemon juice

Blend all ingredients until frothy. Enjoy in good health!

Pear-Cucumber-Mint

Joel Odhner

   4 pears
   1 cucumber
   1 ounce mint juice

Run the ingredients through your juicer and enjoy.

Spicy Pineapple Crush

Brenda Cobb (Founder of Living Foods Institute® and author of *The Living Foods Lifestyle*, www.livingfoodsinstitute.com)
Prep: 10 minutes

   3 cups very ripe, fresh pineapple
   2 teaspoons mint leaves
   1 teaspoon cilantro

   1 teaspoon fresh lemon juice
   Pinch cayenne pepper

Blend ingredients together in the Vitamix®. Serve and refresh yourself.

Water Kefir: A Dairy-Free, Probiotic Beverage

Melissa Miles (Permanent Future Institute)
Prep: 10 minutes

6 cups water, brought just to a boil	2 quart jar
¼ cup organic sugar	½ organic lemon (optional)
¼ cup water kefir grains	Handful unsulphured dried fruit (optional)

Bring water just to a boil, turn off heat, and stir in the ¼ cup organic sugar until it is dissolved. Allow it to cool to room temperature. Place ¼ cup water kefir grains into a 2-quart jar. Pour in the cooled sugar water. Optionally, you can drop in a handful of unsulphured dried fruit and ½ organic lemon.

Cover the jar loosely with a lid or with cheesecloth secured with rubber band, to allow air in but prevent bugs from entering the jar. Ferment out of direct sunlight, at room temperature for 2–3 days. The longer it ferments, the stronger the flavor. When the desired flavor is reached, strain it through a nonreactive (plastic, wood, or stainless steel) strainer into another 2-quart jar. Leave some head space (discard the spent lemon and dried fruit), but reserve the water kefir grains. Enjoy your water kefir beverage immediately or store in refrigerator.

Try a secondary ferment to add more flavor to the brew: Pour either ¼ cup fruit juice of your choice or 1 tablespoon organic cane sugar into two flip-top bottles. Pour the water kefir from the 2-quart jar into bottles, filling them up to within one inch of the opening. Seal the bottles and set them on a countertop to ferment an additional 18–24 hours (keeping in mind that warm temperatures will speed up the fermentation process, and cool temperatures will slow it down). Grains can be immediately re-cultured or stored in water in the fridge for a few weeks, or frozen or dehydrated for longer storage. Probiotics aid you in digesting food, particularly hard-to-digest foods and foods to which some individuals are more sensitive. They enhance the synthesis of B vitamins and improve calcium absorption. They also help to keep a healthy balance of intestinal microflora.

Coconut Water Kefir

Melissa Miles (Permanent Future Institute)
Prep: 10-15 minutes

    4 cups young coconut water
    4 tablespoons water kefir grains

Combine the coconut water and the grains in a jar and let sit for 12–24 hours. Some people like to add a tablespoon of organic cane sugar but this is optional. Coconut water tends to ferment quickly and the flavor will become more intense (sour and tangy). Taste often; when you like the results, just strain the grains out and enjoy. Grains can be stored in refrigerator or start another batch right away.

Basic Kombucha

Melissa Miles (Permanent Future Institute)
Prep: 10–15 minutes

    3 quarts non-chlorinated/filtered spring
        water or distilled water
    5–7 tea bags

    ½ cup organic cane sugar
    1 kombucha SCOBY (Symbiotic Culture
        of friendly Bacteria and Yeast)

In a large, non-aluminum pot, bring water to a simmer. Note: a rolling boil will reduce oxygen and carbon, which are necessary for proper fermentation, so *simmer*, don't boil. Add tea bags. Tea is the herb that it feeds on, so organic black or green teas are best. Steep 5–10 minutes. Add ½ cup organic cane sugar, ½ cup white sugar (white sugar is essential to its survival and no substitution should be made.) Stir with wooden spoon only; ferments hate metal. Allow to cool to room temperature. Keep covered to avoid contamination.

Pour cooled liquid into fermenting container (glass is best; no plastic or metal). Add kombucha SCOBY with 2 cups of previously fermented starter. (If none available, use ¼ cup white distilled vinegar to reduce the pH and protect against all pathogens. Do not use unpasteurized non-distilled apple cider vinegar.)

Cover with clean cloth. Set aside in an undisturbed spot out of direct sunlight to ferment. Ferment for 6–8 days at a constant temperature of 75–80°F. You should notice an apple cider aroma when finished. If you notice any mold or unpleasant smell, discard the entire batch, SCOBY and all. You cannot salvage a moldy SCOBY.

To bottle, choose a glass container in which you will consume the entire amount within 1–2 days, otherwise you'll risk having the tea turn flat. You may choose to filter the tea over cheesecloth. While this may filter possible contaminants, it also reduces some beneficial bacteria and the taste becomes lighter. I do not filter my liquid, but it is your choice. The bottled tea may be left on the counter at room temperature to allow for additional 2–3 days of fermentation. Refrigerate the final brew. Note that kombucha has been known to "contaminate" other ferments, so keep it away from sourdough, kefir, lacto-ferments, etc.

Raw foodists and the health world are really into kombucha and kefirs because of their many health benefits.

We Got the Beet

Strawberry Fields Naturally
Prep: 7 minutes **Yield:** 12 ounce

8 ounces apple juice
4 ounces beet juice

¼ lime
1 large kale leaf or handful of spinach

Juice apple and beet into large measuring cup, pour into blender pitcher. Add 1 large kale leaf or handful of spinach and blend in Vitamix® for 20 seconds or until desired consistency is reached.

Contributor's Note: For larger yields:
- 16 ounces of smoothie requires 10 ounces apple juice, 6 ounces beet juice, and ¼ lime
- 20 ounces of smoothie requires 12 ounces apple juice, 8 ounces beet juice, and ¼ lime

Water Kefir

Annmarie Cantrell
Prep: 10 minutes

    3 tablespoons water kefir grains
    3 tablespoons sugar (organic cane sugar)

Dissolve the sugar in the water. Add kefir grains and cover loosely with the lid. Let sit at room temperature for about 48 hours (in summer, it may only take 24 hours). The longer it ferments, the stronger it will become.

    Strain the kefir through a non reactive strainer (or a strainer lined with cheese-cloth). Pour the liquid back into the jar and add some dried fruit and any flavorings that you desire (vanilla bean, cinnamon stick, star anise, lemon, ginger, clove, and fruit)—be creative! Seal and let sit for an additional 2 days. Watch it carefully, as it can get very fizzy. To prevent it from leaking or rupturing, you can ferment them in grolsch bottles that have the seal on them.

    To keep grains that are not being cultured, keep them in your refrigerator in sugar water. Feed them every 3 days or so. If grains turn dormant (do not culture a batch immediately), try feeding them with molasses, lemon, and ginger. These three seem to "wake" the grains back up. Then proceed as usual.

Contributor's Note: Water kefir is a fermented drink that is full of beneficial acids, beneficial microorganisms, and enzymes. The culture is called a "grain," but is really a SCOBY—Symbiotic Colony of Yeast and Bacteria. The culturing of the water kefir produces a bit of alcohol (about .05-.75%). Kefir grains are best procured from a friend who makes kefir. I find these to be the hardiest, most prolific grains. You can also order grains from www.culturesforhealth.com.

Young Thai Coconut Water

Prep: 5 minutes

1 young Thai coconut

To open a young Thai coconut, place firmly on a chopping board on your countertop. Take the back end of your cleaver or chef's knife, and using the backend, chop a circle around the top of the coconut. Pop open the lid and pour the liquid into your glass. The meat can be removed with an ice cream scoop and saved for another recipe; or, you can combine the coconut water and meat in a Vitamix® high-speed blender and drink.

WORDS FROM LISA:

Coconut water has been used to treat a variety of health problems including dehydration, heat stroke, digestive complaints, constipation, diarrhea, fatigue, hives, low libido, urinary tract infections, jaundice, and nausea. Even your overall health will improve if you regularly drink coconut water!

12

Breads, Crackers, & Chips

Garlic Bread

Joel Odhner
Prep: 15 minutes   **Dehydrate:** 4–8 hours at 105°F

Jicama, peeled and sliced ¼-inch thick
1 cup flax seeds, ground
1½ cups walnuts

4 or 5 cloves garlic
1 teaspoon lemon juice
1 teaspoon sea salt (or to taste)

Peel and slice the jicama and lay out on Teflex sheets. Combine the rest of the ingredients in your food processor and hand-press the mixture onto jicama slices. Dehydrate 4–8 hours.

Contributor's Note: This is one of the first recipes that Joel taught me at his raw cooking classes. This recipe is easy and so good. It is one of those recipes that, once you start eating it, you just keep going. If you would make this recipe as a snack for your family, they will devour it.

Sauerkraut Crackers

Prep: 10 minutes

3 cups raw sauerkraut
1 cup sunflower seeds
1 cup golden flax seeds
½ cup water

½ teaspoon caraway seeds
½ teaspoon sea salt
¼ cup fresh dill
¼–½ teaspoon garlic granules

Mix all of the ingredients in the Cuisinart Food Processor until thoroughly combined. Spread cracker mixture on a Teflex dehydrator sheet at 105°F. Halfway through the drying process, flip the cracker mixture, and remove it from the Teflex sheets. Place on dehydrator tray and dry until desired dryness. Depending on where you live, whether it is hot cold, humid, or not, will determine how long it will take for your crackers mixture to dry.

Leftover Salad Crackers

Prep: 30 minutes

2 cups leftover salad
½ cup flax seeds
⅔ cup water
1 teaspoon sea salt or to taste
1 teaspoon raw honey

1–2 tablespoons cold-pressed olive oil,
    Austria's Finest Pumpkin Seed oil, or
    coconut oil (each of the oils will give
    the cracker a totally different taste)
Seasonings to taste

Grind flax seeds in a nut grinder, coffee grinder Vitamix® High Speed Blender, Tribest® personal blender, or mini food processor. Take ground flax seeds and combine with water. Let sit for 10 minutes. Some people also combine 1 cup of flax seeds with the ground flax seeds for a different texture. If you decide to try this option, make sure to add another cup of water to the mix. Once the flax seeds have soaked up the water, combine the above ingredients in a food processor until they are the desired texture. You can also different seasonings, vegetables, or dried fruit combinations for different textures and flavors. If you don't wish to use two cups of leftover salad, you can use two cups of assorted vegetables or dried fruit. The combination of vegetables, fruits and spices/flavorings are endless.

Horseradish & Dill Crackers/Bread

Barbara Shevkun (Rawfully Tempting)
Soak: Walnuts, overnight   **Prep:** 20–30 minutes
Dehydrate: Approximately 24 hours or as desired, at 115°F

1½ cups walnuts (soaked overnight)
½ cup almond pulp/flour
1½ cups veggie pulp (from juicing), or zucchini, chopped
2½ cups water, or as needed
¼ cup ground flax seeds
3 tablespoons hemp seed
2 tablespoons grated horseradish (optional)
1 garlic clove, minced
1 teaspoon dill, dried (save ½ teaspoon for garnish) or 1½ tablespoons fresh dill

2 tablespoons sesame seeds (may also use some for garnish)
1 tablespoon lemon juice
1 tablespoon honey (or your favorite sweetener)
1 tablespoon Annie's horseradish mustard (optional, not raw)
¼ teaspoon onion powder
¼ teaspoon garlic powder
¾ teaspoon sea salt

In food processor, process walnuts, almond pulp, and veggie pulp.

Add water as needed to mix (if you use more water, the dehydration time will need to be increased). Add remaining ingredients and continue to process until well mixed. Taste and adjust seasoning to your liking. Spread 1 cup of batter onto no-stick dehydrator sheet, rotating the tray in a circle as you spread the batter onto the tray (an offset spatula helps a lot). Repeat this for each tray. Garnish with dill and/or sesame seeds, or poppy seeds, onion flakes, etc. Dehydrate at 115°F for about 3 hours. To flip over, place a mesh tray on top. Holding two trays together, quickly flip over. Remove tray and peel off non-stick sheet. Score batter using a dull-edged knife and continue to dehydrate 12–18 hours, or until crisp.

Note: For bread, spread batter onto two trays, instead of three, making the layers thicker than crackers. Follow directions above, although you may have to wait another hour to flip. Score into squares. Dehydrate until bread is firm, but not crunchy. Freeze in airtight container and use as needed.

Contributor's Note: As part of my recent exploration into my "roots," I prepared fresh horseradish. It was deeply earthy and delicious. From that recipe, I made a horseradish hummus dip, which was lighter in texture, but also fabulous. I needed some crunchy crackers, so what else? Horseradish & Dill Crackers, of course! The horseradish flavor turned out rather mild while the dill seems to permeate the crackers. I love dill, so it works for me, and I can spread either horseradish or the hummus on them. If you're not a fan of dill, replace it with your favorite herb. This recipe may also be prepared as a bread.

Garlic Bread

Elaina Love (Author of *Elaina's Pure Joy Kitchen*, www.PureJoyLove.com)
Prep: 30 minutes **Dehydrate:** 6–8 hours at 105°F

6 cups almond meal (leftover from
making almond milk)
2 cups flax meal (1¼ cups flax seeds
ground in a dry blender)
½ cup Bariani® Olive Oil
2 teaspoons Celtic sea salt

2–3 crushed garlic cloves
½ cup chopped fresh Italian herbs: basil,
oregano, thyme, and rosemary
Pitted and sliced sun-dried olives,
optional

Place all ingredients in a bowl and mix with your hands. Place some of the batter in between 2 Teflex sheets or wax paper, and roll with a rolling pin until the batter is about ¼-inch thick. Cut into bread-sized pieces or use fun cookie cutter shapes.

Dehydrate at 105°F for 6 to 8 hours. Bread should be moist and firm. You can also sun-dry these on a screen or put them in your car to dry on a warm day. Will last 2 weeks in the refrigerator.

Graw Crumbs Magic Crackers

Ken Immer
Prep: 20 minutes

4 ounces Degelet date paste
4 ounces apples, cored (Gala, cameo,
Fuji)
2 ounces filtered water

2½ cups Graw Foods graw crumbs™
1 drop orange oil, cold pressed
Dash cinnamon, ground
⅛ teaspoon Celtic sea salt

Puree dates, apples, and water together in a food processor until well combined. Pour into a bowl. Add the graw crumbs and salt. Mix well until a thick batter forms. Allow to sit for 5 minutes. Spread out thinly on dehydrator non-stick sheets. Dehydrate until crunchy.

Raw Olive Flat Bread (Crackers)

Natural Zing
Prep: 20 minutes

- 2 cups raw, organic Natural Zing® Peruvian dried black olives (pitted), soaked in water for 2 hours, then drained
- 2 cups raw, organic sunflower seeds
- 3 cloves garlic
- 1 carrot
- 1 cup raw, organic Brazil nuts (or chia seeds)
- 1 cup ground flax seeds or Natural Zing® sprouted ground golden flax seed powder
- 1 teaspoon Celtic sea salt

Blend all ingredients in a food processor until smooth. Add ½ cup water and smooth with a spatula onto a Teflex sheet on a dehydrator tray. Dehydrate for 12 hours, or until desired crunch level has been achieved. Serve with hummus, salad, guacamole, or tapenade.

Carrot Ginger Crackers

Brenda Hinton (Rawsome Creations, www.rawsomecreations.com)
Prep: 40 minutes   **Yield:** 25–50 crackers depending on size

- 2½ cups, rough, chopped carrots (approximately 2 large carrots)
- 3 cups, rough, chopped Gala apples (approximately 2 medium apples)
- ¼ cup water (optional—use if necessary to blend)
- 1 teaspoon whole brown flax seeds, soaked 3–4 hours
- 1 teaspoon whole golden flax seeds, soaked 3–4 hours
- 2 tablespoons water
- 1 cup walnuts (soaked and dehydrated preferred but not necessary)
- 1 cup almond pulp
- 1 cup carrot-apple pulp (from step one)
- ¼ cup ground flax meal (approximately 3 tablespoon whole flax seeds)
- 1½ tablespoons lemon juice
- ¼ teaspoon garlic powder
- ¼ teaspoon ginger powder
- ¼ teaspoon salt
- 1 tablespoon nutritional yeast

In a Vitamix® High Speed Blender, place chopped carrots and apples and blend until smooth. Strain blended mixture through the "More Than a Nut Milk Bag" catching the juice in a bowl or a pitcher. Reserve juice for another recipe or drink. You will be saving the pulp in the nut milk bag for use in this recipe. Yields roughly 1 cup pulp.

In a small jar, add the brown and golden flax seeds and water and soak for 4–6 hours, or until thickened and gelatinous. Set aside.

In a food processor, place walnuts and grind to a fine meal, uniform in size, no chunks. Add almond pulp, carrot-apple pulp, ground flax meal, lemon juice, garlic and ginger powders, salt, nutritional yeast, and soaked flax seeds. Process until mixture is well combined and uniform in consistency. (Rocking the food processor helps with the consistency).

Line one dehydrator tray with both grid and Teflex sheets. Use an off-set spatula to spread the full amount of the mixture to ⅛ to ¼ inch thick. Score into desired shapes. Please note that the mixture will be very thick. Dehydrate at 115°F for about 2 hours or until dry to the touch. Flip your crackers and remove the Teflex sheet. Continue dehydration until crackers are completely dry and crunchy approximately 10 hours or more. Crackers can be stored in airtight glass containers for up to 3 months.

Living, Dehydrated Herb Flax Crackers

Elaina Love (Author of *Elaina's Pure Joy Kitchen*, www.PureJoyLove.com)
Prep: 20 minutes   **Soak:** flax seeds, 24 hours   **Dehydrate:** about 24 hours at 105°F
Yield: approximately 100 crackers

½ onion
5 cloves garlic
4 cups flax seeds, soaked (seeds will double in size so put them in an 8-cup container, fill to the top with water, and then store in a dark place)

2 teaspoons sea salt
¼ cup lemon juice
1 cup chopped fresh dill, and/or rosemary, sage, basil, oregano, thyme, cilantro

Puree onions, garlic, and herbs in a food processor until finely ground. In a large bowl, combine sprouted flax seeds, salt, lemon juice, and herb mixture. Place 2 cups in the middle of a Teflex dehydrator sheet using a plastic spatula. Take the corner edge of your firm spatula and score the sheets into 25 squares. You should fill 4 16x16-inch trays. The thicker you make them, the easier they are to dip with. Dehydrate at 105°F until crackers are firm enough to flip. Let crackers remain in dehydrator until crunchy (about 24 hours all together).

Kale Chips

Derek Batman
Prep: 15 minutes

1 clove garlic
1 cup cashews, soaked at least 8 hours, rinsed and drained
¼ cup nutritional yeast
⅓ cup water

2 tablespoons olive oil
½ teaspoon smoked paprika
¼ teaspoon chipotle (spice)
Pinch sea salt

With processor running, drop in garlic and mince. Add the rest of the ingredients and process until smooth. Pour over kale chips in a bowl and massage until kale is coated. Dehydrate on screens at 115°F for 4–6 hours or until crisp.

Contributor's Note: Nutritional yeast is not raw but is used frequently in raw food recipes.

Kale or Beet Leaf Chips

MJ Pangman (Dancing with Water)
Prep: 15 minutes

15–20 kale or beet leaves (depending on size, with middle stem removed from kale)
3 tablespoons extra virgin olive oil
1 tablespoon raw vinegar
3 tablespoons nutritional yeast flakes

¼ cup fresh lemon juice
2 teaspoons bamboo salt (you will need less salt if you use other unprocessed salts)
Seasoning blend (optional)

Mix all ingredients (except leaves) in a large bowl. Add kale or beet leaves and massage the seasoning into the leaves so that all leaves are covered. Lay on open dehydrator trays. Dehydrate at 115°F for 2 hours for kale or 3–4 hours for beet greens.

Corn Tortillas

Brenda Hinton (Rawsome Creations, www.rawsomecreations.com)
Prep: 30 minutes

> Brenda's Sweet Corn Chowder mixture from page 96
> ¼ cup golden flax seeds ground separately in a coffee or spice grinder
> 1 tablespoon psyllium powder

Before removing the Sweet Corn Chowder from the Vitamix® High Speed Blender, add the remaining 3 cups of corn kernels and blend until very smooth. Then add the remaining ingredients while the blades are still turning slowly.

Pulse or blend until well incorporated throughout. Ready five dehydrator trays with grid and Teflex sheets. Using a Teflex-lined dehydrator tray and template (More Than a Wrap Mold, page 97) as a guide, spread a generous ¼ cup of the mixture for each tortilla round. Using a small offset spatula, spread the mixture flat and smooth so that it fills out the entire round evenly.

If not using template: use ¼ cup measure of mixture for each 6-inch tortilla and spread evenly (about ⅛-inch thick) forming four piles for wraps on each Teflex sheet.

Sunny Crisps

Brenda Cobb (Founder of Living Foods Institute® and author of *The Living Foods Lifestyle*, www.livingfoodsinstitute.com)
Prep: 20 minutes   **Soak:** sunflower seeds, almonds, and flax seeds, overnight
Dehydrate: 1–2 days at 100°F

1 cup sunflower seeds, soaked	2 cups carrots
1 cup almonds, soaked	1 tablespoon cumin powder
1 cup hemp seeds	2 teaspoon Himalayan sea salt
1 cup flax seeds, soaked	3 cups fresh tomatoes
7 cups water	1 cup onion
¼ teaspoon cayenne pepper	

Soak the sunflower seeds, almonds, hemp, and flax seeds in 7 cups of water overnight and drain. Place the cayenne pepper, carrots, cumin, salt, tomato, and onion in the food processor, and blend until creamy. Add the seeds and nuts, and continue blending until all the ingredients are mixed together well and the nuts are finely chopped (you want the batter to be creamy and easy to spread).

Spread the mixture on Teflex dehydrator sheets and dehydrate overnight at 100°F. Flip the crackers and continue dehydrating another day until crispy.

Vegetable Chips

Prep: 15 minutes

Green fried tomatoes	Nutritional yeast (optional)
Cold-pressed olive oil (optional)	Assorted seasoning (sea salt, pepper, Herbamare, basil, oregano)

Slice the tomatoes about ⅛ inch thick and set them aside. In another bowl, combine the nutritional yeast, oregano, basil, and sea salt and whatever other seasonings you'd like. On another plate put a little cold-pressed olive oil. Take the tomato slices and coat them in olive oil and then coat them in the seasonings (both sides.) Because tomatoes are juicy, you don't need to roll them in the olive oil for the seasonings to stick. Take the coated tomato slices and dehydrate them at 105°F until desired dryness.

Eggplant or Zucchini Parmesan Chips

Prep: 15 minutes

Sliced eggplant or sliced zucchini
Cold-pressed olive oil (optional)

Nutritional yeast
Basil, sea salt, and oregano to taste

Combine nutritional yeast and seasonings in a plate with rim and set aside. Take sliced eggplant or slices of zucchini and roll in olive oil and then in the nutritional yeast/seasoning mixture and place on Teflex coated dehydrator sheets. You can also add a dollop of tomato sauce on each slice. Dehydrate at 105°F until desired doneness.

Kale Chips

Prep: 10 minutes

Kale, remove leaves from stem
Dressing or mayo

Olive oil
Seasonings

Place kale in large mixing bowl and combine with your favorite dressing, mayo, olive oil, and seasonings until coated thoroughly, and dehydrate on Teflex coated sheets in your dehydrator until crunchy.

Nori Chips

Prep: 10 minutes

Raw nori sheets

Spread your favorite pâté, dressing or mayo on nori sheet and then dehydrate until crisp. Cut or break into desired sizes.

Cheesy Kale Chips

In *Raw Inspiration: Living Dynamically With Raw Foods*, I shared how to make your basic kale chips. This recipe takes it one step farther, and I must confess that it is to die for. I also use the "Cheese" recipe as a dip and dressing.

Prep: 20 minutes   **Dehydrate:** Overnight or 4–8 hours at 105°F

Cheese
⅔ cup cashews
4 tablespoons lemon juice
1 tablespoon agave
6 tablespoons water
½ cup cold-pressed olive oil
1½ teaspoons sea salt

½ cup nutritional yeast
1 teaspoon turmeric
5 cloves garlic, minced
⅛ cup red onion, chopped
Dash Herbamare

Kale Chips
2–4 bunches kale

Cheese
Combine the ingredients in a high-speed blender until creamy and smooth. Add more or less water for desired consistency. I tend to double the recipe so I have plenty to coat my kale, and then keep the rest as a dressing.

Kale Chips
Rip kale off of stems, and place in a bowl. Pour the Cheese over the kale, and, with your hands, make sure that the kale is totally covered. Place on Teflex-coated sheets, and then place in your dehydrator. Dehydrate overnight, and, by the time that you wake up the next morning, they are ready for you to eat. If you make them during the day, one tends to walk by the dehydrator, eating them in the process, and they are good that way, as well.

WORDS FROM LISA:

For basic kale chips, place de-stemmed shredded kale in a mixing bowl, sprinkle sea salt to flavor, and add enough Austria's Finest, Naturally pumpkin seed oil or cold-pressed olive oil to cover the kale. Place on Teflex sheets on trays in a dehydrator for approximately 4–6 hours at 105°F.

Eggplant Rounds

Prep: 10 minutes

Slices of eggplant
Cold-pressed olive oil

Mayo (toasted or untoasted)
Red pepper cheese (optional)

Place slices of eggplant on dehydrator sheet, brush with cold-pressed olive oil and place a spoonful or dollop of mayo, toasted mayo, red pepper cheese, or any of your other favorite dips. Dehydrate until desired consistency. This is another great snack, and I must confess, they are so good that you need to be careful not to eat them all before they're done!

Basic Vegetable Chips

Prep: 10 minutes

Beets
Carrots
Yellow squash

Zucchini
Tomatoes

Slice vegetables and lightly roll in cold-pressed olive oil or coconut oil and dehydrate. You can dehydrate as is, or you can sprinkle with seasonings like salt or Herbamare.

Banana Wrap

Prep: 5 minutes

Bananas, peeled   Vanilla (optional)
Cinnamon (optional)   Flax seeds (optional)

Place bananas in a Vitamix® High Speed Blender and blend well. Spread banana mixture over Teflex sheets and place in dehydrator at 105°F until desired doneness. You can dehydrate them long enough so they are pliable and can be rolled into banana wraps, or totally dehydrate and make them more chip-like.

To kick it up a notch, you can add various flavorings like the vanilla and cinnamon to taste. If you want to add some texture, throw in a few flax seeds.

13

Entrées

Spring Rolls

Brooke Preston
Prep: 30 minutes   **Serves:** 8

5 cups Thai coconut meat (add coconut water as needed)
¾ cup ground golden flax seeds
¼ teaspoon Himalayan sea salt
¼ cup blonde sesame seeds

Blend coconut meat, flax, and salt until completely smooth. Fold in blonde sesame seeds. Spread 2 cups onto each dehydrator tray lined with Teflex sheet. Dehydrate for about 4 hours at 105°F; flip and dehydrate on the other side for about 4 more hours, or until pliable but dry.

Transfer to a surface large enough to cut with a pizza cutter into wrap size. Fill with enoki mushrooms, julienne cut carrot, and julienne green onions. Roll, and serve with Plum Sauce (page 267).

Spicy Hummus Quesadilla with Jacob's Cattle Gold and Poblano Relish

Chili Smith Family Foods, adapted by Lisa Montgomery
Prep: 45 minutes

6 cloves garlic
2 cups canned chickpeas, drained and rinsed
¾ cup Jacob's cattle gold beans, soaked and drained
3 tablespoons freshly squeezed lemon juice
2 tablespoons tahini
½ cup extra virgin olive oil
2 tablespoons finely chopped cilantro leaves
1 poblano chili, roasted, peeled, and finely chopped
2 tablespoons finely chopped fresh thyme
12 (6-inch) flour tortillas
2 cups raw cheese
1 cup julienned zucchini
½ cup crumbled goat cheese
¼ cup chili powder
Salt and freshly ground black pepper

Soak and sprout chickpeas until tails appear. For the beans, either soak in water in a slow cooker set on low, or in a glass dish of water in your dehydrator. Combine ingredients in a food processor. After combining, place filling ingredients on a romaine lettuce leaf or collard leave and wrap it up. You can sprinkle with chili powder if you want to add a little extra heat. Eat raw; do not cook.

Quinoa Collard Wrap

Colin Brett (Kimberton Whole Foods, www.kimbertonwholefoods.com)
Prep: 30 minutes–2 days

1 cup quinoa	½ cup yellow bell pepper
4 collard leaves	¼ cup red onion, diced
4 raw nori sheets	⅛ cup fresh mint, diced
2 cups carrots, shredded	⅛ cup fresh basil, diced
1 cup cucumbers, diced	1 tablespoon fresh lemon juice
½ cup tomatoes, diced	1 tablespoon sea salt

Boil quinoa in two cups water. Combine shredded carrots, diced cucumbers, tomatoes, yellow bell pepper, red onion, fresh mint, and fresh basil with quinoa, along with sea salt and fresh lemon juice after it has cooled. Lay ¾ cup quinoa mixture on each nori sheet. Roll nori sheet, tucking in the sides. Roll the nori wrap in the collard leaf and roll up.

LISA'S RAW VERSIONS:

Option 1: Soak quinoa overnight and sprout for two days until tails appear. Rinse quinoa and then follow directions above.

Option 2: Soak quinoa in water in Tribest® GlasLife dish and dehydrate at 105°F until quinoa is "cooked." The heat helps speed up the process.

Option 3: Place quinoa in a warming lunch crock pot in water until cooked.

Prepare your quinoa in whichever way that works for you where you are in your journey.

"Chick'n" Roll-Ups

Dr. Scott and Raechelle Walker
Prep: 15 minutes

- 1 can (12 ounces) raw chick peas, chopped (or processed)
- 1 tablespoon soaked raw cashews (food processed)
- ½ cup cucumber

- Curry, to taste
- Sea salt, to taste
- Garlic, to taste
- Onion, to taste
- Kale or romaine leaves

Mix ingredients (except kale or romaine lettuce leaves) and blend in a food processor. Roll mix in kale or romaine leaves and wrap. For truly raw chickpeas, please soak and sprout.

Quinoa Burger

Colin Brett (Kimberton Whole Foods, www.kimbertonwholefoods.com)
Prep: 25 minutes

- 1 cup quinoa
- 2 cups water
- 2 cups shredded carrot
- 1 cup chopped green kale
- 2 cups shredded zucchini

- ½ cup red onion
- 1 cup tahini
- 1 tablespoon Italian season
- 1 tablespoon sea salt
- 1 tablespoon dill

Prepare quinoa with one of the options on page 202. Add all ingredients and mix well. Dehydrate burgers in dehydrator at 105°F until desired doneness or eat it cold.

Hemp & Pumpkin Seed Burgers (aka Seed Burgers)

Prep: 15 minutes

- 1 cup Austria's Finest, Naturally® pumpkin seeds
- 1 cup hemp seeds
- 1 teaspoon sea salt
- 1 clove garlic

- ¼ cup golden flax seeds, ground or unground
- ¼ cup red onion
- 1 stalk celery
- ¼ cup fresh dill
- ¼ cup carrot

Combine the above ingredients in a food processor and form into mini burgers or balls. Dehydrate at 105°F in the Tribest® Sedona Dehydrator. If you don't grind the flax seeds, the mini burgers will be seedier. It just depends what consistency you would like them to be. Note that these burgers dehydrate pretty quickly.

WORDS FROM LISA:

Some folks are allergic to nuts but can eat seeds, therefore, this would be a burger alternative for the non nut eaters.

Sun Burgers

Kimberton Whole Foods, www.kimbertonwholefoods.com

Soak: Seeds, 4 hours   **Prep:** 20 minutes   **Dehydrate:** 2–3 hours at 105°F (optional)

- 1 cup ground sunflower seeds
- ½ cup ground flax seeds
- ½ cup water
- ½ medium onion, diced

- ½ red bell pepper, finely chopped
- ¾ cup celery, finely chopped
- Avocado, tomato, and alfalfa sprouts, for garnish

Process the sunflower seeds and flax seeds well in a processor and transfer to a bowl. Mix in ½ cup water, or less, if you prefer your burgers to be dryer. Chop the onions, peppers, and celery into very small pieces and mix in by spoon.

Add remaining water until desired consistency is reached for forming balls and flattening into patties. Dehydrate the patties for several hours (or less if making smaller patties), making sure they are slightly crunchy on the surface. You can even opt not to dehydrate them at all. Garnish with avocado, tomato, and alfalfa sprouts and place on a bed of lettuce. Try some raw catsup or another raw sauce with these burgers.

Taco Meat

Prep: 11 minutes

1 cup sunflower seeds, soaked
1 cup walnuts, soaked
¼ cup sun-dried tomatoes
1 tablespoon taco seasoning
¼ cup water

Pinch sea salt
Dash of pepper
1½ teaspoons Austria's Finest Pumpkin seed oil
1 tablespoon wheat-free tamari

Combine the above ingredients in a Cuisinart Food Processor until taco meat consistency. Pulse-chop. This is a spicy taco meat, so you can back off on the taco spices to your taste buds' liking.

Indian Chickpea Patties

Wendy Landiak
Prep: 20 minutes

¾ cup sprouted chickpeas
½ cup coconut
¾ cup raw soaked sunflower seeds
3 tablespoons coconut oil
1 tablespoon fresh ginger

1 teaspoon cumin seeds
1 teaspoon fennel seeds
⅓ cup nama shoyu
⅓ cup coconut flour
2 tablespoons curry powder

Mix chickpeas, coconut, sunflower seeds, coconut oil, and fresh ginger in food processor. After mixing, blend the remaining ingredients in by hand. Eat as is, or dehydrate at 115°F for 24 hours.

Bruschetta Bowl

Jenny Ross
Prep: 20–25 minutes   **Serves:** 2–4

Bowl
2 cups chopped romaine lettuce leaves
2 cups spinach
2 cups chopped kale

Bruschetta
4 Roma tomatoes, diced
½ cup chopped basil
3 cloves garlic, minced

1 teaspoon Himalayan salt
3 tablespoons dulse flakes
3 tablespoons hemp seeds
3 tablespoons capers
3 tablespoons extra virgin olive oil
1 tablespoon lemon juice
Assorted toppings (olives, spicy peppers, or avocado slices), to taste

In a medium bowl, toss together the lettuce leaves, spinach, and kale; separate into desired bowls to form the simple base of the dish. In a medium size bowl, mix together the tomatoes, basil, garlic, salt, dulse flakes, hemp seeds, capers, and olive oil, saving the lemon for last. Toss together well. Divide evenly over the four bowls. Top with additional ingredients as desired.

Note that the bruschetta mixture can be refrigerated for up to 4 days.

Contributor's Note: A living foods spin on a restaurant classic, this dish combines spices, superfoods and sea vegetables. Enjoy this crisp, refreshing, and nutritionally powerful option as an entrée or a side dish.

Raw Samosas

Wendy Landiak
Prep: 30 minutes

Filling
1 cup coconut meat
1 cup sprouted chickpeas
½ cup hemp seeds
1 cup cilantro, chopped
2 tablespoons ginger
1 teaspoon cumin
1 teaspoon turmeric

1 teaspoon ajwain
Salt, to taste

Wrap
6 huge collard leaves
3 teaspoons coconut oil
Pinch sea salt

Rub each collard leaf with ½ teaspoon of coconut oil and sprinkle it with sea salt. Pulse filling ingredients in food processor. Soak collard green leaves, and lightly brush with coconut oil and sea salt. Place 2 tablespoons of filling inside leaves and fold into a triangle. Use chutney and sriracha as dipping sauces or spread them on your dehydrated crackers.

Mac & Cheese

Prep: 15 minutes

Cheese
2 cups raw cashews
¼ cup pine nuts
2 tablespoons nutritional yeast
1 teaspoon sea salt
¾ cup water
¼ cup cold-pressed olive oil
1 clove garlic

Mac Options
Spiralized zucchini
Mung beans
Mung beans fettuccine
Black bean spaghetti
Kelp noodles
Hemp seeds (optional)

Place the cheese ingredients in a Vitamix® high-speed blender until well blended. If you want a thinner consistency, add more water (a little bit at a time).

When I made this dish, I combined spiralized zucchini with kelp noodles. I poured the cheese over the noodles and sprinkled a few hemp seeds on top.

WORDS FROM LISA:

Sometimes, life can get very busy. What I have started to do is, whenever I make a pesto, pâté, or sauce, I freeze some of it in containers. That way, when I just don't have the time to make it fresh, I can pull out one of my pre-made containers and thaw it out in the refrigerator.

Cauliflower Casserole

Richard Golden (BleepCancer.org)
Prep: 30 minutes

2 teaspoons olive oil
½ teaspoon Celtic sea salt
1 pinch cayenne pepper
2-4 teaspoons cumin
1–2 teaspoons turmeric
½ yellow or red onion, finely chopped
1 red bell pepper
½ cup water

1 large or 2 small heads cauliflower
  (about 4 or 5 loose cups)
4 tablespoons fresh parsley
2 tablespoons raw pine nuts
7–8 pieces sun-dried tomatoes, soaked
  in olive oil
1 tablespoon fresh squeezed lemon juice
2 cloves garlic, minced (optionally
  crushed)

Mix the lemon juice, cayenne, salt, cumin, and turmeric with the oil. Stir vigorously in a small bowl or cup. Heat up ½ cup of water just to the point of boiling, let sit for a couple minutes.

Chop up the pepper, onion, and parsley into desired pieces—small is good! Set to the side. In a food processor fitted with an S-blade, process water, garlic, cauliflower, and sun-dried tomatoes into small pieces (similar in size to couscous). Add about half of your seasoned oil mix while food processor is running. Pour these ingredients into your serving bowl. With a large spoon, stir in the parsley, peppers, and onion. Then, stir in the rest of your seasoned oil mix. Sprinkle pine nuts on top and garnish with parsley, sweet pea, or sunflower shoots.

Cortido

Annmarie Cantrell
Prep: 25 minutes

1 large head cabbage, shredded
2 medium onions, sliced
¼–½ teaspoon red pepper flakes
1 cup shredded carrots

2–3 medium garlic cloves
2 teaspoons dried oregano
1–2 tablespoons sea salt

Combine all ingredients in bowl and mash together. Stuff into containers, making sure liquid rises above the vegetables. Leave to ferment for 2–3 weeks at room temperature (out of direct light) and refrigerate.

Unroasted Broccoli

Prep: 15 minutes (plus warming if desired)

3 bunches broccoli heads
½ cup red pepper, chopped
¼–½ cup red onion, chopped

¾ cup Austria's Finest, Naturally® pumpkin seed oil
1 clove garlic, minced
1 teaspoon sea salt (or to taste)

Toss the above ingredients in a bowl to make sure all the vegetables are covered with the oil and salt. Place in a glass dish and dehydrate at 105°F until desired consistency.

WORDS FROM LISA:

This recipe is good whether you warm it up, or unload in your dehydrator and eat right away. When I make this I either prepare it the night before so it is ready to go, or in the morning so it is ready to eat by lunch time.

Eggplant and Spinach Parmesan

Barbara Shevkun (Rawfully Tempting)

Prep: This is one of those dishes you want to make on a Saturday . . . all day

Eggplant
2 small eggplants, peeled and sliced
   thinly (I use one white eggplant and
   one graffiti eggplant. They are small
   and very tender)

Coating
¼ cup pine nuts
¾ cup raw almonds
Dried Italian herbs, to taste
Sea salt, to taste

Cheese
½ cup cashews
½ cup macadamia nuts
1–2 tablespoon lemon juice
Onion powder, to taste
½ garlic clove, crushed
Sea salt, to taste
Water to blend
3–4 cups fresh spinach, chopped
Your favorite marinara sauce

Sauce
2–3 large tomatoes
1 clove garlic
Italian herbs, to taste
2 dates, pitted and chopped
½ avocado
¼ red bell pepper
Olive oil for desired consistency
Salt, to taste
Pepper, to taste
Cayenne (optional)
½ cup sun-dried tomatoes
Onion, to taste
Chopped olives, to taste

Greens (Spinach)
3–4 cups spinach
Olive oil
Sea salt, to taste

Eggplant
Soak eggplant slices in salted water for 2–3 hours. Drain and spread on dehydrator trays and dehydrate for 30–45 minutes at 105°F.

Coating
In a food processor, blend all ingredients until almost smooth, but don't over process. Keep mixture thick.

Cheese
In a high-speed blender, combine all ingredients and blend until creamy.

Sauce
Combine sauce ingredients in a high-speed blender.

Greens (Spinach)
Clean and trim stems. Chop into smaller pieces. In a large bowl, drizzle a bit of olive oil and sea salt onto greens and massage with fingers to soften. Set aside.

Assembly
Lightly oil the bottom of a small glass baking dish. Arrange slices of eggplant in base of dish. Sprinkle and press on some coating mix to each slice with your fingers. Spread marinara sauce on top. Spread cheese mixture on top of sauce using an offset spatula. Add a light layer of spinach.

Continue layering in same order until all ingredients are used. Top with thin layer of cheese mixed with some of the under layer of marinara and don't go all the way to the edge, so that it looks like melted cheese on top when done.

Garnish top with a bit of chopped spinach and some of the coating mixture. Sprinkle with crushed red pepper and oregano. You could also use marinated and dehydrated mushroom slices and slivered olives to top off the dish as well. Or try adding a layer of Rawsages (page 253).

Dehydrate for several hours until eggplant is soft.

Veggie Medley

Joel Odhner
Prep: 20–30 minutes   **Stand:** 30 minutes

½ pound asparagus, chopped into 1-inch
   pieces
1 cup tomatoes, diced
1 red or yellow pepper, diced
½ cup broccoli florets, chopped

¼ cup basil, julienned
¼ cup parsley, chopped
⅛ cup cold-pressed olive oil
⅛ cup lemon juice
Sea salt to taste

Combine all the ingredients in a bowl and let stand for 30 minutes. Lasts 2–3 days refrigerated.

Tofu Portabello

Prep: 11 minutes

1 package tofu, drained and diced
1 portabello heads, diced
1–2 tablespoons toasted sesame oil
½ cup wheat-free tamari

2 tablespoons Austria's Finest Pumpkin
    Seed Oil
¼ cup red onion, finely chopped
½ teaspoon garlic powder

Combine the above ingredients in a mixing bowl making sure the tofu, portabello, and onions are thoroughly coated with the liquids. You can eat as is, or warm in the dehydrator at 105°F for desired heat.

Wild Rice & Chickpea Salad

Prep: 20 minutes

2 cups natural wilderness rice
    (blossomed)
1½ cups chickpeas, sprouted and pulse-
    chopped in food processor to desired
    consistency
2 teaspoons ground cumin seeds
1 medium red onion, chopped
2½ tablespoons cold-pressed olive oil
2 teaspoons cumin powder

1½ teaspoons curry powder
⅔ cup dried blueberries or raisins
2 tablespoons parsley, chopped
1 tablespoon cilantro (If you don't like
    cilantro, just replace the cilantro with
    extra parsley)
1 tablespoon dill, chopped
Salt and ground black pepper to taste

How to blossom natural wilderness rice
Take rice and place in glass jar or bowl with water and place in dehydrator at 105°F until rice has blossomed or sprouted. By blossoming the rice, you are cooking it the raw foodist way! If you don't have a dehydrator, you can place the rice in water in a jar on your counter and sprout it as you would sprout seeds. Cover for 24 hours, pour off the water; then rinse twice a day and lay jar on its side until the rice sprouts. This is a slower but still very effective way to blossom your rice.

Sprouting chickpeas

Place chickpeas in a Ball® jar; cover with water, and let sit overnight. The next day pour off the water, rinse, and let jar sit with chickpeas on its side, continuing to rinse twice a day until chickpeas sprout. This should take between one and three days, depending on how sprouted your want your chickpeas.

Combine cold-pressed olive oil and chickpeas in food processor, pulse-chopping until desired consistency. Place olive oil/chickpea combo in large mixing bowl along with Natural Wilderness Rice and the rest of the ingredients and toss well. This salad is great just as it is but if you want to meld the flavors a little more or warm up the salad, place it in a large glass bowl and heat in dehydrator at 105°F until desired warmth and/or flavors meld.

Asian Vegetable Medley

Prep: 30 minutes

Marinade
½ cup wheat-free tamari
1 teaspoon toasted sesame oil
1 tablespoon cold-pressed olive oil
1 tablespoon olive oil
1 clove garlic, minced
Pinch sea salt
¼–½ teaspoon grated ginger

Vegetables
Assorted Asian vegetables (such as shitake mushrooms, snow peas, mung bean sprouts, Asian cabbage or bok choy, scallions, cauliflower florets, and jicama)

Marinade
Combine the ingredients in a high-speed blender and set aside.

Vegetables
Slice and chop the vegetables into bite-sized pieces. If using jicama, you can peel and grate it for a rice-like effect.

Combine vegetables with marinade, making sure the vegetables are totally coated. Transfer coated vegetables to a glass dish and place in Tribest Sedona Dehydrator for 1 hour at 105°F. You can also add pieces of raw cashews to add a little more Asian flair.

Unmacaroni Salad

16 ounces mushrooms, sliced
1 head cauliflower, chopped into bite-
     sized pieces
1½ cups raw mayonnaise (see page 148)
3 tablespoons lemon juice
½ teaspoon celery seed

2 cups celery, chopped
1 small jar pimento, finely chopped
1 red pepper, finely chopped
Sea salt to taste
Agave to taste

Combine the ingredients in a large mixing bowl, making sure that the Raw Mayonnaise thoroughly coats all of the ingredients. You can either eat as is or serve on a bed of greens.

Fennel Apple Salad

Prep: 15 minutes

1 fennel, chopped into bite-size pieces
1 green apple, cored and chopped into
     bite-size pieces
1 cup raisins
½ cup celery, chopped into bite-size
     pieces

1 red apple, cored and chopped into
     bite-size pieces
Balsamic vinegar or freshly squeezed
     orange juice

Combine the above chopped ingredients in a large bowl. Drizzle with balsamic vinegar or freshly squeezed orange juice to taste.

Happy Harvest Mushroom Tomato Salad

Prep: 20 minutes   **Dehydrate:** 4–6 hours at 105°F

8 ounces crimini mushrooms, sliced

8–16 ounces heirloom cherry tomatoes, quartered

2 tablespoons red onions, chopped

2 tablespoons pine nuts

2 tablespoons raisins

1 tablespoon raw honey (I use honey from my own bees)

3–4 tablespoons Austria's Pumpkin Seed Oil (enough to thoroughly cover all ingredients)

1 tablespoon wheat-free tamari

Sea salt and ground pepper, to taste

Combine all of the above ingredients in a bowl until thoroughly covered. Place ingredients in glass dish and place on the bottom tray of your dehydrator. Set dehydrator at 105°F and dehydrate until all of the ingredients and flavors have melded. This should take approximately 4–6 hours. (I use this method when I want my "casserole" to come out like it has been baked in a conventional oven.) Periodically, throughout the dehydrating/heating process, take the dish out and use a spoon to remix the ingredients, making sure all the ingredients are covered with the sauce so as not to get dried out.

WORDS FROM LISA:

I was inspired to create this recipe after having bought fresh crimini mushrooms at my local farmers market. I excitedly brought the mushrooms and then simply added what I already had at home and this is what I came up with.

Zucchini Spaghetti

Arnold Kaufman
Prep: 15 minutes

Sauce
2 tomatoes
½ red bell pepper
2 dates, pitted and soaked in water

1 cup mango, diced

Spaghetti
2 medium zucchini

Place all sauce ingredients in a Vitamix® high-speed blender or a food processor until well blended. Pulse for a short period of time.

To make the spaghetti, spiralize two zucchini. Place spiralized zucchini in a bowl and pour the sauce over your spaghetti and serve.

Good Faith Farm's Fresh and Simple Pasta

Karen Handman (Good Faith Farms)
Prep: 20 minutes   **Serves:** 4

Juice of 1 lemon
3 tablespoons brown rice vinegar
1 small bunch green onions, chopped
    fine (or chives)
2 large garlic cloves, chopped fine
1 teaspoon sea salt

1 pound spiralized zucchini
1 cup pitted raw sevillano or Kalamata
    olives
½ cup fresh herbs (such as basil or
    parsley), chopped

Combine the first five ingredients in a small bowl and let it marinate while spiralizing zucchini. Pour dressing over spiralized zucchini pasta. Fold in the olives, chopped tomatoes, and fresh herbs, mixing gently but thoroughly. When I serve pasta (spiralized zucchini) I serve the spiralized zucchini on one plate and the sauce on another. That way, the guests can put as much or as little on their "pasta" as they wish. Also, if you are packing your lunch each day, the dish will keep longer and won't get soggy by the end of the week.

Singapore Kelp Noodles

Natural Zing
Prep: 25 minutes

Noodles
2 pounds kelp noodles

Singapore Sauce
½ cup coconut aminos
¼ cup nama shoyu
½ cup olive oil
¼ teaspoon red pepper cayenne powder
½ teaspoon sea salt
1 teaspoon garlic powder or 3 cloves
    fresh garlic
¼ cup water

1 tablespoon raw, organic agave nectar
    (optional)

Shredded Vegetables
Red bell pepper (optional)
Carrots (optional)
Mushrooms (optional)
Broccoli (optional)
Napa cabbage (optional)
Green cabbage (optional)
Celery (optional)

Soak noodles for 1–8 hours, and then cut into smaller pieces. Blend all sauce ingredients together. Toss noodles and sauce and serve cold with your choice of shredded vegetables.

Contributor's Note: The best part about these noodles is that they are raw and gluten-free, so you don't have to feel guilty about eating noodles!

Raw Mung Bean Noodles or Black Bean Spaghetti

Prep: 2 minutes

Mung bean noodles
Water, enough to cover the noodles

Place the noodles in a glass dish and cover them in water. Then, place the water-covered noodles in a dehydrator at 105°F. You can put anything on these noodles: tomato sauce, un-cheesy sauce, or an alfredo sauce. Let your imagination run wild!

> ## WORDS FROM LISA:
>
> I learned about these raw mung bean noodles from a friend who had purchased them from Matt Monarch's web site. I tried them and loved them. By placing the noodles in the water while you dehydrate them, it rehydrates the noodles and becomes a raw foodist version of un-cooking them.

Basic Raw Spaghetti Noodles

Assorted vegetables (zucchini, yellow squash, red beets, etc.)

A spiralizer is a machine that will spiralize and make spaghetti, alfredo, and curly-cue noodles (depending on what type of spiralizer you use). You can spiralize zucchini, yellow squash, red beets and yams with a spiralizer. You can also use a mandoline or a peeler, running it down the side of a zucchini to make lasagna-style noodles.

I Can't Believe This Isn't Pasta

Drew Hunt
Prep: 35 minutes   **Soak:** cashews, overnight

2 cups raw cashews
Juice of 2 lemons
2 tablespoons chickpea miso
1 tablespoon coconut oil
2 tablespoons nutritional yeast (optional, not raw)
8 generous cups spiralized zucchini
2 ⅓ tablespoons sea salt

3–4 ripe tomatoes
3–4 sundried tomatoes
Cold-pressed virgin olive oil
1 clove garlic
Few sprigs fresh basil
¼ small red onion (or 1 shallot)
1 teaspoon black pepper

Soak 2 cups of raw cashews overnight. Put 1¾ cups of soaked nuts into food processor with lemon juice, chickpea miso, coconut oil and 2 tablespoons nutritional yeast (optional). Process until smooth. Remove from processor and then use the processor to crumb the remaining nuts. Mix the smooth nut mixture with the crumbed nuts. Preferably set aside at room temperature for a few hours before proceeding as this will allow flavors to mature. If you don't have time, just continue to next step.

Using a spiralizer with a linguini or spaghetti blade, spiralize about 8 cups of zucchini. Using two tablespoons of sea salt toss the zucchini noodles with the salt to evenly distribute. Set to the side while making the sauce and occasionally return to hand toss the zucchini (the salt will wilt the zucchini which is intended).

Core and roughly chop several ripe tomatoes. (If tomatoes are out of season use vine-ripened Roma tomatoes.) Put tomatoes in blender. Add a few sundried tomatoes, a healthy splash of cold-pressed virgin olive oil, garlic, a few sprigs of fresh basil, red onion or shallot, black pepper, and sea salt. Blend until smooth. Add olive oil to reach desired consistency.

Return to zucchini noodles. When they are limp, pliable and roughly the consistency of cooked pasta, fill the bowl with cold water, drain and repeat until the salt has been removed. (The only way to be sure the salt has been sufficiently removed is to taste the noodles.) Toss the zucchini noodles with the tomato sauce. Liberally sprinkle the nut cheese on top. Garnish generously with chopped tomatoes (different colors are nice) and chopped fresh basil or cilantro.

Lasagna La Zelinda

Linda Leboutillier
Prep: 45–60 minutes   **Soak:** 12 hours
Dehydrate: warm in dehydrator 1–2 hours before serving (optional)   **Serves:** 8

Artichoke Mixture
½ cup cold-pressed extra virgin olive oil
4 tablespoons fresh-squeezed lemon juice
1 teaspoon Himalayan sea salt
1 tablespoon Italian seasoning
½ teaspoon freshly ground pepper
⅛ teaspoon cayenne pepper
3 (12 oz.) packages frozen artichoke hearts, thawed and torn apart

Sunflower Seed Mixture
2 cups fresh basil
⅓ cup cold-pressed extra virgin olive oil
4 tablespoons fresh-squeezed lemon juice
1 teaspoon Himalayan salt
3½ cups sunflower seeds, soaked 12 hours, then drained
½ teaspoon freshly ground pepper
⅛ teaspoon cayenne pepper

Lasagna
6 large plum tomatoes, thinly sliced
¼ cup fresh basil leaves, minced
2 cups green olives, pitted
1 large red bell pepper, cleaned and diced

Artichoke Mixture
Mix together all the ingredients and marinate for 30 minutes.

Sunflower Seed Mixture
Mix together all the ingredients in a food processor until finely chopped.

Lasagna
Spray a 9- by 13-inch casserole dish with coconut or olive oil. Line the bottom of the casserole with the sunflower seed mixture, and then distribute the artichoke mixture evenly over the sunflower seed mixture.

Layer the tomatoes and basil over the artichoke mixture. Place the green olives and bell pepper in a food processor, pulse slightly, and then spread evenly over the tomato layer. Serve.

Pasta Primavera with Alfredo Sauce

Barbara Shevkun (Rawfully Tempting)
Prep: 60 minutes

Alfredo Cream Sauce
1 cup cashews
½ cup macadamia nuts
½ water, or more to blend
2 cloves garlic, crushed
1 teaspoon miso
1 tablespoon olive oil
3 tablespoons onion
1 teaspoon raw honey or agave
Sea salt to taste

Marinade
2 tablespoons olive oil
½ teaspoon salt
Fresh basil, chopped
Italian herbs, to taste

Vegetables (such as carrots, Portobello mushrooms, onions, scallions, tomato, zucchini, baby eggplant, and yellow squash), sliced in thin strips and chopped

Parmesan Cheese
½ cup mixed almonds, pine nuts, and sesame seeds
Sea salt, to taste
Nutritional yeast (optional), to taste

Spaghetti Noodles
1 (12 oz.) package sea kelp noodles
Warm water
Lemon juice

Alfredo Cream Sauce
Mix ingredients in high-speed blender until creamy.

Marinade
Massage the first four ingredients into the assorted vegetables and let sit for 2 hours (or marinate for 1 hour and dehydrate for 1–2 hours at 110°F, placing in a glass bowl on bottom of your dehydrator).

Parmesan Cheese
Pulse process nuts and seeds in food processor. Add salt and nutritional yeast (optional). Mix.

Spaghetti Noodles
Rinse and soak kelp noodles in warm water with lemon juice for at last 30 minutes (the longer the better). Cut kelp noodles in half and mix with a bit of alfredo sauce. Massaging the cream into the noodles by hand is easier (and therapeutic).

You can top the creamy noodles with vegetables or you can mix some of the alfredo sauce into the vegetables first. You can also add a dollop of cream sauce to garnish the dish. It depends on how rich you like it.

Top with a sprinkle of Parmesan cheese and serve. Warm in dehydrator or lowest oven setting, if desired.

If you don't have kelp noodles readily available, you can spiralize zucchini for your pasta. Remember, the rule of thumb is to use one zucchini per person.

Raw Vegan Lasagna Vegetable Stacks

Kimberton Whole Foods, www.kimbertonwholefoods.com
Prep: 45–60 minutes

Lasagna Sheets
2 large zucchinis
3 yellow squash or yellow zucchini
6 large tomatoes, sliced
Basil leaves
Olive oil
Cherry tomatoes (optional)
Gomasio (optional)

Raw Tomato Sauce
2 cups sundried tomatoes
1 cup chopped tomatoes (2 medium tomatoes)
¼ cup cold-pressed extra-virgin olive oil
2 teaspoons fresh garlic
¾ teaspoon Celtic sea salt
1 teaspoon dried basil
¼ teaspoon red pepper flakes

Basil Pesto
5 cups tightly packed fresh basil leaves
1½ cups raw macadamias, soaked (optional)
½ cup olive oil
1½ teaspoon Celtic sea salt
2 tablespoons lemon zest
3 tablespoons lemon juice
6 tablespoons garlic

Macadamia Ricotta
2 cups raw macadamias, soaked (optional)
¾ cup–1 cup filtered water for desired consistency
2 tablespoons fresh lime juice
2 tablespoons finely chopped serrano chili (chillier to taste)
1 tablespoon finely minced fresh garlic
2 teaspoons yellow mustard powder
½ teaspoon Celtic sea salt
¼ cup finely chopped cilantro/coriander

Lasagna Sheets

Hold each zucchini and, using vegetable peeler (or mandolin), peel off large thin strips of the zucchini. Peel the yellow squash and cut the tomatoes into ¼-inch or ½-inch thick slices. Set aside on layers of paper towel to remove any excess liquid while you make the sauces.

Raw Tomato Sauce

Throw all the ingredients in a food processor and pulse until well combined. Season to taste. (You want this sauce to be mild in order to blend with the pesto and the ricotta.)

Basil Pesto

Throw all the ingredients in a food processor and pulse until well combined.

Macadamia Ricotta

Throw all of the ingredients (except cilantro) into a food processor and pulse until well combined and fluffy. Stir through the chopped cilantro.

To assemble, lay out six large plates. Lay three slices of zucchini side by side to make a wide rectangle lasagna sheet base. Spread some red sauce on top of each base. Lay three slices of yellow squash or zucchini on top of the sauce. Place two tomato slices on top of the ricotta. Now place three more pieces of zucchini to make another sheet of pasta. Spread a layer of green pesto and top with two more pieces of tomato. Garnish with large fresh basil leaves and drizzle the whole plate with a bit of olive oil. You could also surround the lasagna with some chopped cherry tomatoes tossed in olive oil or garnish with some gomasio.

Spaghetti alla Puttanesca, Alfredo, or Pink Sauce with Parmesan Cheese

Sheryll Chavarria (Raw Can Roll Café and Pure Body Spa, Douglassville, PA, www.rawcanrollcafe.com)

Sheryll taught us this recipe in a raw cooking class and it is to die for. You can choose to serve the pasta with the puttanesca, alfredo, or pink sauce. Then top with Parmesan cheese.

Spaghetti Prep: 15 minutes   **Puttanesca Sauce Prep:** 20 minutes
Alfredo Sauce Prep: 15 minutes   **Serves:** 4

Spaghetti
4 zucchini, peeled (spiralized or shredded with a vegetable peeler)
1 lemon, juiced

Puttanesca Sauce
1 red bell pepper, chopped
5 tomatoes, chopped (preferably plum or Roma)
Handful sun-dried tomatoes (to create medium thickness), optional
Bunch fresh basil, oregano, parsley
Thyme and rosemary (optional)
Pinch cayenne pepper or finely chopped hot peppers
2 cloves garlic, minced
Celtic sea salt to taste or 2 tablespoons white mello miso

½ cup black olives, sliced
¼ cup olive oil, adder after sauce is prepared

Alfredo Sauce
1½ cups raw pine nuts, soaked
1½ cups raw cashews, soaked
2 cloves garlic, minced
2 tablespoons lemon, juiced
½ cup water (add more if necessary)
Celtic sea salt to taste

Parmesan Cheese
1 cup sesame seeds, soaked
1 tablespoon fresh parsley, finely chopped
Pinch Celtic sea salt

Spaghetti
After zucchini is prepared, place in bowl. Pour lemon juice on zucchini and work through well (tossing carefully so as not to break the zucchini). The lemon works to break down the zucchini so it becomes softer. You may place the zucchini (pasta) and the sauce in a dehydrator for about 1 hour to warm.

Puttanesca Sauce

Combine all the ingredients (except olive oil) in blender until smooth (or chunky if you prefer). If sauce is not thick enough, add more sun-dried tomatoes. Place in serving bowl, then add olive oil and stir. Do not blend olive oil in blender. To make a chunkier sauce, you may put all the ingredients into a food processor instead of using a blender. Serve on top of zucchini or summer squash spaghetti.

Alfredo Sauce

Combine all ingredients together in a high-speed blender until smooth. Serve on top of zucchini or summer squash spaghetti.

Pink Sauce

Combine ¾ parts alfredo sauce to ¼ part puttanesca sauce. Mix both together and serve on top of zucchini or summer squash spaghetti.

Parmesan Cheese

Finely grind sesame seeds in coffee grinder. In a small bowl, add the rest of the ingredients and mix well. Serve on top of pasta dish.

Spaghetti with Sausage and Peppers

Barbara Shevkun (Rawfully Tempting)
Barbara is an upcoming star who has her own raw product line and is a great teacher.
Prep: 60 minutes

Veggie Marinade
1 large tomato
¼ red or orange bell pepper
½ cup onion, chopped
1 tablespoon olive oil
1 teaspoon each fresh basil, parsley, dried oregano (or to taste)
Pinch cayenne pepper
Pinch sea salt

Veggies
1 red bell pepper, sliced thin
1 orange bell pepper, sliced thin
½ large onion, sliced thin
½–1 cup mushrooms, sliced
½ zucchini, sliced thin

Spaghetti
½ package kelp noodles (kelp noodles come in 12–ounce packages)
Zucchini, spiralized (1 zucchini per person)

Veggie Marinade

Blend ingredients until smooth. Set aside.

A sneaky way to add more greens into your family's diet is to add a bit of chopped kale to the marinade as well.

Veggies

Place all sliced vegetables in a large bowl and mix with marinade. Let sit for at least 1 hour. Spread on a non-stick dehydrator sheet and dehydrate at 110°F for two hours, mixing and stirring halfway through).

Spaghetti

Rinse kelp noodles and cut in half. Soak in warm lemon water at least 1 hour or more, while preparing the rest of your meal. Spiralize zucchini shortly before serving and let sit in a strainer to remove some of the excess liquid.

Three Nut Basil Pesto Pasta

Prep: 10–15 minutes   **Pesto Prep:** 10 minutes

4 medium zucchini, spiralized

Toppings
Cherry tomatoes, quartered or whole
(quantity as desired)—approximately
½–1 cup
6 asparagus stalks, thinly sliced on
an angle
½ cup fresh chopped cilantro

Pesto
2 cups raw pine nuts
½ cup raw cashews
½ cup raw macadamia nuts
4 garlic cloves, minced
6 tablespoons fresh lemon juice
4 teaspoons Himalayan sea salt
1 cup fresh basil, chopped

Pasta

Spiralize zucchini and set aside.

Pesto

Combine ingredients in a Cuisinart Food Processor until well blended and set aside.

Now it's time to build your dish. Place the zucchini in a large bowl and combine with the pesto and top with the cherry tomatoes, asparagus, and cilantro. Alternately, you can serve all parts of the recipe separately, so when you have guests over you allow them to build the dish themselves! Place the zucchini on a plate (of greens if desired), add a spoonful of pesto (amount depends on how much they like pesto), and top with the tomatoes, asparagus, and cilantro.

Ratatouille

Prep: 40 minutes

16 ounces Roma tomatoes
1 yellow squash, chopped
1 zucchini, chopped
1 red bell pepper, chopped
1 yellow pepper, chopped
1 orange pepper, chopped
1 eggplant, cubed
1–2 large Portobello mushrooms, chopped

1 red onion, chopped or ringed
2 cloves garlic, minced
2 teaspoons dried parsley
2 teaspoons dried oregano
2 tablespoons olive oil
½ cup orange juice
Sea salt, to taste
Ground pepper, to taste

Pulse-chop tomatoes in food processor so they look like stewed tomatoes, and set aside. Chop remaining vegetables and combine with tomatoes in a large mixing bowl. Add seasonings to mixture and thoroughly coat. Add more olive oil to make sure that all vegetables are covered. Place ratatouille in large glass dish and place in dehydrator until warm. Stir occasionally to make sure the flavors are all melding together. Serve on a bed of greens.

Cauliflower Sushi Rolls

Kimberton Whole Foods, www.kimbertonwholefoods.com
This is a very easy recipe but the assembly just takes a little extra time until you get the trick of rolling your own sushi.
Prep: 30 minutes

Cauliflower Rice
½ head of cauliflower
2 diced spring onions
¼ cup pine nuts
1 teaspoon tamari sauce
Juice of ½ lemon
Salt, to taste

Sushi Assembly
1 nori sheet
¼ ripe avocado, sliced
Handful of sprouts
Greens of your choice
Tamari or nama shoyu, for dipping

Cauliflower Rice

Pulse cauliflower until it reaches a rice-like consistency. Add the remaining ingredients and pulse again until combined. Adjust salt and tamari sauce to taste.

Sushi Assembly

Place one nori sheet shiny-side down on a sushi mat (if available). Cover bottom half of nori with cauliflower "rice." Layer on sliced avocado, sprouts, and greens. Roll sushi mat away from you and tighten roll. Seal edge with water. Slice roll into bite-size pieces with a sharp knife.

Repeat the process until all the filling is used up. Dip in tamari or nama shoyu sauce and pop into your mouth!

Nori Rolls

Joel Odhner
Prep: 30 minutes

Rice

4 cups jicama, chopped
½ cup cashews or pine nuts
¼ cup rice wine vinegar or apple cider vinegar
3 tablespoons agave nectar

Filling

4–6 sheets raw nori
1 red pepper, julienned
3 celery ribs, julienned
1 zucchini, julienned
4–6 marinated shitake mushrooms (optional)
1 avocado, sliced (optional)
Handful of your favorite sprouts

Rice

Place jicama and nuts in a food processor, and process until rice-sized. Place the mixture in a nut milk bag and squeeze the moisture out. Place in a bowl and mix in the remaining ingredients.

Filling

Lay out nori sheets on a clean, dry surface. Place ½ cup of rice on nori and spread evenly over the bottom third of the sheet. Place vegetables on the rice. Carefully roll the nori. Wet the top edge of the nori with a little water to seal. Let the nori roll stand for 5 minutes. Cut with a sharp knife.

Enjoy plain, or you can use Braggs, chopped ginger, or agave mixture.

Spinach Wraps

Brenda Hinton (Rawsome Creations, www.rawsomecreations.com)
Prep: 30 minutes

- 2 batches of Brenda's Green Giant Juice pulp (page 175)
- ½ cup olive oil
- 1 cup coconut meat
- 2 tablespoons Irish Moss paste (or equivalent amount kelp noodles)
- 2½ cups spinach, packed measure
- 2 tablespoons spinach powder
- ½ teaspoon onion powder
- ¼ teaspoon garlic powder
- ½ teaspoon ground pepper
- ½ teaspoon salt
- ¼–½ cup water to blend

Blend all ingredients in Vitamix® High Speed Blender, in the order listed, utilizing as much water as needed to blend. Using a Teflex-lined dehydrator tray and template ("More Than a Wrap Mold," page 96) as a guide, spread a heaping ¼ cup mixture for each wrap round. Using a small spatula, spread the mixture flat and smooth so that it fills out the entire round evenly.

If not using Brenda's "More Than a Wrap Mold," which can be purchased at her website, www.rawsomecreations.com, use ¼ cup measure of mixture for each 6-inch tortilla and spread evenly (about ⅛-inch thick) forming 4 circles for wraps on each Teflex sheet. Repeat until all the mixture is distributed. Place trays in the dehydrator and dehydrate at 155°F for 3 to 4 hours or until firm to the touch. Flip wraps and remove Teflex sheets. Continue to dehydrate wraps at 105°F until dehydrated all the way through, yet still flexible and pliable—about 5 to 6 more hours. Allow to cool all the way through before storing. Wraps can be stored in the refrigerator in a sealed container for up to one week.

Spinach powder: Make your own spinach powder by dehydrating and grinding spinach in a spice grinder, available for purchase from Frontier Foods.

Extra flavors: Tomato powder and nutritional yeast add great flavors to these recipes.

Spring Roll

Joel Odhner
Prep: 30 minutes   **Soak:** nuts, 2–4 hours

Wrap
1 head Napa cabbage

Filling
1 cup Brazil nuts, soaked
1 cup walnuts, soaked
¼ teaspoon sea salt
½ tablespoon sage
⅛ cup lemon juice
½ cup olive oil

½ clove garlic
½ cup cilantro, chopped

Spicy Mustard
½ cup mustard seed, soaked, with
   soaking water
⅛ cup lemon juice
½ cup agave nectar
¼ teaspoon sea salt

Filling
Place all the ingredients (except the cilantro) in a food processor and blend until smooth. Gently mix in the cilantro.

Spicy Mustard
Place the mustard ingredients in a high-powered blender, and blend until smooth.

Place ¼–½ cup of filling on a Napa cabbage leaf and drizzle with spicy mustard. Roll up and enjoy. Lasts 3–5 days refrigerated.

This is another great dish to pack in your lunch each day.

Summer Wrap

Joel Odhner
Prep: 30 minutes

Wrap
1 large collard leaf
½ avocado, diced
1 plum tomato, diced
¼ cup Vidalia onion, diced

Honey Mustard
¼ cup cold-pressed olive oil
¼ cup fresh lemon juice
¼ cup apple cider vinegar (optional)
1 tablespoon ground mustard
1 clove garlic, minced
2 teaspoons agave nectar
½ teaspoon cumin
Pinch sea salt

Wrap
Combine avocado, plum tomato, and Vidalia onion. Place the mixture in collard leaf, drizzle with Honey Mustard, and add sea salt and pepper to taste. Fold top and stem ends of the collard leaf in, and roll up burrito style.

Honey Mustard
Blend all the ingredients in a high-powered blender. Add water to reach desired consistency.

Sushi Roll

Bruce and Marsha Weinstein (Awesome Foods, Bridgeport, PA, www.awesomefoods.com)
Bruce and Marsha's veggie nori rolls were the hit of the potluck.
Prep: 40 minutes   **Dehydrate:** 3 hours at 115°F   **Yield:** 3 (3 ounce) rolls

Veggies
1 ounce carrots, shredded
1 ounce yellow pepper, thinly sliced
1 ounce red pepper, thinly sliced
1 ounce celery, thinly sliced
½ ounce scallions, thinly sliced
0.3 ounce olive oil
0.2 ounce lemon juice
⅛ teaspoon sea salt

Sushi Rice
26 ounces jicama
0.4 ounce apple cider vinegar
1.1 ounces extra virgin olive oil
0.7 ounce agave nectar
½ ounce Himalayan sea salt

Veggies
Combine veggies in a bowl so they are thoroughly coated with the olive oil, lemon juice, and sea salt, and set aside.

Sushi Rice
Shred the jicama in a food processor until it is the consistency of rice grains. Press the chopped jicama in batches into thick towels inside a colander to remove the juice. Combine the jicama with the other ingredients in a bowl. Spread out on parchment paper or Teflex sheets, and place in your dehydrator for 3 hours at 115°F. After you dehydrate, you should have about 5 ounces (by weight).

Assembly
Spread 1.4 ounces (by weight) of rice on bottom half of nori sheets. Nori weighs 0.1 ounces, so now you have 1.5 ounces. Lay 1.5 ounces of marinated veggies on rice. Roll up and put face down on paper towel or sushi bamboo mat. Total weight is 3 ounces. Cut each roll into 6 pieces.

Veggie Collard Wraps

Sheryll Chavarria (Raw Can Roll Café and Pure Body Spa, Douglassville, PA, www.rawcanrollcafe.com)

Prep: 30 minutes

Marinade
1 tablespoon ginger, ground fresh
2 cloves garlic, pressed
2 tablespoons tamari
2 tablespoons lemon juice
2 tablespoons sesame oil

Wrap
1 Portobello mushroom, sliced and
   marinated
4 collard greens, de-stemmed
4 snow peas
2 carrots, ribboned
2 cups Napa cabbage, cut fine
1 cucumber, julienned

Marinade
Combine all ingredients.

Wrap
Marinate the mushrooms for about 15 minutes. Squeeze out excess marinade back into bowl and set aside to use later as a sauce.

Place the remaining ingredients in the collard leaf and roll. Wrap and secure the roll with a strip of carrot and a toothpick.

Use the remaining marinade for dipping or pour on wrap before you wrap the collard.

Collard Wrap

Prep: 10 minutes

Hummus (see page 261)
Assorted vegetables cut in long sticks, (carrots, celery,
   pepper, tomatoes, avocado wedges, mushrooms)
Sprouts

Place your collard wrap on the counter; fill with hummus, sprouts, and assorted vegetables; and roll it up. You can pick this up and eat it like a sandwich or you can cut it. I tend to cut mine; otherwise I end up wearing it.

Nori Rolls

Prep: 30 minutes

Filling
3 tablespoons white miso
¼–½ teaspoon toasted sesame oil

Assembly
Raw nori sheets
Assorted vegetables, thinly sliced

Filling
Combine the miso and toasted sesame oil and set aside. This keeps in a sealed container for a week.

Assembly
Spread the filling on a raw nori sheet which you lay out (shiny side down) on a bamboo sushi mat. Spread the miso filling over the first inch of the nori sheet. Then fill with your favorite vegetables (such as carrots, celery, cucumber, mushrooms, onion, sprouts, red pepper, and avocados). Lay the thinly sliced vegetables across the nori sheet then roll up starting with the end closest to you. Seal the end of the nori roll with water. Cut the long nori roll into 1-inch pieces.

   I use wheat-free tamari as a dipping sauce.

WORDS FROM LISA:

When I make this, I tend to store the filling in a sealed plastic container. I also store the sliced vegetables in another plastic container so that way if I am packing this for lunch several days in a row, I just build my nori rolls each day to save time and to keep them fresher when I don't have the luxury of making the dish right before I eat it.

BAT Cereal (Banana, Apple, and Tahini)

Karen Ranzi (Author of *Creating Healthy Children*)
Prep: 5 minutes   **Serves:** 1

   2 bananas
   1 apple
   1 teaspoon raw tahini

Mash two bananas, mix in a scoop of raw tahini, and top with small, coarsely-chopped apple pieces.

Contributor's Note: In my house, this has been a most satisfying cereal in the fall and winter. In summer, we would substitute the apples with peaches or nectarines. This delicious cereal was eaten by my kids for years and years. They love it and so do many kids who have attended my class "Raw Food Fun for Families."

"Dill-licious" Breakfast

Marina Grubic
Prep: 7 minutes

   4 sweet oranges, peeled
   ⅓ cup fresh dill

Combine the dill and peeled oranges in a high-speed blender.

"Ooeey-Gewy" Blueberry Swirled Oatmeal

Tiffany Robbins
Prep: 10 minutes   **Soak:** blueberries, 6 hours; almonds, 8 hours; oat groats, 8–12 hours
Serves: 1–2

Blueberry Swirl
1 cup dried blueberries
8 ounces grape juice (enough to cover blueberries)
3 tablespoons raw agave or coconut nectar

3 drops lavender essential oil

Oatmeal
1 cup oat groats or steel cut oats
½ cup So Delicious® almond milk
1 teaspoon coconut oil

Place dried blueberries in shallow bowl, cover with grape juice. Water can be used to top it off, if you don't have enough grape juice (depends on the depth of the bowl). Soak overnight or at least 6 hours. Strain blueberries and keep soaking liquid. Blend blueberries, agave, and essential oil until smooth. You can add a little of the soaking water to make blending easier, but not too much. You want a smooth, thick puree. Set aside to swirl into oatmeal.

Soak oat groats or steel cut oats overnight in water. Strain oat groats and discard soaking water. Blend oats with almond milk, and coconut oil until desired consistency. Swirl in mango puree. An optional topping is raw granola.

Raw Baby Food

Jinje's (The GardenDiet.com) seven-year-old daughter **Shale** came up with this recipe for her one-year old sister Yarrow to eat. It is a delicious green baby food that has purslane in it, which is a green herb that has both a wonderful sour flavor that kids love, and an awesome essential fatty acid content that their growing brains need.

Prep: 15 minutes

> ½ bunch purslane
> 1 pear
> A few peas, leaves of basil, and sprig of dill (or alternate a few pinches of whatever other yummy greens or veggies that you might have around)

Blend all of the above in a high-speed blender until baby-food consistency.

Yarrow could not get enough of this lovely dark-green and tasty treat, which any baby should love.

So, if little Shale can be creative in creating raw food from her garden, so can you.

Cream of Cauliflower Curry

Wendy Landiak
Prep: 15 minutes

> 1 teaspoon curry powder
> 1 cup cauliflower, chopped
> 1 cup coconut milk
> 1 tablespoon nama shoyu

> 1 date
> ¼ cup cilantro stems
> 1 tablespoon fresh ginger

Purée in a Vitamix® blender and top with fresh cilantro and chopped tomato.

Sprouted Bean Curry over Cauliflower Rice

Wendy Landiak
Prep: 30 minutes

Bean Curry
1 cup coconut milk (or 1 cup coconut water)
1 tablespoon date paste
1 tablespoon fresh ginger
1 tablespoon curry powder of choice
2 tablespoons fresh cilantro
½ red pepper, chopped

Rice
4 cups crunchy sprouts
½ cup basil
¾ cup fresh coconut
1 head of cauliflower

For the bean curry, make a coconut milk curry sauce with 1 cup coconut milk, 1 tablespoon date paste, 1 tablespoon fresh ginger, 2 tablespoons fresh cilantro, and 1 tablespoon curry powder. Use coconut water to thin to desired consistency (or in place of coconut milk) to lighten up the recipe. Vitamix® the mix, then toss into your sprouts and add chopped red pepper.

For the rice, pulse cauliflower florets in your food processor until they are of rice consistency. Add curry, cilantro, ginger and your choice of ingredients for a touch of sweet, a touch of heat and a touch of tang. Serve curry over rice and top with fresh cilantro and coconut.

Contributor's Note: When looking for good combinations to meet your need for sweet, heat, and tang, consider the following:
- Sweet: maple syrup, agave, coconut sugar
- Heat: cayenne, fresh habañero, red chili
- Tang: vinegar, lemon, lime

Fresh Tomato Curry

Wendy Landiak
Prep: 15 minutes

1 teaspoon dried cumin
1 teaspoon fennel
½ onion
1 tablespoon fresh grated ginger
Squeeze of lemon
2 cups chopped tomato

½ cup fresh cilantro
½ cup curry spices
Finely diced tomato
Fresh cilantro
Black pepper, to taste

Start with 1 teaspoon each of dried cumin and fennel, and blend in a Vitamix®
into a powder. Add half an onion, 1 tablespoon fresh grated ginger, a squeeze
of lemon, black pepper, 2 cups chopped tomato, ½ cup fresh cilantro, and curry
spices. Top with finely diced tomato and fresh cilantro.

Kurry Kraut

Annmarie Cantrell
Prep: 30 minutes

5 pounds green cabbage
3 tablespoons curry powder
3 tablespoons sea salt

Either chop vegetables by hand or put through grater option of the food processor.
(The more finely the vegetables are chopped, the more surface area is present
for the bacteria to infiltrate. The vegetables will also ferment more quickly when
chopped more thinly.) Place vegetables in a large bowl. Sprinkle salt over and
begin to massage salt into the vegetables. You can either use your hand or a
pounder to do this. As you pound, you are breaking up the cell wall and allowing
the liquid to be released. This liquid will serve as your brine.

   Pack vegetables into a clean jar and push them down so that there are no air
bubbles. Be sure that the liquid rises above the vegetables and covers them. If the

brine does not cover, add water with a pinch more salt. Let vegetables sit on the counter (out of direct sunlight) for anywhere from 5 days to 3 weeks taste it as time goes on and see how you like it! When it suits your taste, transfer to the refrigerator. Consume within 8–12 months.

Unstir Fry

Prep: 20–30 minutes

1 cup shitake mushrooms, sliced
1½ pounds assorted vegetables
   (miniature corn cobs, chopped red
   onions, carrot sticks, mung bean
   sprouts, red/yellow pepper slices,
   snow peas, etc.)

Stir Fry Marinade
¼ cup sesame oil
⅓ cup wheat free tamari
¼ cup toasted sesame oil
¼ cup Austria's Finest, Naturally® pumpkin seed oil
Sea salt, to taste

Combine the marinade ingredients and pour over vegetables. Toss the vegetables until they are totally covered with the liquid. Place in a glass dish and set in your dehydrator at 105°F until reaching desired warmth. The vegetables will warm and soften in the dehydrator.

WORDS FROM LISA:

If you don't have a dehydrator, this dish will taste good as is. I just like it better in the dehydrator! Note that the bulk of the prep time for this dish is preparing the vegetables.

Live Un-Stir-Fry with Cauliflower "Rice"

Kimberton Whole Foods, www.kimbertonwholefoods.com
Prep: 30 minutes   **Serves:** 4

Vegetable Medley
2 cups chopped Napa cabbage
1 cup thinly sliced red bell pepper
¾ cup raw unsalted cashews (optional)
½ cup chopped red cabbage
½ cup thinly sliced carrots
½ cup thinly sliced snow peas
¼ cup thinly sliced green onion
2 tablespoons chopped cilantro

Spicy Vegetable Dressing
½ cup sesame oil
1 fresh stalk lemongrass, outer leaves removed, finely chopped (optional)
3 tablespoons raw agave nectar or maple syrup
3 tablespoons nama shoyu or soy sauce

2 tablespoons umeboshi plum vinegar or raw apple cider vinegar
1½-inch piece peeled fresh ginger
1 tablespoon dehydrated onion flakes
1 tablespoon tamarind paste (optional)
1 tablespoon grated lime zest
1 clove garlic, peeled
1 teaspoon minced Thai or jalapeño chili
1 small kaffir lime leaf

Cauliflower Rice
4 cups cauliflower florets
½ cup macadamia or pine nuts
1 tablespoon dehydrated onion flakes
½ teaspoon sea salt
½ teaspoon garlic powder

Vegetable Medley
Combine all ingredients in large bowl.

Spicy Vegetable Dressing
Place all ingredients in blender or food processor, and blend until creamy. Add to vegetable medley, and toss well.

Cauliflower Rice
Place all ingredients in food processor, and pulse-chop to rice-like consistency. Serve topped with the vegetable medley.

Raw Thai Curry

Kimberton Whole Foods, www.kimbertonwholefoods.com
Prep: 20 minutes

2 avocados
2 (dried) lime leaves
¼–½ fresh chili
1 teaspoon lime juice
¾ inch lemongrass stem

¾ inch cube fresh ginger
½ loosely packed cup fresh coriander (cilantro)
½–1 cup pure water (or as needed for desired consistency)
½ tablespoon curry powder

Simply blend all ingredients together, either in a blender or food processor until everything is fully blended. Taste test. Add more water if you'd like it runnier. Add more lemongrass and a tomato, and/or avocado if it's too hot.

Middle Eastern Sauerkraut with Curry

Prep: 30 minutes

1 green cabbage head, cut into bite-size pieces
3 medium carrots, peeled and cut into bite-size pieces
2 small cucumbers cut into bite-size pieces

¼ small cauliflowers cut into bite-size pieces
2 celery stalks, cut into bite-size pieces
1 tablespoon curry powder
1 teaspoon ground allspice
6 cloves garlic, minced
3 tablespoons sea salt

Combine ingredients in a large mixing bowl. Using a wooden mallet or potato masher, keep pounding the vegetables until they release the juices from the pounding and the salt. When you start, the bowl will be filled with vegetables; by the time you get done pounding the vegetables, the amount of vegetables decreases or shrinks down by about half. Place vegetables in Ball® jar pushing vegetables firmly into the jar, leaving no air pockets. Leave 1 inch at the top and either place cheesecloth on top with a rubber band, or a Ball® jar lid on top. Push down on the mixture twice a day until mixture ferments. Fermentation in the summertime can take a matter of 2 to 3 days, whereas it could take a week or so in the wintertime. Taste the vegetables for desired tartness.

Southern Style Vegetable Chili

Chili Smith Family Foods
Prep: 25 minutes   **Serves:** 10

- 2 chopped medium onions (red, sweet, Walla Walla, Maui, or your favorite)
- 2 diced medium carrots (organic, with tops still attached)
- 1 small butternut squash (or sweet potato), peeled, seeded, and medium-diced
- 2 cups organic collard greens, chopped (may substitute kale or mustard greens)
- 3 cups diced tomatoes, canned or fresh
- 3 cups cooked black-eyed peas
- 1 garlic clove, minced
- 3 tablespoons chili powder
- 1 tablespoon canola oil
- 1½ cups water
- 1 teaspoon hot sauce

Combine carrots and onions in a crock pot slow cooker, setting the temperature on low so it is below 118°F. Cook until onion is soft. Add the butternut squash and stir to mix with carrots and onions. Add the collards and garlic and cook until collards are wilted. Add the tomatoes, chili powder, water, salt and hot sauce.

Let simmer 30 minutes; or, until the vegetables are tender. Soak beans in a glass dish in water in your dehydrator and then combine with the vegetables. Let simmer to blend the flavors. Add water as necessary, and adjust seasonings to taste.

Contributor's Note: Beans are naturally low in fat and filled with nutrition, high protein, and soluble fiber. Beans have been grown on planet earth for at least 7,000 years; like water, air, and other common requirements, beans have served humanity for all that time. There is no culture and no location on earth where beans have not been used. Beans and bean stories are a part of everyone's story and all people have their own "Bean Stories." Chili Smith's beans are heirloom organic. Not only can you eat them but you can plant them and grow your own bean plants.

Tiger Eye Chili

Chili Smith Family Foods, adapted by Lisa Montgomery
Prep: 25 minutes

1⅔ cups tiger eye beans
1 large white onion
2 small fresh tomatoes
1 teaspoon salt
⅛ teaspoon paprika

⅛ teaspoon cayenne pepper
3 whole cloves
1 bay leaf
1–2 tablespoons chili powder

Place the ingredients in a slow cooker with the temperature at less than 118°F. Simmer until reaching desired doneness. Add water if necessary to maintain desired consistency. Add additional salt and chili powder until the flavor is correct.

South of the Border Bean Bake

Chili Smith Family Foods, adapted by Lisa Montgomery
Prep: 35 minutes

Olive oil
1 chopped onion
2 eggs
2 cups coconut milk
1 cup shredded raw cheese
1 cup cooked arikara yellow beans

1 cup cooked hidatsa red beans
1 (4 ounce) can diced green chiles
6 corn tortillas, cut into strips
½ cup grated jack or cheddar cheese
1 cup chopped tomatoes

Soak beans in water in your slow cooker at 118°F until cooked. Once beans are cooked (or uncooked), combine beans with raw milk, chilies, and onion. Place in glass dish. Sprinkle top with grated raw cheese and tomatoes. Place in a dehydrator at 105°F until warm and flavors have melded.

Rocky Mountain Baked Beans

Chili Smith Family Foods, adapted by Lisa Montgomery
Prep: 25 minutes

- 1 pound black calypso beans
- ¾ cup sliced green onions (including tops)
- ¾ cup diced green peppers
- ½ cup homemade or commercial chili sauce
- 8 ounces tomato sauce
- 1½ teaspoons dry mustard
- 1 package corn bread mix
- 1 (4 ounce) can chopped green chilies

Pre-soak beans in water for 24 hours, changing the water every 6 to 8 hours. Cook in a slow cooker/crock pot on low, so that the temperature is below 118°F. One pound of beans will yield 2.5 pounds of beans after cooking. Drain and rinse beans with a fresh water bath. Beans can be stored in the refrigerator. Combine remaining ingredients in Vitamix® high-speed blender and combine with the beans in your slow cooker at 118°F until desired doneness. You can eat this dish warm or cool.

Sort of Chili

Prep: 25 minutes

- 1 cup black beans
- ¼ cup corn kernels
- ½ cup red pepper, chopped
- ¼ cup green pepper, chopped
- ¼ red onion, chopped
- 1 clove garlic, minced
- 1 teaspoon chili powder
- 1 teaspoon dried basil
- 1 teaspoon dried oregano
- ½ teaspoon lemon juice
- Large juicy tomatoes, chopped
- ¼ teaspoon dried mustard
- ¼ cup date paste
- Chili peppers (optional)
- Sea salt, to taste
- Black pepper, to taste

Combine the ingredients in a glass dish and set in dehydrator at 105°F until beans have softened and warmed. You want the beans to soak up all of the flavors of the other ingredients. Make sure when you chop the tomatoes you use the tomato juice in the dish.

> ## WORDS FROM LISA:
>
> I have added a little green pepper for flavor. I realize that green peppers are not ripe and are harder for some to digest, so you can remove it, or replace it with an equivalent amount of red pepper.

Chili Con Amore

Sheryll Chavarria (Raw Can Roll Café and Pure Body Spa, Douglassville, PA, www.rawcanrollcafe.com)
Prep: 30 minutes   **Dehydrate:** Several hours at 105°F (optional)

1 cup zucchini, chopped	1 tablespoon chili powder
1 large portobello mushroom, chopped	2 tablespoons tamari
2 cups corn, cut off the cob	2 cloves garlic
1 cup fresh tomatoes, chopped	3 tablespoons olive oil
½ red bell pepper, chopped fine	1 red bell pepper, chopped coarsely
½ cup onion, chopped fine	1 cup tomato, chopped coarsely
1 tablespoon cumin powder	1 cup sundried tomatoes

Soak sundried tomatoes in water, keeping approximately 1 cup soaking water.

Mix the zucchini, mushroom, corn, tomatoes, bell pepper, and onion in a bowl and set aside. Blend remaining ingredients. Add reserved soaking water to blended ingredients as needed if the mixture is too dry. (Do not pour all in at once.) Mix into bowl with chopped vegetables. Serve. This can also be warmed in a dehydrator for several hours at 105°F to allow the flavors to meld.

Portobello Mock Meatloaf

**Sheryll Chavarria (Raw Can Roll Café and Pure Body Spa, Douglassville, PA,
www.rawcanrollcafe.com)**
Prep: 20–30 minutes   **Soak:** 2–4 hours   **Dehydrate:** 1–2 hours at 115°F

Meatloaf
2½ cups sunflower seeds, soaked
2 cups walnuts, soaked
3 cups portobello mushrooms
1 cup yellow or red bell pepper
½ cup onion
½ cup parsley (can substitute rosemary
   or use ¼ cup parsley and ¼ cup
   rosemary)
2–3 cloves garlic, pressed
1 cup celery

1 tablespoon cumin
¼ cup wheat-free tamari
½ cup olive oil

Tomato Paste Sauce
1 cup tomato
¼ cup fresh basil
2 sun-dried tomatoes
1 tablespoon agave or raw honey
Salt to taste

Meatloaf
Place soaked nuts, seeds, and mushrooms into a food processor, and process until smooth. Add the rest of the ingredients to the food processor, and process to desired "meatloaf" consistency. Form into a meatloaf shape and dehydrate for 1–2 hours at 115°F, cut into thin slices, and serve. Can also top with a tomato-paste sauce.

Tomato Paste Sauce
Combine the ingredients in a high-speed blender until well-blended. Paint the top of the mock meatloaf.

Mock Taco Meat

Sheryll Chavarria (Raw Can Roll Café and Pure Body Spa, Douglassville, PA, www.rawcanrollcafe.com)
Soak: Seeds, 4 hours   **Prep:** 15 minutes   **Dehydrate:** 1 hour at 105°F

2 cups sunflower seeds, soaked for
    4 hours
2 tablespoons nutritional yeast

2 tablespoons cumin
2 tablespoons chili powder
Tamari, to taste

Put all ingredients into food processor and blend well. Place ingredients onto dehydrator sheets (do not use Teflex sheets, only use the mesh plastic). Dehydrate for about 1 hour at 105°F.

Un-"Meatloaf"

Joel Odhner
"Meatloaf" Prep: 30 minutes   **Soak:** nuts and seeds, 4–5 hours
Dehydrate: 1 + 2–3 hours at 115°F   **Barbeque Sauce Prep:** 10 minutes

"Meatloaf"
¾ cup walnuts
1 cup sunflower seeds
1 cup almonds
Filtered water, for soaking seeds and
    almonds
2 cloves garlic
½ cup parsley, chopped
½ cup celery, chopped
1 cup red bell pepper, chopped
1 cup portabella mushroom, marinated
    (optional)
1 tablespoon onion, chopped
2 tablespoons rosemary

1 tablespoon tarragon
1 tablespoon jalapeño
1 teaspoon cumin

Barbeque Sauce
1 cup tomatoes
½ cup sun-dried tomatoes
¼ cup onion, chopped
1 clove garlic
½ teaspoon jalapeño or chili powder
4 fresh basil leaves
¼ cup Braggs or sea salt
¼ cup cold-pressed olive oil

"Meatloaf"

Homogenize seeds, nuts, and garlic in a food processor. Pour the homogenized seeds, nuts, and garlic in a large mixing bowl. Stir the remaining ingredients with the nuts, seeds, and garlic mixture. Form into a loaf. Dehydrate for 1 hour.

Barbeque Sauce

Blend together in a high-speed blender and spoon over the "meatloaf" after it has dehydrated for 1 hour. Then put the "meatloaf" back in the dehydrator for another 2–3 hours.

Walnut Steak

Brenda Cobb (Founder of Living Foods Institute® and author of *The Living Foods Lifestyle*, www.livingfoodsinstitute.com)

Prep: 25 minutes **Soak:** walnuts, sunflower seeds, and almonds, overnight
Dehydrate: 2 hours at 100°F

1 cup walnuts, soaked
½ cup sunflower seeds, soaked
½ cup almonds, soaked
3 Medjool dates, pitted and soaked
5 cups water
3 cloves garlic
¼ tablespoon Himalayan salt
¼ cup onion

1 tablespoon fresh rosemary ½ cup red bell pepper
1 teaspoon fresh jalapeño pepper, seeded
¾ teaspoon cumin
1 cup fresh tomatoes
2 tablespoons fresh basil leaves

Soak the walnuts, sunflower seeds, almonds, and dates in 5 cups of water overnight, and then drain. Combine the remaining ingredients in the food processor using an "S" blade. Then add the walnuts, sunflower seeds, and almonds to the mixture in the food processor, and blend into a chunky mixture.

Form into patties, dehydrate at 100°F for 2 hours, and serve warm.

Pad Thai

Joel Odhner
Prep: 30 minutes

Noodles
Green and red cabbage, julienned
Zucchini, julienned
Young Thai coconut meat, julienned
Red and yellow peppers, julienned

Sauce
1 cup young Thai coconut meat
½ cup young Thai coconut water
½ cup macadamia or Brazil nuts
1 clove garlic
⅛ cup lime or lemon juice
½ teaspoon sea salt
½ teaspoon ginger chopped
Pinch of cayenne

Noodles
Combine all the ingredients and set aside.

Sauce
Place all the ingredients in a high-speed blender, and blend until smooth. Mix the sauce with the noodles, and let stand for 30 minutes. Lasts for 2 days in the refrigerator.

Picadillo

Linda Leboutillier

When Linda made this for lunch for me one day, I was blown away. The serving says that it yields 4–6, but this is so good that you could eat it all yourself. I just loved it.

Prep: 40 minutes   **Soak:** pecans, 6 hours; walnuts, 6 hours

Nut and Spice

2½ cups pecans, soaked, drained, and dehydrated

2½ cups walnuts, soaked, drained, and dehydrated

4 tablespoons Frontier™ Pizza Seasoning

¾ tablespoon paprika

2 teaspoons dried oregano

½ teaspoon clove garlic, minced

Pinch of cayenne

1 tablespoon of kelp powder or 3 tablespoons Bragg® Liquid Aminos

2 teaspoons mesquite

½ teaspoon cumin

½ teaspoon black pepper

Vegetables

2½ cups red pepper, diced

2½ cups yellow squash, diced

1 cup red onion, diced

¼ cup lime juice

½ cup fresh parsley, chopped

1 cup green olives, chopped

1 cup corn, cut from cob

1½ cups tomatoes, chopped

2 bay leaves (remove upon serving)

¼ cup raisins

2 teaspoons capers

1 (2¼ ounce) can black olives, drained and chopped

Nut and Spice

Pulse all ingredients in a food processor.

Vegetables

Combine all ingredients in a large mixing bowl with the first mixture.

Serve on a bed of greens.

Sprouted Sunflower Seed Pâté (Tuna-less Salad)

Barbara Shevkun (Rawfully Tempting)

When Barbara brought this dish to our raw potluck, it was the hit of the night. It was the first dish to be eaten so you know that it was a huge success.

Prep: 25 minutes   **Soak:** sunflower seeds, 4–6 hours; almonds, overnight

1½ cups sunflower seeds, soaked
½ cup almonds, soaked overnight
¼ cup water (or more as needed)
1 clove garlic, crushed
½ cup celery, chopped
¼–½ cup red onion, finely chopped

2 tablespoons fresh parsley, chopped
1 teaspoon dried dill
2 tablespoons olive oil
1 tablespoon coconut water vinegar
  (or your favorite vinegar)
1 tablespoon dulse flakes (optional)
¼ teaspoon sea salt (or to taste)

Rinse and drain soaked nuts and seeds, and then process in a food processor, adding water as needed. Mix until mixture is similar to tuna-salad consistency. Transfer to a bowl and add remaining ingredients. Serve on raw flax crackers, bread, or lettuce wraps. Garnish with sliced tomato, avocado, and red onion.

Rawfully Tempting Marinara Sauce and Rawsages

Rawsages are optional in this dish, but add a wonderful texture and flavor.

Marinara Sauce
3 tomatoes
½ cup kale, chopped
1 clove garlic, chopped
¼ red onion
¼ red or orange bell pepper
½ avocado
2 teaspoon lemon juice
Fresh basil, to taste
Sea salt, to taste
Cayenne pepper, to taste
Pinch of dried oregano

Rawsages (optional)
¾ cup walnuts (soak overnight, towel dry, may dehydrate a bit)
¼ cup pecans (soak overnight, towel dry, may dehydrate a bit)
Dash crushed red pepper
2 Medjool dates, pitted and chopped
½ teaspoon fennel seeds, crushed or ground
Dash cayenne
¼ teaspoon each salt, pepper, oregano, basil, sage, thyme

Marinara Sauce
Blend ingredients. Taste and season to your liking. Set aside.

Rawsages
Process the nuts until well chopped in a food processor. Add remaining ingredients, and process until it begins to come together but still has texture.

Roll into small balls and dehydrate at 110°F for 6–8 hours. To store, freeze in an air-tight container and use for raw pizzas and other Italian-style dishes.

Assembly
Place a mixture of kelp and zucchini noodles on each plate. Top with marinated veggies. Add marinara sauce and garnish with rawsages and chopped fresh parsley or basil.

You can warm veggies and marinara in dehydrator prior to serving.

You can serve this as an amazing Main Event or make each of it in parts and combine with other dishes . . . Mix it up.

Asian Slaw

Prep: 30 minutes

2 cups shredded Napa cabbage
1 large carrot, shredded or cut into matchsticks
4 scallions, thinly sliced
1 pear, peeled and cut into bite-size pieces
1 cup jicama, peeled and cut into bite-size pieces
1 small red onion, thinly sliced

¼ cup cilantro, chopped
1 tablespoon sesame seeds
2 cups daikon, shredded
Zest and juice of 2 limes (If this is too tangy for you, back off on the zest. Start with just the juice and then add zest to taste as you go)
1 teaspoon sea salt
2 tablespoons raw honey

Combine ingredients in a large bowl and serve. This is one of those dishes that you start eating while you are making it!

14

Spreads, Sauces, & Dips

Junior's Guacamole

Arnold Kaufman
Prep: 2 minutes

  1 avocado
  2 tomatoes

Cut avocado in half, take out the pit, and spoon out the green avocado meat into a bowl. Next, chop or process tomatoes with avocado to a creamy consistency.

Almond Hummus

Kimberton Whole Foods, www.kimbertonwholefoods.com
Prep: 15 minutes   **Soak:** almonds, 8 hours

  2 cups almonds, soaked
  ½ cup tahini
  1 large garlic clove, minced
  Juice of 2 large lemons

  ¼ to ½ teaspoon sea salt
  1 tablespoon fresh chopped parsley
  1 teaspoon basil

Break down the almonds using a homogenizing juicer with the blank plate, or even better, a high-powered food processor such as the Cuisinart®. If you have neither, with sufficient time and patience you can use a hand blender, but take care with it as this is hard work. Put the broken-down almonds into a food processor along with all the other ingredients. Try to achieve a smooth consistency, adding a little water if necessary. Process until desired consistency is reached. Some people like chunky bits of nut to remain, while others like it smooth, or you could take half of the mixture out of the food processor while still chunky and process the rest to smoothness to create two different textures—they actually do taste a little different! Serve with green vegetables (such as lettuce, cabbage, and kale) or spread on flax crackers. This is also good as a dip and is great for taking on board a plane as it remains stable on a long flight, and is good for car trips.

Annie's Guacamole

Annie Marshall (Fante's Kitchen Ware Shop, Philadelphia, PA)
Prep: 20 minutes

3 ripe avocados
¼-½ cup onion (approximately), chopped
1 clove garlic, chopped
½ lime, juiced

10 springs fresh cilantro, chopped
1 fresh whole tomato, chopped
1 jalapeño pepper, chopped (seeded if
    you do not want it to be too hot)
Salt and pepper to taste

Mix all of the ingredients together in a bowl, but not too much. The guacamole is meant to be lumpy. To store, place plastic wrap directly on top of the mix to keep the guacamole from oxidizing and turning brown. I have read that keeping 1 of the pits from the avocado in the dip will also help to keep it from turning brown.

Brazil Nut Pâté

Kimberton Whole Foods, www.kimbertonwholefoods.com
Prep: 10 minutes

1 cup Brazil nuts
1 clove garlic

1-inch fresh ginger
Sea salt, to taste

Place all ingredients into a high-speed blender or food processor, adding a little water if needed. Process until desired consistency is reached. This goes perfectly with crudités.

Cashew Cheeseless Spread

Bruce and Marsha Weinstein (Awesome Foods, Bridgeport, PA, www.awesomefoods.com)
Prep: 30 minutes

15 ounces Cashew Cream (10 ounces cashews, 5 ounces water)
4½ ounces yellow pepper
2½ ounces fresh lemon juice
2 teaspoons dried parsley
1½ tablespoons dried dill

1⅔ teaspoons dried basil
1 teaspoon black pepper
1 teaspoon granulated garlic
1 teaspoon granulated onion
½ teaspoon sesame seeds
1/6 teaspoon Himalayan sea salt

Grind cashews in a food processor, and then add water and process to make the cream. Add the rest of the ingredients until smooth.

Contributer's Note: In addition to being used as a cheese spread, you can dehydrate it, and turn it into crackers or cashew-dill cheese sticks.

All ounces are measured by weight. They are not to be measured in a measuring cup.

Chipotle Sour Cream

Sheryll Chavarria (Raw Can Roll Café and Pure Body Spa, Douglassville, PA, www.rawcanrollcafe.com)
I made this recipe on air on WFMZ TV, Channel 69, in Allentown, PA, on April 1, 2011, and the crew loved it.
Prep: 25 minutes

3 tomatoes, chopped (preferably plum/ Roma tomatoes)
1 mango, peeled and pitted
¼ cup onion, chopped fine
½ bunch cilantro, chopped fine

½ lemon or lime, juiced
½ jalapeño pepper, chopped fine (optional)
1–2 cloves garlic, minced
Sea salt, to taste

Combine all ingredients together in a Vitamix® high-speed blender.

Serve as a sauce on the Chili Con Amore (see page 246). This can also be used as a dip. You can even dehydrate the mixture, turn it into crackers or pour it over broccoli cut into bite-sized pieces, place in a glass Pyrex® dish, and dehydrate until warm.

Curried Carrot Pâté

Kimberton Whole Foods, www.kimbertonwholefoods.com
Prep: 15 minutes

  2 organic carrots, grated and chopped   1 teaspoon curry powder
  1 tablespoon raw organic peanut butter

Place all ingredients in a food processor and blend until pâté is formed. Pair with raw veggies for dipping or use as topping for other dishes. This pâté can also be placed with veggies on greens for lunch or in a wrap with veggies for a meal.

Curry Dill Pâté

Joel Odhner
Prep: 20 minutes   **Soak:** nuts; 2–4 hours

  2 cups pecans, soaked   1 tablespoon cold-pressed extra virgin
  2 cups cauliflower, chopped   olive oil
  1 tablespoon curry powder   1 tablespoon lemon juice
  1 tablespoon dill weed   1 teaspoon Celtic sea salt

Combine all of the ingredients in a food processor until smooth.

Pine Nut-Dill "Cheese" Spread

Elaina Love (Author of *Elaina's Pure Joy Kitchen*, www.PureJoyLove.com)
Prep: 20 minutes

2 cups soaked and peeled (optional) almonds (1½ cups before soaking)

¼–½ cup purified water (amount needed may vary)

½ cup pine nuts, chopped

½ cup red onion, minced

2 green onions, minced

2 tablespoons raw, light miso (look for unpasteurized in the refrigerator section)

1 tablespoon nutritional yeast (not a raw food)

2 cloves garlic, crushed

4 tablespoons parsley, chopped

2 teaspoons fresh dill, chopped

Peel almonds by soaking in hot water for 20–30 seconds, then draining and removing the skins. The almonds should slide out of the skins with this method. This is optional for a lighter textured paste.

Run almonds through the juicer using the blank blade or put in food processor. Alternate water with nuts to keep them moving through the machine. If using a food processor, add water after the nuts are pureed well. Add remainder of ingredients and mix well. Form into a round or square shape. Garnish with a sprig of dill or parsley and chopped dehydrated almonds. Serve with fresh vegetables or flax crackers. Makes 3 cups.

Spinach Basil Pesto

Bruce and Marsha Weinstein (Awesome Foods, Bridgeport, PA, www.awesomefoods.com)
Prep: 15 minutes   **Soak:** walnuts, 4 hours; sunflower seeds, 6 hours

2.2 ounces soaked raw walnuts

2.2 ounces soaked raw sunflower seeds

2.3 ounces cold-pressed olive oil

2 ounces fresh basil (please wash)

2.3 ounces spinach

0.3 ounces fresh garlic

0.6 ounces fresh lemon juice

0.9 ounces water

Pinch dried basil

¼ teaspoon Himalayan sea salt

Combine ingredients in a Vitamix® and blend well.

Contributer's Note: This pesto can be used as a dip, as a pesto on spiralized pasta, as a dressing on a salad, as a coating for kale chips, as a spread on crackers, or as a pesto on pizza.

Sunflower Zuke Hummus

Prep: 10 minutes

½ teaspoon garlic granules
2 garlic cloves, minced
½ cup water
½ cup tahini
¼ teaspoon cumin

2 teaspoons curry
½ cup lemon juice
1 tablespoon raw honey
2 cups zucchini, chopped
1–2 tablespoons fresh dill

Blend ingredients in a Vitamix® High Speed Blender or a Cuisinart food processor until smooth. Hummus is great as a dressing, dip, pâté, or filler in a wrap.

Toasted Sesame Mayo

Prep: 10 minutes

½ teaspoon toasted sesame oil
1 teaspoon black sesame seeds

Follow the Basic Mayo recipe on page 262, and during the blending process blend in the toasted sesame oil. Remove mayo mixture from blender/food processor and pour into your bowl. Stir in the sesame seeds.

Either of these recipes can be used as dips, dressings, or spread.

Avocado Mash

Prep: 5 minutes

1 avocado
Splash of lemon juice

Sea salt to taste
Ground black pepper to taste

Remove the avocado from its skin (remove pit as well) and mash it on a plate. Squeeze a touch of lemon juice on the avocado, along with Celtic Sea Salt® and ground black pepper to taste.

Basic Mayo

Prep: 7 minutes

1 cup raw cashews
½ cup water
½ teaspoon sea salt

1 teaspoon freshly squeezed lemon juice
½ teaspoon agave or raw honey

Blend all ingredients in a Vitamix® High Speed Blender or CuisinartTM Food Processor until creamy smooth.

Guacamole

Prep: 7 minutes

2 avocados
½ red onion, chopped fine
Juice of 1 lemon

1 tablespoon cilantro (optional, substitute parsley)
Sea salt to taste

Combine ingredients in a Vitamix® High Speed Blender or Cuisinart Food Processor until desired thickness.

Olive Tapenade

Prep: 7 minutes

1 cup pitted olives
1 tablespoon cold-pressed olive oil

½ teaspoon lemon juice
1 teaspoon raw honey

Combine the above ingredients in your Vitamix® High Speed Blender or Cuisinart Food Processor. Store in Ball® jar with lid in your refrigerator. Tapenade is great as a cracker topping, topping on your salad, or filler in a wrap or nori roll.

Apple Ginger Sauerkraut

Betti-Lou Kramer
Prep: 20 minutes

1 small cabbage, thinly sliced (save a few leaves)
2 apples, thinly sliced
1 teaspoon grated fresh ginger

½ cup NOW Foods® Probiotic-10 50 Billion
1½ tablespoons Himalayan salt
Water, as needed

Wash and sterilize 2-quart sized jars and lids. Place cabbage in a bowl and sprinkle with salt. Using a wood tamper (or a wooden spoon), work salt into the cabbage for about 3 minutes or until cabbage starts giving off some liquid. Add apples, ginger, and probiotic (emptied out of capsule); mix well. Place into jars and press down with the tamper firmly.

The mixture should be giving off enough liquid to fully cover cabbage and apples; if not, add some water. Top with saved cabbage leaves, making sure it is completely covered with liquid. Let ferment (sit at room temperature) for several days; depending on the temperature in the house, it could take up to a week.

Eric's Guacamole

Dr. Eric Benedetti
Prep: 10 minutes

2 ripe avocados
½ clove fresh garlic
2 tablespoons lime juice
½ teaspoon salt

½ teaspoon pepper
1 teaspoon chopped cilantro
¼ teaspoon cayenne pepper

Peel ripe avocados and add to a small bowl. Coarsely mash. Smash garlic and mince; add to avocado. Add lime juice, salt, pepper, cilantro, and cayenne pepper to bowl. Gently fold ingredients together. Serve within two hours with your favorite chips.

Dandelion Marmalade

Sue Hess (Farm at Coventry)
Prep: 30 minutes

2 cups dandelion flower petals
  (all green bits removed)
2½ cups organic sugar
¾ cup fresh squeezed orange juice
3 tablespoons organic orange zest,
  slivered

2 tablespoons organic lemon zest,
  slivered
¾ cup water
1 packet Sure Jell® pectin

Pulse dandelion petals, sugar, orange juice, and zests together in food processor until well blended and leave mix in processer bowl. In a small saucepan over medium heat, mix ¾ cup water and one packet of Sure Jell® pectin, stirring constantly until well blended. Bring to a hard boil for one minute. Remove from heat and immediately add to the flower mix while the processer is running. Jam sets up very fast, so have six 4-ounce sterilized jam jars and lids ready. Fill, seal, and refrigerate. Enjoy!

Cranberry Apple Relish

Annmarie Cantrell
Prep: 20 minutes

3 cups cranberries
1 apple, diced
Juice of 1 orange
2 teaspoons grated ginger

⅓ teaspoon cinnamon
2 tablespoons honey
¼ cup water kefir or whey
2 teaspoons salt

Combine cranberries, apple, orange juice, ginger, cinnamon, and honey in a food processor. Remove to a bowl and stir in salt and kefir or whey. Spoon into jar and make sure the mixture is covered with liquid. If it is not covered, add some water. Keep at room temperature for 2 days before transferring to cold storage. Eat within 2 months.

Red Almond Pâté

Prep: 15 minutes

1 cup raw almonds, soaked and drained
¼ cup Austria's Finest, Naturally® pumpkin seeds
⅓ cup red peppers, chopped

1–2 oranges, remove seeds and skin
¼ cup red onion, chopped
½ teaspoon sea salt
Raw honey, to taste

Combine the above ingredients in a Vitamix® high-speed blender or food processor until well blended.

WORDS FROM LISA:

Pâtés are great as dips, as a filling in a wrap (whether a nori sheet or collard leaf), as a spread on raw crackers, or even as a dip. Try it spread on celery sticks!

Red Pepper Pesto

Prep: 15 minutes

1 cup fresh basil, chopped
2 cups raw cashews
1 cup red pepper, chopped

4 cloves garlic
2 teaspoons sea salt
2 tablespoons lemon juice

Combine the above ingredients in a Vitamix® high-speed blender or a food processor until desired consistency is reached. Some people like their pesto smooth, while others prefer it chunky. Make your pesto to the consistency that you like!

Hemp Pesto

Prep: 15 minutes

2 cups hemp seeds
1 cup fresh basil
3 tablespoons lemon juice

2 teaspoons sea salt
2 cloves garlic
Cold-pressed olive oil or water (optional)

Combine the above ingredients in a Vitamix® high-speed blender or a Cuisinart® food processor until well blended. If the pesto is a little dry, add a little cold-pressed olive oil to make the pesto smoother. For a light-weight alternative, add a touch of water.

This pesto can be used as a dip, a filling, or served over noodles. Noodles can be spiralized out of zucchini or squash. Kelp noodles or mung bean noodles are another alternative, or better yet, combine all four options for a very colorful dish.

Avocado Mash

1 avocado, pitted
Splash of lemon juice

Sea salt, to taste
Ground black pepper, to taste

Remove the avocado from its skin. Run the avocado through the mincing feature of your juicer so that it mashes your avocado. Combine with seasonings and serve.

Elijah Apple Sauce

Arnold Kaufman
Prep: 5 minutes

2 apples, cut and cored

3 dates, pitted and soaked

Mix apples and dates in a food processor until the mixture becomes a sauce-like consistency.

Plum Sauce

Brooke Preston
Prep: 25 minutes

3½ ounces umeboshi plum paste
3 ounces brown rice vinegar
3 tablespoons turbinado sugar
1 ounce toasted sesame oil
½ cup coconut sugar
3 tablespoons onion powder

3 cloves peeled garlic
1 tablespoon red chili flakes
2 tablespoons ginger juice
2 tablespoons lime juice
1½ cups water

Blend together in a high-speed blender. Store in airtight glass container.

Healthy Lime Vinaigrette

Dr. Eric Benedetti
Prep: 10 minutes

¼ cup red wine vinegar
¼ cup lime juice
½ cup olive oil
1 clove garlic, minced

½ red onion, minced
½ teaspoon salt
½ teaspoon pepper
1 teaspoon spicy brown mustard

Add red wine vinegar, lime juice, garlic, red onion, salt, pepper, and mustard into a small mixing bowl. Using a small food processor, whisk, or hand blender, slowly add olive oil while mixing.

Raw Cranberry Sauce

Sheryll Chavarria (Raw Can Roll Café and Pure Body Spa, Douglassville, PA, www.rawcanrollcafe.com)
Prep: 15 minutes

2 cups fresh cranberries
1 teaspoon lemon or orange zest

4 tablespoons pitted dates
1 medium apple, chopped medium-fine

Blend all ingredients (except the apple) until it reaches desired consistency. Mix in the apple and serve.

Sun-Dried Tomato Marinara

Ultimate Superfood
Prep: 45 minutes   **Serves:** 4

3 cups chopped soaked sun-dried
tomatoes
1 cup spring water
4 cloves garlic, chopped
1½ cups Ojio™ organic hemp seeds

1½ cups organic extra virgin olive oil
1 tablespoon Ojio™ organic clear
agave nectar
Pinch of Ojio™ Himalayan salt
Pinch or two of black pepper

First, soak the sun-dried tomatoes for 20 minutes. Place all ingredients in a high-speed blender. Blend on high until creamy; add more water if necessary. Blend until smooth.

Contributor's Note: A slightly sweetened update to a classic easy-to-make marinara recipe, this tomato marinara is packed with hemp seed protein and Omega chain fatty acids with the added minerals of Himalayan salt.

Raw Sriracha

Wendy Landiak
Prep: 15 minutes

1 cup dehydrated tomatoes
½ cup vinegar
½ cup maple syrup
1 teaspoon paprika

1 teaspoon cayenne
1 whole red habanera
Salt, to taste

Purée in Vitamix®, adding water until desired consistency is reached. Add an Indian twist with ginger and curry powder!

Apple Waldorf Sauce

Prep: 25 minutes

Puree
1 Gala apple, cored and cubed
1 tablespoon date paste
1 tablespoon lemon juice
¼ cup water

Waldorf
Gala apples, cored and cubed

¼ cup raisins
¼ cup shredded coconuts
¼ cup celery, chopped
Cinnamon, to taste
Raw cacao and almond slivers, to taste
or garnish (optional)

Combine puree ingredients in a Vitamix® high-speed blender and puree. Start with a little water at a time, just enough to puree the apples. If the puree is too runny, drain through a sieve. Set the pureed apple mixture aside in a bowl.

Combine pureed portion with the Waldorf portion. Sprinkle with cinnamon to taste and add raw cacao nibs and almond slivers (optional) to taste or to garnish.

Tomato Sauce

Prep: 10 minutes

4 large heirloom organic tomatoes
1 cup red onion, chopped
½ cup softened dates, pitted
1 red pepper, cleaned and chopped

1 teaspoon cinnamon
¼ teaspoon oregano
1 clove garlic
¼ cup cold-pressed olive oil

Combine ingredients together in a Vitamix® high-speed blender until blended well. This tomato sauce can be used as a pasta sauce, whether you serve it over spiralized zucchini, kelp noodles, or mung bean noodles. It can also be used as a dressing. You can warm the tomato sauce in a glass dish in your Tribest® Sedona Dehydrator.

Fast Alfredo Sauce

Kimberton Whole Foods, www.kimbertonwholefoods.com
Prep: 15–20 minutes   **Serves:** 2–3

1 cup water (the original recipe called for soy milk)

⅓ cup raw cashews (or a wee bit more to compensate for soy milk omission)

¼ cup nutritional yeast

3 tablespoons tamari or nama shoyu

2 tablespoons margarine (in the original recipe; I simply omit this)

1 tablespoon tahini

1 tablespoon lemon juice

2 teaspoons mustard (ideally Dijon)

½ teaspoon paprika

1 pinch nutmeg

2–4 cloves garlic

Black pepper, to taste

Add all the ingredients to a blender and blend until smooth. Pour over spiralized zucchini noodles.

The cooked version (in addition to the soy milk mentioned): Drain the pasta and return it to the hot empty pan. Pour the sauce over, place on medium heat, and stir until heated through. Serve with lots of fresh cracked black pepper, and steamed broccoli, if desired.

Contributer's Note: The whole sauce is made in a blender, so the faster you can toss ingredients into a blender, the faster it's done. This also makes it super easy for additions. Try adding red peppers, for instance.

Mushroom Gravy

Joel Odhner

1 cup portobello mushrooms, chopped

1 cup olive oil

¼ cup Bragg

¼ cup onion, choppd

½ red pepper, chopped

Place all of the ingredients together in a high-speed blender and blend until smooth. Add just enough water to reach the desired consistency. This dressing will last for 2–3 days in the refrigerator.

Raw Prepared Mustard

Rhio (author of *Hooked on Raw*)
This is a good substitute for cooked Dijon mustard.
Prep: 10 minutes

7 tablespoons whole brown mustard seeds

1½ tablespoon whole yellow mustard seeds

3 tablespoons raw apple cider vinegar

3 ounces filtered water

1½ tablespoons raw unheated honey

½ teaspoon Celtic sea salt

In a pint glass jar combine the whole mustard seeds, apple cider vinegar, and water and give the mixture a gentle stir.

Cap the jar, but not tightly, and let sit at room temperature for 24 hours.

After 24 hours, put the mixture into a blender, add the honey and Celtic sea salt, then blend well. You will have to stop the machine and push the mustard down a few times. You might also have to add a little more filtered water, but do this one tablespoon at a time until it becomes a mustard consistency.

Store in a glass jar in the refrigerator. Makes 1 cup. Keeps for months.

Contributer's Note: If you close the jar too tightly, some pressure might build up in the jar…mustard is potent.

The first time you make this recipe, try making it as stated above to see if it suits you. To make a hotter mustard, simply increase the ratio of yellow mustard seeds. To make a milder mustard, increase the brown mustard seeds and decrease the yellow.

To make a simple salad dressing, add ½ teaspoon of Raw Prepared Mustard to olive and flaxseed oils, fresh lemon juice, fresh prepared garlic, and Celtic sea salt. I also use this as a condiment with raw veggie burgers. Use it anywhere you would use Dijon mustard.

Red Sauce

This sauce can be used as a pasta sauce, dressing, or salsa.
Prep: 7 minutes

1 cup Roma tomatoes, chopped
1 cup sun-dried tomatoes
¼ red onion, chopped
1 clove garlic

1 red pepper, seeded
1 teaspoon sea salt
½ teaspoon fresh basil
½ teaspoon oregano

Combine the above ingredients in a Vitamix® High Speed Blender or Cuisinart Food Processor until desired thickness. For a red sauce or dressing, blend until creamy. For a salsa, pulse-chop in your food processor for a chopped texture.

Dipping Sauce

This is a great dipping sauce for bok choy, celery, collard roll-ups, or zucchini roll-ups. It also makes a great dressing.

1–2 cloves garlic, chopped
1 tablespoon ginger, grated
4 tablespoons water
4 tablespoons wheat-free tamari
2 tablespoons cold-pressed olive oil or sesame oil

1–2 dates
2 tablespoons sesame tahini
Dash pepper
Dash curry
Dash sea salt

Using a small blender (or mix by hand), blend all of the ingredients together.

Sweet Vegetable Marinade

Prep: 30 minutes

Marinade
½ cup orange juice, freshly squeezed
1 tablespoon agave
1 tablespoon cold-cold pressed olive oil
Sea salt to taste

Vegetables
Assorted vegetables, sliced into bite-sized pieces

Marinade
Combine ingredients in a high-speed blender and set aside.

Vegetables
Toss the vegetables into the marinade. You can even add dried cranberries and pineapples to add pop as well. Place marinated vegetables in a glass dish and place in Tribest Sedona Dehydrator at 105°F for 1 hour. This dish tastes great warm as well as chilled. You can serve this as a stand-alone dish, on greens, or as a side dish.

Portabella Marinade

Sheryll Chavarria (Raw Can Roll Café and Pure Body Spa, Douglassville, PA, www.rawcanrollcafe.com)
Prep: 80 minutes

2 portabella mushrooms, cut into
    medium thick slices
1 large onion, peeled and sliced thinly

¼ cup wheat-free tamari
1 cup water

Place mushrooms and onion in a glass bowl and cover with the water-tamari marinade and stir frequently for 20 minutes. Then place the mixture in the dehydrator at 105°F for approximately one hour and serve.

Snappy Bean Dip

Chili Smith Family Foods, adapted by Lisa Montgomery
Prep: 25 minutes   **Yield:** about ½ cup dip or 24 servings

2 cups cooked Flor de Mayo beans
Juice of ½ lemon
2 tablespoons raw cashews
1 teaspoon wheat free tamari

1 teaspoon chopped and seeded canned
  jalapeño peppers, fresh
¼ teaspoon salt
3 tablespoons chopped green onions,
  divided
Daiya coconut cheese, to taste

Place beans in slow cooker, covering with 2 inches of water at 118°F until beans are uncooked. Blend beans and remaining ingredients (except 1 tablespoon of the green onion) in a Vitamix® high-speed blender. Place in a small bowl and garnish with 1 tablespoon chopped green onion. Serve as a dip with raw vegetables or raw kale chips. Can be used as filler for a wrap made out of romaine lettuce leaves or collard leaves. If you use raw butter, raw cheese, or Daiya coconut cheese, you can sprinkle or add to the wrap.

Cashew-Based Nacho Cheese Dip

Will Eddy
Prep: 25 minutes

11–16 ounces cashews
1 teaspoon salt
⅓ medium tomato
2 garlic cloves
¼ red pepper flesh
1 medium carrot, for color
Juice of one lemon
1 tablespoon nutritional yeast
1 tablespoon taco seasoning
1 teaspoon cumin

1 teaspoon oregano
Your choice of spices (onion powder,
  garlic powder, chipotle, smoked
  paprika)
1 jalapeño with inside removed
½ tomato, deseeded and dehydrated
¼ red pepper
½ onion
2 peeled garlic cloves
Handful of chopped cilantro
Tabasco sauce, to taste

Ensure Vitamix® container, lid, and tamper are completely dry. Blend 11–16 ounces of cashews with 1 teaspoon salt. Use tamper on high until runny/ smooth, which should take about one minute. It is important that the cashews are extremely smooth before adding any wet ingredients. Add the following ingredients to the container: ⅓ medium tomato, 2 garlic cloves, ¼ sweet onion, ¼ red pepper flesh, 1 medium carrot (for color), and juice of one lemon.

Add 1 tablespoon nutritional yeast, 1 tablespoon taco seasoning, 1 teaspoon cumin, 1 teaspoon oregano, a splash (or five!) of Tabasco sauce, and any other spices you think will taste good, like onion powder, garlic powder, chipotle, or smoked paprika. Blend on high with tamper until smooth. If it gets clumpy, that means you put too much watery stuff in there; better luck next time, but it'll still taste good.

Cut into strips and add a jalapeño with inside removed, ½ tomato with liquid and seeds removed, ¼ red pepper, ½ onion, 2 peeled garlic cloves, and a handful of chopped cilantro. Set the blender to chop, using tamper vigorously. Leave it chunky.

Contributor's Note: If you put a bowl of this dip on the table in the room with a bunch of cheese junkies, they'll say it is the best nacho cheese dip they've ever tasted. The basic combo is salty cashew butter with some lemon juice, but this is the version I make at home. If you're missing a couple ingredients, make it anyway! Also, I don't measure at home and it's different every time. This is a lot more filling than real cheese dip, and it's probably a lot healthier, too.

Easy Mac Nut Nacho Cheese

Natalie Norman
Prep: 15 minutes

1 cup raw macadamia nuts
¼ cup water, added slowly and
as needed
½ teaspoon probiotic powder (optional)
¼ teaspoon salt, or to taste

2 tablespoons lemon juice
2 tablespoons nutritional yeast
⅓ of a small red bell pepper
1 teaspoon chipotle chili powder

Blend to creamy consistency in high-speed blender such as a Vitamix®. Do not overblend; just go until the cheese is uniformly smooth. Enjoy!

Contributor's Note: This recipe is quick; no soaking of the nuts is required. You can play with this recipe, adding other seasonings if you like (such as onion or garlic) or folding in some minced cilantro. Use it as a spread, in wraps, as a dip for veggies, or even thin it out with additional water or nut milk for a creamy/spicy salad dressing.

Vegan Cheddar Cheesey (Better Than Velveeta)

Janice Inella
Prep: 20 minutes

2½ cups raw cashews (soak for 1 hour)
6 sun-dried tomatoes
1 red pepper
1 tablespoon chipotle spice (or more, if
you like it hot)
3 tablespoons red onion or a small to
medium red onion

2 tablespoons olive oil
1 teaspoon sea salt, or to taste
Juice from 1 lemon (Meyer when
in season)
½ cup pure water (more if needed)

In a high-speed blender, add all ingredients and blend until smooth. Serve as a veggie dip or dressing. A great crowd pleaser at any party!

Hot Artichoke Dip

Prep: 15 minutes

1 cup parmesan cheese
1 cup mayonnaise
1 cup artichoke hearts

Paprika, to taste
Cayenne pepper (optional), to taste

Combine the above ingredients in a food processor or combine manually by hand, until desired consistency is reached. I used to make this by hand, but the consistency is much smoother, and combines better when you pulse the mixture in your food processor or Vitamix® high-speed blender. Sprinkle the top with paprika. If you like heat, also sprinkle with cayenne pepper. Bake at 350°F until it begins to bubble.

WORDS FROM LISA:

When I was in my 20's I started making the Hot Artichoke Dip at every gathering because everyone (including me) just loved it. I hadn't made this recipe in 25 years because of the cheese (I'm allergic to dairy) and because it doesn't fit within my raw diet. On pages 279–280, I have shared with you 3 different variations of this recipe, starting with this original recipe and then taking you through the transitions that get you to where I am today. I understand that not everyone is allergic to dairy, and I know many people may eat raw cheese, so I've given you that version as well. With these recipes, I am showing you the progression of where I started with standard American diet and how I have transitioned to a raw diet. I want you to see this progression so that you can learn how to do it for yourself with your recipes, wherever you are in your journey.

Hot Artichoke Dip–Transition No. 1

Prep: 15 minutes

1 cup Daiya cheese, Jack style (made from coconut meat and contains no dairy)
1 cup Vegenaise®

1 artichoke heart
Paprika, to taste
Cayenne pepper (optional), to taste

Combine the ingredients in a Vitamix® high-speed blender or food processor. Sprinkle with paprika and cayenne pepper, if desired. Bake in a conventional oven at 350°F until bubbly.

WORDS FROM LISA:

Option No. 3 on page 280 involves making this recipe by dehydrating it in a Tribest® Sedona Dehydrator at 105°F until warmed.

Hot Artichoke Dip–Transition No. 2

Prep: 15 minutes

1 cup raw cashews
1 cup artichoke hearts
1 cup pine nuts
2 tablespoons nutritional yeast

1 tablespoon lemon juice
Paprika, to taste
Cayenne red pepper (optional), to taste
Water, enough to blend

Combine the above ingredients (except for one tablespoon nutritional yeast) in a Vitamix® high-speed blender or food processor. Be careful to pulse, or you will end up having an artichoke smoothie. Place the mixture in a glass dish, stir in the remaining tablespoon of nutritional yeast, and sprinkle with paprika and cayenne pepper, if desired.

Hot Artichoke Dip–Transition No. 3

Prep: 15 minutes

1 cup young Thai coconut meat
1 cup pine nuts
1 cup artichoke hearts
1½ tablespoons nutritional yeast
1 tablespoon lemon juice

2 pinches sea salt
Paprika, to taste (shake on finished dip
   to add garnish and flavor)
Cayenne pepper (optional), shake on top
   to add zip

Combine the young Thai coconut meat, pine nuts, artichoke hearts, nutritional yeast, lemon juice, and sea salt in a Vitamix® high-speed blender or a food processor and pulse-chop. You want the mixture to be blended, yet choppy in consistency. Place mixture in a glass dish big enough for the dip to be approximately ½–1 inch in depth. Sprinkle with paprika and cayenne pepper, if desired.

    Place in Tribest® Sedona Dehydrator at 105°F until warm; serve cool. Goes great on top of greens or as a sauce on your raw version of pasta, whether that be spiralized zucchini, kelp noodles, or mung bean noodles.

Creamy Beet and Horseradish Dip

Barbara Shevkun (Rawfully Tempting)
Prep: 20 minutes

Horseradish
1½ cups horseradish root, chopped
½ medium red beet, chopped
½–¾ cup water (or more as needed)
2 tablespoons vinegar (or coconut water
   vinegar)
3 tablespoons maple syrup (grade B or
   your favorite sweetener)
⅛ teaspoon sea salt

Dip
3 tablespoons horseradish (see above)
¼ cup cashews, soaked 1–2 hours
¼ cup water (or as needed for
   consistency)
2 tablespoons Irish moss paste
   (optional)

Horseradish

Clean, peel, and chop horseradish root.

Add horseradish, beet, and water to blender or food processor to blend.

Add vinegar, maple syrup, and salt. Process until well blended.

Transfer to a glass jar or airtight container.

Dip

Blend cashews and water.

Add Irish moss paste, if available (optional, but it gives a little more body).

Transfer to a bowl and stir in horseradish (the more you use, the hotter the mix will be).

Serve with sliced cucumbers or other veggies, on raw vegan crackers, over salad, or use as a condiment in wraps. Delicious!

Creamy Spinach Dip

Elaina Love (Author of *Elaina's Pure Joy Kitchen*, www.PureJoyLove.com)
Prep: 25 minutes **Serves:** 8

2 zucchinis, chopped
¼ cup water
1½ cups cashews
⅓ cup light miso
1 teaspoon Himalayan crystal salt
1 tablespoon lemon juice

1 tablespoon onion powder
3 cloves garlic
½ teaspoon white pepper
¼ teaspoon nutmeg
Pinch of cayenne
2–3 heads of spinach (about 10 cups)

Place the zucchini and water in a blender, and blend until smooth. Add the remainder of the ingredients (except the spinach). Blend until creamy. You may need to use a spatula or celery stick to get the mixture to blend. Pulse the spinach in a food processor until it is well-chopped. Mix all the prepared ingredients together in a bowl. This dish will keep 3 or more days in the refrigerator.

Contributer's Note: I prefer South River miso, as it is gluten-free.

15

Desserts

Coconut Chocolate Truffles

Natalie Norman

Prep: 60 minutes (includes 25 minutes to chill batter)

50 deglet noor or other medium-sized
    dates* (soaked/softened in water,
    then strained)
1 tablespoon raw cacao powder
2 tablespoons raw cacao butter

½ teaspoon pink salt
5 cups raw dried shredded coconut
½ teaspoon raw vanilla bean powder
¼ cup warm water (if needed)

In your food processor, process dates, cacao powder, cacao butter, and vanilla bean powder until a very creamy and even consistency is achieved. If needed while processing, conservatively drizzle water and pause occasionally to scrape down bowl as you go. Add salt and 4 cups of coconut, cup by cup, pulsing and scraping down bowl until cookie dough consistency is achieved. Set the remaining cup of coconut aside in a large bowl for rolling your truffles later.

Scoop out truffle mixture into bowl and refrigerate for around 25 minutes until it hardens slightly. It should still be pliable enough to roll into balls. Remove from refrigerator and roll into balls that are roughly 2 tablespoons of mixture each. Roll each ball in your bowl of coconut. When you're done rolling all your truffles, place them back into the refrigerator to harden. They will last in the fridge for about two weeks; frozen, they'll last for a month if well-sealed. Enjoy!

Contributor's Note: *If you use Medjool dates, you will only need around 25, since they are generally twice the size of other dates.

Here's my treat for you: *candy*. Yes, you can eat sweets when following the raw foods lifestyle. And here's the biggest secret—they taste *better* than processed junk or flour-filled recipes. Not only will you be taking better care of your precious body, but you'll also get to be a total food snob as you enjoy truly haute gourmet.

Start practicing these kinds of recipes now so that you can have them perfected in time for the holidays. Bring them to parties and impress your friends and start conversations when you tell them these are 100% raw and vegan. Just be sure to tell them *after* they eat them. People get a little apprehensive when they know in advance that something is raw/vegan. Best of all, you won't ever find yourself stuck at a party without a raw food dessert option. Win-win all around!

Almond-Coconut Macaroons

Sheryll Chavarria (Raw Can Roll Café and Pure Body Spa, Douglassville, PA, www.rawcanrollcafe.com)
Prep: 20 minutes   **Dehydrate:** 6 hours at 115°F

2½ cups coconut (unsweetened and dried)
1¼ cups almond flour (finely ground dried raw almonds)

¾ cup agave
¼ cup coconut butter/oil, melted
1 tablespoon vanilla
1 pinch Celtic sea salt

Mix all ingredients together in a mixing bowl. Form into small balls and place on dehydrator sheets (you may eat them un-dehydrated, as well). Dehydrate at 115°F for up to 6 hours.

Feel-Good Fudge

Sally Bowdle (Sally B Gluten Free, www.sallybglutenfree.com)
Prep: 20 minutes

¼ cup almond butter
¼ cup agave syrup
2 tablespoons coconut oil

¼ cup cacao powder
Pinch salt

In a double boiler, gently warm the almond butter, agave syrup, and coconut oil, and melt together until smooth. Remember to warm the chocolate at less than 118°F. Sift in the cacao powder and salt. Mix until smooth.

Contributer's Note: This can be used as a sauce over a dessert or can be poured into tiny candy-cup liners set in a mini-muffin tray. Freeze for 1 hour, and you have the perfect one-bite dessert treat. You can also pour into an 8-x-8-inch pan lined with parchment, freeze, and cut into squares.

Coconut Fudge

Annmarie Cantrell
Prep: 15 minutes

3 tablespoons creamed coconut (melted or easily stirred)
Pinch well-ground sea salt
1 tablespoon coconut oil (melted)
Coconut flakes (optional)
Cinnamon (optional)

Sweetener, such as honey (optional)
Lemon zest (optional)
Coconut, almond, or vanilla extract (optional)
Cocoa nibs (optional)

Combine all ingredients in a bowl and pour into a mold or a baking dish and let it firm up in the refrigerator.

Contributor's Note: Coconut products are extremely healing. This is a fun snack for children, which provides good fat, lauric acid (a key component for immunity), and a touch of sweetness.

Coconut products like creamed coconut and coconut oil are very forgiving, as they firm up with refrigeration. You can add as many things as you like to the fudge. If your child can eat chocolate, raw cacao nibs gently melted down would make this a chocolate-coconut fudge!

Superfood Fudge Brownies

Ultimate Superfood
Prep: 1 hour **Serves:** 10–12

4 cups raw pecans
¾ cup Medjool dates, pitted and packed
¾ cup Ojio™ cacao powder
1 teaspoon Ojio™ chlorella (or Ojio™ spirulina powder)
1 teaspoon Ojio™ maca powder
½ teaspoon Ojio™ Himalayan salt

¼ teaspoon raw organic cinnamon
1 teaspoon Ojio™ vanilla ground
¼ cup dried Ojio™ golden berries
½ cup crushed raw pecans
Ojio™ coconut oil (for greasing a baking dish)

In a food processor, process the pecans until slightly chunky and mealy. Do not over-process into pecan butter. Slowly add the dates while the food processor is running and rock the base of the food processor to combine evenly. Then, add all remaining ingredients, except golden berries and some pecans. Process again until well combined.

When finished, spoon the almond butter into a bowl and add the rest of the ingredients on top.

Take an 8- by 8-inch glass baking dish and gently grease with coconut oil. Add the brownie mixture and fold in the reserved golden berries and pecans. Press down with your palms to spread the mixture evenly and refrigerate for 30 minutes to set. Cut brownies into squares and serve with warm fudge sauce or non-dairy ice cream. Add the brownie mixture and fold in the reserved golden berries and pecans. Press down with your palms to spread the mixture evenly and refrigerate for 30 minutes to set. Cut brownies into squares and serve with warm fudge sauce or non-dairy ice cream.

Contributor's Note: Hiding in these chewy brownies is the amazingly beneficial green nutrition of protein and vitamin rich microalgae. We added in maca for extra energy; these rich cacao chocolate morsels are spiked with mystical goodness. Trick a friend into eating healthy!

Pecan Crust

Sally Bowdle (Sally B Gluten Free, www.sallybglutenfree.com)
Prep: 20 minutes

½ cup pecans
¾ cup rolled oats
¾ cup brown rice flour
½ teaspoon cinnamon

Pinch of salt
¼ cup coconut oil
3 tablespoons maple syrup

Toast pecans in the oven for just a few minutes. Watch closely, so that they don't burn. Cook until they smell rich and nutty. Let cool slightly and put in food processor. Pulse a few times, then add flour, oats, cinnamon and salt to food processor. Pulse until you reach a sandy consistency.

While the machine is running, quickly add oil and syrup and process until the ingredients are incorporated. You can process longer to make a smoother crust, or shorter to make a more textured crust.

Turn contents of food processor into a pie tin and press out a smooth thin crust. It will be a little crumbly. Bake crust in oven at 350°F for about 10 minutes, until dry and set.

Contributor's Note: Please note this is *not* a raw recipe. It is a gluten-free recipe and is good for those transitioning from a standard American diet to a raw diet. It's the step in between.

Sweet Potato Pie

Sally Bowdle (Sally B Gluten Free, www.sallybglutenfree.com)
Prep: 25 minutes

1 cup canned coconut milk
¼ cup arrowroot powder
1¾ cup steamed and pureed sweet
    potato
⅓–½ cup brown rice syrup or maple
    syrup

1 teaspoon cinnamon
½ teaspoon ginger
½ teaspoon nutmeg
Pinch clove
Pinch salt

Blend arrowroot and coconut milk in the food processor or blender until smooth, which should take just a few seconds. Add in the remainder of the ingredients and process until smooth. Taste and adjust salt and seasonings. It needs to taste good raw, for it to come out good baked! Fresh cooked vegetables will vary in sweetness, so adjust sweetener to match. I find steamed, peeled sweet potatoes to be the most consistent vegetable to use, however any winter squash would work here too.

Pour pie filling into a prebaked crust. Bake at 375°F for 40–50 minutes. The top will be dry, and the center just a little jiggly. Eat while warm and gooey right out of the oven, or allow the pie to set overnight in the refrigerator for a firmer texture.

LISA'S RAW VERSION: RAW SWEET POTATO PIE

Prep: 45–50 minutes

Crust
2 cups raw pecans
2 cups Mejdool dates, pitted
½ teaspoon cinnamon

Pie Filling
1¾ cup sweet potatoes or butternut squash
½ teaspoon ginger
½ teaspoon nutmeg
Pinch cloves
Pinch salt
¾ cup soaked, softened, pitted dates
1 teaspoon vanilla
1 teaspoon coconut oil

Crust

Combine crust ingredients in a Vitamix® high-speed blender or food processor until well blended. Take crust batter and spread over the bottom and sides of a 9-inch pie plate. Place pie crust in refrigerator to chill.

Pie Filling

In a food processor or Vitamix® high-speed blender, blend together sweet potato with spices, coconut oil, and vanilla extract until well blended. Pour the water off of the soaked dates. Blend in the soaked, softened dates with the sweet potato, spice batter. Blend well and pour into the crust. Refrigerate the pie.

Chocolate Cheesecake

Jenny Ross
Prep: 20 minutes   **Serves:** 8

Crust
2 cups walnuts or pecans
1 tablespoon cinnamon
1 teaspoon sea salt
½ cup raw agave or raw honey

Filling
1 cup coconut water (regular water will also work)
1 cup raw cacao nibs
2 avocados
1 tablespoon cinnamon
1 teaspoon sea salt
2 tablespoons green superfoods (optional)

In a food processor with the S-blade, combine the nuts, cinnamon, and sea salt for the crust. Pulse until a meal is formed. While processing, add the agave (or raw honey) and process until a dough ball forms. (Be careful not to over process; with the nuts the oil will separate.) Line a 10-inch glass pie dish with the crust.

In a blender, combine coconut water, raw cacao, avocado, cinnamon, sea salt, and optional superfoods, loading the liquid first for easier blending. Layer the rich, thick and creamy mixture into the crust for this recipe. (This mixture is delicious as is as a pudding.) Place the cheesecake into the freezer until firm. Remove, slice and serve.

Contributor's Note: The crust can be prepared in advance and frozen until use. The entire recipe can be frozen up to 14 days. Thawing takes approximately 15 minutes.

The most popular recipe in our household to date, Chocolate Cheesecake delivers more than 8 grams of protein per slice along with essential fatty acids, potassium, and vitamin E! Wow! Nutrients make this dessert a winner for Sunday dinner and the entire week.

Raw Chocolate Fantasy Pie

Natural Zing
Prep: 30 minutes

Crust
1½ cups raw, organic Natural Zing® Brazil nuts or almonds

1½ cups raw, organic Natural Zing® dates, pitted

Filling
1 cup raw, organic Natural Zing® cacao nibs or cacao paste

½ cup raw, organic, virgin Natural Zing® coconut oil

½ cup raw, organic Natural Zing® cashews (soak for a couple hours for a creamier consistency)

1 raw, organic Natural Zing® vanilla bean (or 1 teaspoon vanilla bean powder)

½ cup raw, organic Natural Zing® agave nectar

Chocolate Sauce
1 cup raw, organic Natural Zing® agave nectar

2 tablespoons raw, organic Natural Zing® cacao powder

A dash of Natural Zing® Celtic sea salt

For the crust, blend nuts and dates in a food processor until sticky, then press into pie plate using wax paper and a mini dough roller. For the filling, blend nibs, coconut oil, cashews and vanilla bean in a high-powered blender until smooth. Use a spatula to work mixture into blade. As the mixture warms up, it will blend together easier. Add agave and blend briefly until mixed. Pour into crust, smooth with spatula. Drizzle with chocolate sauce or top with your favorite fresh fruit. Refrigerate or freeze for 3 hours. Thaw it for 5 minutes before cutting. This recipe is a cult classic at Natural Zing. People who don't even eat raw food love this recipe! Enjoy!

Apple Cobbler

Linda Cooper (a. k. a. Linda Louise Cakes)

Linda is one of my long-time potluckers, and she comes up with amazing and spectacular desserts. We have been encouraging her to do more with her talents so, in addition to her and her husband's roofing business (Cooper Roofing), she has started Linda Louise Cakes. If you live in southeast Pennsylvania, you will be able to buy her products locally. If you are not local to us, then she will be able to ship to your home.

Prep: 30–45 minutes   **Dehydrate:** 4 hours

Cobbler
4 medium apples, cored and peeled
    (keep 1 separate)
½ soft dates, pitted
½ teaspoon ground cinnamon
1 tablespoon lemon juice
2 tablespoons raw honey or agave

1 teaspoon vanilla
½ teaspoon ground nutmeg
½ teaspoon sea salt

Topping
2 apples, peeled and cored
1 tablespoon raw caramel

Cobbler
Combine 1 peeled and cored apple, pitted dates, cinnamon, lemon juice, raw honey, vanilla, nutmeg, and sea salt in a food processor or high-speed blender. Puree until completely soft and creamy. Set aside. Peel, core, and thinly slice the 3 remaining apples. Place slices in a large bowl and toss with the pureed mix. Place in a medium-sized glass or ceramic dish.

Topping
Combine the peeled and cored apples with 1 tablespoon of raw caramel, spread over the apples, and sprinkle currants on top. Dehydrate for 4 hours at 105°F.

Apple Pie

Joel Odhner

By now, you have noticed that we have a thing for apples. I live in Pennsylvania, which is a mid-Atlantic state in the United States, and we have apples here all year round (thank God). As you can see, the apple is very diverse.

Prep: 20–30 minutes   **Chill:** 30 minutes

Crust
2 cups shredded coconut
1 cup dates, pitted

Filling
3 apples, peeled, cored, and sliced
10 dates, pitted
1 teaspoon cinnamon
2 tablespoons psyllium

Crust
Place shredded coconut in a food processor for about 30 seconds. Then add dates and process until sticky. Press into a pie pan.

Filling
Blend all of the filling ingredients in your food processor, and add the psylium last. Process to desired consistency.

Pour the filling into the crust. Chill for ½ an hour and enjoy.

Lasts 3–5 days refrigerated: that is, if you do not eat it all up by then.

It will take you longer to wash the food processor than it will to make this recipe.

Banana-Strawberry-Nut Cobbler

Brenda Cobb (Founder of Living Foods Institute® and author of *The Living Foods Lifestyle,* **www.livingfoodsinstitute.com)**

Prep: 25 minutes   **Soak:** walnuts, overnight

1 cup walnuts, soaked and drained
4 ripe bananas
6 pitted Medjool dates

3 cups strawberries
1 tablespoon fresh lemon juice
2 cups shredded coconut

Soak the walnuts in 3 cups water overnight and drain. Chop the bananas, dates, 2 cups of the strawberries, and walnuts, and then toss with the lemon juice. Add in the coconut and blend together. Serve in small dessert dishes and decorate the top with the remaining sliced strawberries.

Blueberry Cheeseless Cake

Bruce and Marsha Weinstein (Awesome Foods, Bridgeport, PA, www.awesomefoods.com)
Prep: 30 minutes   **Dehydrate:** overnight   **Yield:** 8 (4 oz.) slices

Filling
10½ ounces raw cashews
2.8 ounces filtered water
2.3 ounces coconut butter, melted
2.2 ounces agave nectar
1 ounce lemon juice
5.6 ounces fresh or frozen blueberries
¾ teaspoon Himalayan sea salt
1⅓ tablespoons apple pectin

Crust
6.6 ounces almonds, soaked (4.7 ounces dry)
6.6 ounces sunflower seeds, soaked (4 ounces dry)
16.7 ounces Gala apples
0.3 ounce agave nectar
4¾ teaspoons cup cinnamon
¼ teaspoon Himalayan sea salt
¼ teaspoon ginger
1–2 ounces water

Crust
Combine the crust ingredients together in a food processor. Take the dough and mold into a dehydrator tray in a 12- by 12-inch square. Dehydrate overnight. The next day, take the crust, process again with 1–2 ounces of water, and put the crust in a 9-inch pie plate.

Filling
Combine the filling ingredients together in a high-speed blender and pour into the crust. Place in a refrigerator to set.

Contributer's Note: All ounces are measured by weight. They are not to be measured in a measuring cup.

Carrot Cake

Joel Odhner

Soak: 2–4 hours   **Prep:** 20–30 minutes   **Icing Soak:** 4 hours   **Icing Prep:** 15 minutes

Cake
2 pounds carrots
2 cups coconut, shredded
2 cups dates, pitted and soaked
¼ cup ginger
1 cup raisins (optional)
2 cups walnuts, soaked and chopped
   (optional)
1 teaspoon cinnamon

½ teaspoon ground cardamom
1 teaspoon nutmeg
Water, enough to blend

Icing
1 cup cashews, soaked at least 4 hours
2 tablespoons agave nectar
A few drops of alcohol-free vanilla extract
Water for desired consistency

Cake
Place carrots in a food processor and process until fine. Place in a mixing bowl. In a high-speed blender, blend coconut, dates, ginger, and enough water to get it to blend. Transfer the contents into the carrot pulp bowl. Mix in raisins, walnuts, cinnamon, cardamom, and nutmeg. Press into the pie plate or spring pan.

Icing
Place all the ingredients into a high-speed blender, and blend until smooth. Spread on the carrot cake. Keeps 3–5 days in a refrigerator.

Chocolate Cheesecake

Sheryll Chavarria (Raw Can Roll Café and Pure Body Spa, Douglassville, PA, www.rawcanrollcafe.com)

Prep: 30 minutes   **Soak:** cashews, 1 hour

Crust
2 cups raw walnuts
½ cup dates, pitted
¼ cup dried coconut

Cheese
2 cups cashew, soaked

½ cup agave
½ cup coconut oil, warmed
1 tablespoon vanilla
Pinch–¼ teaspoon Celtic sea salt
¼ cup warm water
½–¾ cup cacao nibs
1 tablespoon cacao powder

Crust
Process the walnuts and dates in a food processor. Sprinkle dried coconut onto bottom of pie plate (the dried coconut keeps the crust from sticking to the pie plate, which makes it easier to get the pie out of the plate). Press crust onto the coconut.

Cheese
Blend cashews, agave, gently warmed coconut oil (see note), vanilla, sea salt, and water in a high-speed blender. Blend until smooth. Mix in the cacao nibs. Pour the mixture onto the crust. Remove air bubbles by tapping the pan on the table. Sprinkle cacao powder over top of pie. Place in the freezer until firm. Defrost in the refrigerator.

Contributer's Note: Warm coconut oil by placing in a glass Pyrex® dish, and place in a bowl of hot water.

Coconut Silk/Chocolate-Lined Pie with Strawberries

Sheryll Chavarria (Raw Can Roll Café and Pure Body Spa, Douglassville, PA, www.rawcanrollcafe.com)
Prep: 20 minutes

2 cups young Thai coconut meat
1 tablespoon vanilla
¼–½ cup agave
¼ cup coconut oil

Pinch Celtic sea salt
Coconut milk/water (as much as needed, but not much)
2 cups strawberries (ornamentally sliced and fanned with tops on)

In your Vitamix® high-speed blender, blend coconut meat starting with 1 cup, add all other ingredients (except strawberries) until creamy, and then add the rest of the coconut meat and continue blending until creamy. Fill pie crust, top with fanned strawberries, and refrigerate or put in freezer for about 20 minutes to set.

Mango Cheesecake

Joel Odhner
Prep: 20–30 minutes   **Serves:** 2–3

Filling
1 large mango, really ripe and mushy
1½ cups Brazil nuts
⅛ cup agave or less (if mangoes are really sweet, you may not need as much agave; taste first before adding agave, and add a little at a time)
½ cup water

Crust
1 cup almond pulp

Filling

Blend all the ingredients until smooth, and set aside.

Crust

In a glass pie plate, cover the bottom with the almond pulp, and press down to make a crust. If you want your crust to be sweeter, you can add shredded coconut and pitted dates.

Spread the filling over the almond pie crust and chill. You can decorate the top of the cheesecake with strawberries, blueberries, or goji berries to make a nice presentation.

Contributer's Note: When you make almond milk, the left-over pulp is known as almond pulp. If you do not want to make almond milk to get to the pulp, then grind up the raw almonds with a little water.

Mango-Kiwi Soufflé

Sheryll Chavarria (Raw Can Roll Café and Pure Body Spa, Douglassville, PA, www.rawcanrollcafe.com)
Prep: 15–20 minutes   **Chill:** 20 minutes in freezer (or 1 hour in refrigerator)

3 mangos, seeded and chopped
¼ cup agave
½ cup meat young Thai coconut

2 kiwis, peeled and sliced into rounds
Pinch sea salt

Blend mangos, salt, agave, and coconut meat together in a high-speed blender until creamy. Pour into a large bowl and stir in the kiwi, leaving some of the kiwi to garnish the top of the soufflé. Pour into individual bowls, and then place in the freezer for about 20 minutes (or in the refrigerator for about 1 hour) until it sets. Because this is so good, I typically end up eating it right away without waiting for it to chill, but you can serve it either way.

Raw Chocolate Crust

Sheryll Chavarria (Raw Can Roll Café and Pure Body Spa, Douglassville, PA, www.rawcanrollcafe.com)
Prep: 15 minutes

¾ cup cacao
½ cup agave
Pinch Celtic sea salt

½ teaspoon vanilla, mint, or any other
flavoring you would like
¼ cup coconut oil, melted

Place all ingredients into a bowl and stir, adding the coconut oil last. Chocolate will set up quickly, especially in cooler weather. Pour raw chocolate into a pie dish and let set in freezer for 20 minutes. Take crust from freezer, pour in coconut-cream filling (see Coconut Silk/Chocolate-Lined Pie on page 296), top with sliced straw-berries, and sprinkle with coconut flakes.

Pumpkin Pie Cheesecake

Sheryll Chavarria (Raw Can Roll Café and Pure Body Spa, Douglassville, PA, www.rawcanrollcafe.com)
Crust Prep: 10 minutes   **Filling Prep:** 15 minutes

Crust
2 cups raw walnuts
½ cup date paste

Cheese Filling
2 cups cashews

2 tablespoons agave
2 tablespoons pumpkin pie seasoning
¼ cup coconut oil
2 tablespoons lecithin
1–1½ cups water (add water slowly
until very creamy)

To make the crust, process the walnuts and dates in a food processor. For the cheese filling, blend cashews, agave, melted coconut oil, vanilla, and water. Blend until *very smooth*. Layer the bottom of an 8 inch spring pan with wax paper. Put spring form together and close. Press in the crust on the bottom only. Pour in cream, and then top it with a little nutmeg and or cinnamon. Put in the freezer and let set for a few hours. Enjoy!

Incan Berry Oatmeal Cookies

Natural Zing
Prep: 25 minutes   **Yield:** 24 cookies

1 cup almonds (soaked for 6 hours)
2 oranges (juiced)
1 date
1 cup raisins
3 cups fresh rolled oats

4 tablespoons agave nectar
2 teaspoons cinnamon
2 cups Incan berries
2 tablespoons lemon juice
2 teaspoons lemon zest

Blend almonds, orange juice, dates, cinnamon, lemon juice, agave nectar and half of the raisins in a food processor. Add Incan berries and pulse chop until Incans are in small pieces. Stir in zest, oats and the other half of raisins. Blend well and let stand for 5 minutes. Form cookies using spatula and ¼ cup Place onto Teflex sheets and dehydrate 6–8 hours. Remove from Teflex, turn over and dehydrate on other side for 6 hours.

Persimmon Nut Cheese Delight

Tonya Zavasta
Prep: 45 minutes

4 ripe Hachiya persimmons, peeled or
   unpeeled according to preference
1½ cup macadamia nuts, soaked for 2-4
   hours

½ teaspoons raw probiotic powder
   (optional)
½ –1 teaspoon Celtic sea salt, or to taste
1½ teaspoons fresh lemon juice
¾ cup water

Prepare nut cheese by blending together soaked and drained macadamia nuts, water, and probiotic powder in a high-speed blender until smooth. Transfer the mixture into a strainer placed over an empty bowl (line it with cheesecloth if the holes in the strainer are big), place a clean plate on top, and place some weight on that plate, like a small bowl with water, to create enough pressure to slowly squeeze extra water from the cheese during the culturing process. Leave at room temperature to culture the cheese overnight or up to 24 hours if using the probiotic. Once this process is complete, mix in the sea salt and lemon juice.

For casual eating, spread the nut cheese over persimmon pieces, or combine with cut persimmons in a bowl. For a special occasion, use a couple of 4-inch mini spring-form pans or a larger bowl to arrange cheese and persimmon pieces in layers. Blend some persimmon flesh in a food processor, pour on a plate, and flip the pan over the blended fruit. Decorate the top, and serve.

Contributor's Note: This recipe uses Hachiya (Japanese) persimmons, which are very soft when fully ripe. They are combined with macadamia nuts to make a filling meal, which can be as humble or as festive as you prefer.

White Chocolate "Tapioca" Pudding with Glazed Strawberries

Tiffany Robbins
Prep: 20–25 minutes

Pudding
4 tablespoons white chia seeds
1 Thai coconut (meat and water)
2 tablespoons coconut nectar (or agave, honey, or maple syrup)
1 tablespoon tocotrienols
1 tablespoon lucuma
1 tablespoon reishi powder

1 tablespoon shredded cacao butter (or 2 drops Medicine Flower® white chocolate extract)
1 teaspoon vanilla extract or powdered bean

Glazed Strawberries
½ pint strawberries
2 tablespoons palm or coconut sugar
1 tablespoon balsamic vinegar

Blend coconut meat, coconut water, sweetener of choice, tocotienols, lucuma, reishi, cacao butter/white chocolate extract, and vanilla until creamy. Spoon in chia seeds and mix well. Let sit 15 minutes.

Slice strawberries with an egg slicer. Sprinkle with sugar. Let them sit to exude liquid. Stir in balsamic vinegar. Place strawberries on top of pudding.

Contributor's Note: I have made several variations of this recipe. Try layering with raw granola or raw candied nuts for a trifle. Or, place raw granola or candied nuts in a plastic bag and pound with a rolling pin, place strawberries on the bottom, next pudding, then sprinkle with crushed granola or nuts. Reminds me of crème brûlée!

Almond Pudding

Annmarie Cantrell
Prep: 10 minutes

2 cups almonds, soaked overnight in
    water with sea salt

1–2 cups water
Water kefir or whey

Drain almonds from soaking liquid. Add to blender with 1 cup water to start.
Blend to break it up. Add more water as necessary. When a smooth consistency is
reached, pour into jar. Add ¼ cup whey or kefir and leave on counter overnight. To
serve, stir well and sweeten with raw honey.

Blackberry Preserves

Annmarie Cantrell
Prep: 20 minutes

6 cups fresh or frozen blackberries
1 tablespoon grated ginger
2 teaspoons dried lavender

2 tablespoons honey
¼ cup whey or water kefir
1 teaspoon sea salt

Cook blackberries over medium heat. Add ginger, lavender, and honey. Remove
from heat and let cool. Add salt and whey and pour into quart container. Let sit for
1–2 days and serve with Almond Pudding (page 301).

Cashew Crème

1 cup raw cashews
1 tablespoon raw honey

1 tablespoon vanilla
Water, as needed

In a Vitamix® High-Speed Blender blend the cashews, raw honey, and vanilla and adding enough water so the mixture blends smoothly. Add as you go. This crème is an absolute wonder.

Cinnamon Coconut Pudding

Prep: 15 minutes

1 cup young Thai coconut meat
¼ cup water
½ cup Medjool dates, pitted

1 teaspoon vanilla
½ teaspoon cinnamon

Combine ingredients in a Vitamix® High Speed Blender and serve. If you love chocolate, you can add raw cacao powder to taste.

Blueberry Compote

Prep: 10 minutes

2 cups fresh blueberries, cleaned
1 tablespoon water
2 tablespoons raw honey

2 teaspoons fresh lemon juice
1 tablespoon fresh basil, chiffonaded
Cinnamon (optional)

Clean the blueberries and set aside in a glass bowl. In a Vitamix® High Speed Blender, combine the water, raw honey, and lemon juice. Hand stir in the basil and pour over blueberries. Place Blueberry Compote in dehydrator at 105°F until warm. Make sure you keep coating the blueberries with the sauce. If you don't like basil, add cinnamon. By adding cinnamon you totally change the flavor.

Dates & Crème

Prep: 5 minutes

Medjool dates, pitted
Cashew Crème recipe (page 302)

Cut open dates and remove the pits, spoon Cashew Crème into the dates, and eat. It's that simple. You can also fill the dates and freeze or refrigerate them so they are ready to pop into your mouth when you are in the mood for a sweet treat.

Dates are also a great sweet treat when you want something quick and easy.

Coconut Yogurt

Annmarie Cantrell

Meat from 2–3 young coconuts
2–3 tablespoons water kefir

Flavorings of choice (vanilla, cinnamon, lemon, etc.)

Blend coconut meat in blender until smooth. Add optional flavorings and water kefir. Let sit on counter overnight. The coconut will ferment quickly!

The Berry Custard

Antanas Vainius

Prep: 45 minutes   **Refrigerate:** 30+ minutes   **Serves:** 4–5

3 tablespoons extra virgin coconut oil
    (at room temperature)
1 teaspoon raw sunflower lecithin
2 tea bags, Earl Grey
2 acai berry packs (unsweetened)
1 pack (10 ounces) blueberries,
    raspberries, blackberries, strawberries
    (semi-thawed)

½ teaspoon chocolate powder
1 tablespoon vanilla powder or high-
    quality rum
¼ cup small wild strawberry or other
    wild exotic berry puree
Raw dairy cream

First, make an Earl Grey concentrate (about ½ cup of hot water for 2 tea bags). Steep for 3–5 minutes, making sure to remove tea bags before bitterness sets in.

Emulsify coconut oil and sunflower lecithin with some warm water. Blend in berries. Add Earl Grey tea, chocolate powder, pinch of salt, and blend again until smooth.

Pour in individual serving dishes and refrigerate for at least 30–60 minutes. Before serving, spoon raw cream and top with exotic berry puree.

Violet Jam

Sue Hess (Farm at Coventry)
Prep: 20 minutes

1 cup violet blossoms
1½ cups water
Juice of half a large lemon

2½ cups organic sugar
1 package pectin

In a blender combine ¾ cup water and lemon juice. Add the sugar until it well blended. Heat remaining ¾ cup water in a pan, stir in the pectin with a whisk and boil hard for 1 minute while stirring constantly. Pour this mixture into the blender with the other ingredients, blend 30 seconds, throw in violets and pulse 15 seconds more. Pour into sterile jars, and seal in a water bath for ten minutes. Work quickly to fill the jars. This jam sets up fast!

Contributor's Note: You may also use young spruce tips in place of violet flowers for a delicious change. This jam is fantastic served over goat cheese during the winter holidays…if it lasts that long!

Carob Pudding

Arnold Kaufman
Prep: 5 minutes

3 yellow bananas, peeled
2 tablespoons carob

Combine the bananas and carob in a food processor and pulse until it has a pudding consistency. Place a few banana slices on top for decoration.

Contributor's Note: Other fruit options: Mango or peach

Chocolate-Vanilla Pudding Parfait

Barbara Shevkun (Rawfully Tempting)
Prep: 15 minutes   **Serves:** 4

Vanilla Pudding
⅔ cup young Thai coconut meat
1⅓ cups young coconut water or filtered water
½ cup cashews (soak for 2 hours)
3 tablespoons chia seeds (or more, to thicken)
⅔ teaspoon vanilla extract
3 tablespoons maple syrup (grade B)
Pinch sea salt
½ teaspoon lucuma powder (optional)
Water (only as needed to thin)

Chocolate Pudding
4½ tablespoons cacao powder
1½ tablespoons almond butter (optional)
2 tablespoons cacao nibs (optional)
½ teaspoon maca powder (optional)

Garnish
Banana
Chopped cacao nibs
Coconut
Nuts

Vanilla Pudding

Blend coconut meat, water, and cashews. Add remaining ingredients and blend until creamy. Pour less than half the vanilla pudding mixture into a small bowl and set aside.

Chocolate Pudding

Add cacao powder to remaining mixture in blender, and mix. Add nut butter and maca and blend until creamy. Adjust sweetness and pour mixture into small bowl. Layer chocolate and vanilla pudding in a dessert/parfait bowl. Add garnish, chill, and serve.

Butter Pecan Ice Crème

Brooke Preston
Prep: 20 minutes **Yield:** approximately 1 quart

2 cups soaked cashews
2 cup soaked pecans (1 cup dry, 1 cup soaked for 6–8 hours, rinsed, and drained)
¼ cup chickpea miso
¾ cup coconut sugar

¾ cup turbinado sugar
½ cup pitted Medjool dates
½ cup coconut oil
1 vanilla bean
Pinch green stevia

Blend all ingredients (except the dry pecans) until completely smooth. Test sweetness; it should be "too sweet" before freezing. Fold in dry pecans. Freeze in an ice cream maker according to the manufacturer's directions. Enjoy!

Nut Ice Cream: Carrot Cake Flavor

Will Eddy
Prep: 15 minutes

4 cups nut butter (made from one part almonds½ and one part pecans)
¼ cup agave nectar
Sprinkle of cinnamon (optional)

Splash of vanilla (optional)
1 teaspoon lemon juice (optional)
2–3 baby carrots
3 cups ice

Fill your blender with 3 cups of ice. Turn Vitamix® to high, using tamper vigorously to facilitate blending. The aim is to get just enough ice so as to see a good freeze, so that the flavor is nice and concentrated. Serve when it is velvety smooth.

Contributor's Note: Years ago, I was lucky enough to be one of the first few Vitamix® demonstrators in Whole Foods. One day in the basement of a Manhattan store, I had made nut butter and became spontaneously inspired to use the leftovers to make ice cream. Here is the first version of nut ice cream to be used in a Vitamix® demonstration (as far as I know), a recipe which I taught to many demonstrators. This recipe went on to make many people very happy, with its wide variety of iterations. What versions can you come up with?

Maple Pecan Ice Cream

Kimberton Whole Foods, www.kimbertonwholefoods.com
Prep: 25 minutes   **Freeze:** 6 hours or overnight

3 ripe bananas
½ cup raw almond butter
½ cup raw tahini (sesame butter)
¾ cup dark agave nectar

¼ cup raw honey
1 teaspoon vanilla extract
1 tablespoon ground cinnamon
1 cup pecans, chopped (optional)

Combine all ingredients (except the pecans) in a food processor. Process until creamy. Stir in pecans. Freeze in an airtight container for 6 hours or overnight.

Papaya-Banana Swirl Ice Cream

Barbara Shevkun (Rawfully Tempting)
Prep: 25 minutes

2 frozen bananas
½ frozen papaya, cut into chunks
¼ cup shredded coconut (for topping)

1 tablespoon hemp seed (for topping)
Almond cream (optional, see below)

Using your juicer's blank plate, press the frozen fruit through the juicer. (If you are using a blender, cut the frozen fruit into chunks and add to blender.) You may have to add some coconut water or liquid to get it to blend. If it becomes too thin, pour into a casserole dish or bowl and chill. Cut in chunks and run through blender or food processor again. It's a bit of work, but still very yummy! Alternate ingredients though the juicer: frozen fruit, frozen bananas, frozen almond cream. The amounts are up to you, but this gives you a wonderful, creamy ice cream. Top with shredded coconut and hemp seed.

Note: Usually when I make ice cream in the blender, I'll add other ingredients like Sunflower Lecithin and Irish Moss Paste which helps to emulsify the mixture.

Sugar-Free Coconut Ice Cream

Janice Inella
Prep: 1 hour

6 young coconuts
6 tablespoons coconut oil
½ cup lucuma (South American superfood)

1 cup pecan milk or any unsweetened nut milk
3 droppers Omica Organics® butterscotch toffee stevia (this is the best stevia on the planet)

Crack the coconuts with a sharp butcher knife and clip off the top. Pour out the coconut water. Whittle off the husk until you can get into the coconut much easier. Split in half and scrape out the meat. Clean the meat well.

To make the pecan nut milk, blend 2 cups pecans and ¾ cup pure water in a high-speed blender and then squeeze through a nut milk bag. Alternatively, you can use your favorite nuts for nut milk.

Add all ingredients to a high-speed blender and blend until creamy. Add mixture to an ice cream maker and blend for 20 minutes. Or, put the mixture in a bowl and place in a freezer. Take it out every 10 to 15 minutes and mix well until thick.

Serve with your favorite toppings, like chopped nuts or raw cacao nibs.

Cacao Nib Cookie Dough

Ultimate Superfood
Prep: 30 minutes **Serves:** 12–14

3 heaping cups Ojio™ extra-fine cut shredded coconut
6 tablespoons Ojio™ extra virgin raw coconut oil, or more to taste
6 tablespoons Ojio™ vanilla flavored agave nectar, or more to taste

¾ cup Ojio™ lucuma powder
2 teaspoons organic cinnamon powder
1½ teaspoons Ojio™ Himalayan crystal salt
½ cup Ojio™ raw cacao nibs

In a large food processor, add the shredded coconut and lucuma powder and start processing. Slowly add one tablespoon of the coconut oil at a time, waiting for the mixture to thicken and start to "ball up." If the mixture becomes too oily, you can add more coconut shreds and lucuma to balance it out. Gradually add the agave nectar and pay attention to the consistency and thickness of the mixture. The agave will help to bind the dough.

When you have the right doughy consistency, add the cinnamon powder and salt to process one last time. Taste and adjust salt and spice level as needed. Transfer the dough to a large mixing bowl and add in the cacao nibs. Mix well. Use a spoon, melon baller or small ice cream scoop to form the dough into bite-size balls. Serve immediately.

Contributor's Note: This mixture keeps for up to 7 days in a covered container in the fridge. These classic raw chocolate cookie dough treats will melt with delectable goodness on the tongue with the added chunk of raw cacao nibs. A party favorite these little morsels are perfect for a get together with friends of all sorts.

Raw Oatmeal Cookie Dough

Lany Wenke
Prep: 20 minutes

⅔ cup raw pecans (or cashews)	1 tablespoon maple syrup
⅓ cup oats	1 teaspoon vanilla extract
2 tablespoons agave syrup	¼ cup chocolate chips

Mix the oats and pecans (or cashews) in a food processor until smooth. Add the agave, maple syrup, and vanilla into the food processor and mix until smooth. Add in the chocolate chips and mix on low in the food processor (just enough to spread them around). Roll the mix into dough balls and enjoy now, or refrigerate for later!

Contributor's Note: This is a recipe for all those with a sweet tooth! It is a tasty and healthy dessert that is easy to make and will taste just like oatmeal cookie dough!

Banana/Grape Ice Cream

MJ Pangman (Dancing with Water)
Prep: 5 minutes   **Serves:** 2

1 large banana (sliced into ¾ inch pieces and frozen)

½ cup red or green grapes (frozen whole)

½ cup coconut water

2 tablespoons shredded coconut meat (optional)

Combine in personal blender until thick and smooth.

Cinnamon Sorbet

Terrina Kramer
Prep: 10 minutes

½ cup raw cashews

¼ cup agave

½ teaspoon cinnamon

3 cups ice

Combine the above ingredients in your Vitamix® High-Speed Blender until thoroughly combined and you have an instant desert. This is a great solution when you need to prepare a last minute desert for you or your guests.

Butter Pecan Sorbet

Terrina Kramer
Prep: 10 minutes

¼ cup raw agave nectar
½ cup raw pecans

¼ teaspoons cinnamon
3 cups ice

Load all ingredients, in order, into the Vitamix® container. On high speed, blend ingredients until smooth, using the tamper to help get the ice down to the blades. Let it run on high until a consistent color is reached and you see four mounds form.

Peach Sorbet

Prep: 7 minutes

1 cup frozen peaches, pitted and skin removed
1 cup almond milk

2 tablespoons raw honey
1 tablespoon alcohol free vanilla

Combine ingredients in a Vitamix® high-speed blender until well blended. Bon appetit!

WORDS FROM LISA:

You can make this dish by swapping out the fruit with your favorites, like raspberries or strawberries. You can also throw in a frozen banana if you'd like.

Gulab Jaman

Wendy Landiak
Prep: 25 minutes

1 cup raw cashews	Cinnamon to taste (about a teaspoon)
1 cup raw coconut	Cardamom to taste (about a teaspoon)
½ cup dates	Rose water to taste (about a teaspoon)
½ cup sweetener	Cloves to taste (about a teaspoon)
½ cup coconut flour	1 cup maple syrup

Combine cashews, coconut, dates, sweetener, and coconut flour in a food processor, pulsing until able to form into a ball. Roll about 2 tablespoons of the mixture into a ball, repeating until all the mixture is used up. Combine maple syrup and any combination of spices listed in a Vitamix® blender, and drizzle over the balls. Complete with coconut shreds and pretty rose petals as a garnish.

Blueberry Cashew Bars

Prep: 3-4 days   **Yield:** 16 (1.6 ounce) bars

18 ounces frozen blueberries	1 tablespoon vanilla extract
11 ounces dried blueberries	1/10 teaspoon Himalayan salt
4.7 ounces agave nectar	15 ounces cashews (coarsely ground)
1 tablespoon cinnamon	

Puree frozen blueberries, 5 ounces dried blueberries, agave nectar, cinnamon, vanilla extract, and Himalayan salt. Add cashews and remaining dried blueberries and stir in with a spoon or spatula.

Using a large bar mold, fill 48 ounces per bar mold. Dehydrate at 105°F. Flip it the next day and cut into 16 squares, then dehydrate for 2 to 3 more days. If soft, refrigerate.

Blueberry Cashew Bar

Bruce and Marsha Weinstein (Awesome Foods, Bridgeport, PA, www.awesomefoods.com)
Prep: 20–30 minutes   **Dehydrate:** 4 days at 105°F   **Yield:** 16 (2 oz.) bars

20½ ounces frozen or fresh blueberries
5 ounces dried blueberries
1 tablespoon cinnamon
1 tablespoon vanilla extract

⅟₁₀ teaspoon Himalayan sea salt
21½ ounces raw cashews, finely ground
6 ounces dried blueberries, chopped

Puree the above ingredients, adding the 6 ounces of chopped dried blueberries last. Stir in with a spoon or spatula. On the dehydrator tray, make a 12- by 12-inch square of the mixture and then to cut it into 16 pieces.

Dehydrate at 115°F. On day 2, flip the bars over and turn temperature down to 105°F. Then dehydrate for 2–4 more days. If soft, refrigerate.

Contributer's Note: All ounces are measured by weight. They are not to be measured in a measuring cup.

Lemon Squares

Sheryll Chavarria (Raw Can Roll Café and Pure Body Spa, Douglassville, PA, www.rawcanrollcafe.com)
Prep: 25 minutes

4 cups walnuts or pecans, un-soaked
2 cups raisins or pitted dates, un-soaked

3 bananas
2 lemons

Process walnuts and raisins in food processor. Process until the walnuts and raisins stick together. Take out and press the walnut-raisin mixture into the dish.

Slice bananas and set aside. Juice lemons and grate the peel of 1 lemon. Put banana slices on top of crust and pour the lemon juice on top of bananas. Garnish with the lemon peel. Refrigerate, cut into squares, and serve.

Love Child Dessert Candy

Denise DiJoseph (www.miaura.com)

The "Raw Love Child" tastes of dark chocolate, Raisinets, Mounds, and Almond Joy.

Prep: 30 minutes

1 Haas avocado
¼ cup raisins (or more to taste)
3 heaping tablespoons cacao powder
2 tablespoons (or more to taste) agave or scant-powdered stevia (I use Sweet Leaf)
2 tablespoons chia gel

¼ cup (or more to taste) sun-dried or dehydrated flaked coconut
½ tablespoon Amazing Grass Chocolate Supergreen Powder
½-1 tablespoon (or more to taste) Health Force Vita Mineral Green Powder
Whole raw almonds (presoaked 8 hours and towel dried), to garnish

Place the ingredients into a small food processor. If necessary, adjust the recipe by adding more cacao powder or coconut to make a thick dough-like consistency. Use a spring-hinged melon baller, drop portions into miniature fluted muffin papers. Top each candy (optional) with a whole raw almond (presoaked and paper towel-dried). Then if you are already going to use your dehydrator for something else, you can pop these muffin cups into the dehydrator to partially form an outer crust. This is optional, as you can simply eat as is or refrigerate them. Makes about 30 bite-sized portions.

Contributer's Note: Start with these measurements and adjust according to your taste. All the ingredients are raw and organic.

Nutty Almond Caramel Apple Slices

Sheryll Chavarria (Raw Can Roll Café and Pure Body Spa, Douglassville, PA, www.rawcanrollcafe.com)

Raw Can Roll Café in Douglassville, PA, is a new raw restaurant near me, and this is one of the recipes from owner/chef Sheryll Chavaria.

Prep: 30 minutes **Soak:** nuts; 2–4 hours **Dehydrate:** nuts; 4–8 hours

3 apples (whichever you desire), cored and sliced, but with peel on (set aside)

1½ cups date paste or 10–16 dates, pitted (room temperature or slightly warm)

1 tablespoons maca (malty flavor)

¾ cup almond milk (see page 165)

½ teaspoon vanilla

Pinch sea salt

Pinch cinnamon

1 cup mashed nuts (any type), set aside (previously soaked and dehydrated)

Combine all the ingredients (except for the apples and nuts) in a food processor to make the caramel. You may have to open the lid and scrape down the sides of the food processor to make sure that everything is mixed well together. Dip the apples into the caramel, and then into the nuts. Serve.

Raw Chocolate Candies

Sheryll Chavarria (Raw Can Roll Café and Pure Body Spa, Douglassville, PA, www.rawcanrollcafe.com)

Prep: 20 minutes

½ cup cacao

¼ cup agave

Pinch Celtic sea salt

½ teaspoon vanilla

¼ cup coconut oil, melted and warm

2 drops mint, lavender, orange, or any other flavoring you like (optional)

Place all ingredients into a bowl and mix, adding the coconut oil last. Chocolate will set up quickly, especially in cooler weather. Immediately pour into candy mold forms and place in freezer for 20 minutes.

Contributer's Note: You can get creative and place a dab of almond butter or cashew butter in the center for a creamy filling.

Winter Citrus Zippies

Denise DiJoseph (www.miaura.com)

These cashew and pine nut cookies have a zip of citrus flavor.

Prep: 45 minutes   **Soak:** cashews, 4 hours

Dehydrate: cashews, 5 hours (or until dry) at 105°F; cookies, 8 hours at 105–110°F or until you reach a desired soft/chewy texture without making them dry and/or crunchy

Yield: 24–30 cookies

Cookie Base

2 cups raw cashews, ground to a fine powder in grinder (soaked and dehydrated in advance)

¼ cup agave nectar

2½ tablespoons finely grated peel from organic lemon

3 tablespoons lemon juice

1 organic vanilla bean, cut into pieces and ground up in a grinder (reserve half for cookie centers)

¼ teaspoon natural salt (I use Redmond Natural™)

Cookie Center

About ⅛ cup lucuma powder

2 tablespoons maca powder

About ⅛ cup mesquite powder

1 tablespoon Amazing Grass® Green SuperFood Powder™

1 tablespoon cacao powder (optional)

Remainder of ground vanilla bean from cookie base

About ⅛–¼ cup pine-nut butter (or other nut butter: I use raw pine nuts and a grinder to make pine-nut butter)

Filtered water, as necessary

1 soft raisin to top each cookie

Cookie Marinade

1 organic orange and rind

Cookie Base

Combine all ingredients in a small food processor to form a dough-like consistency. Using a hinged melon baller, scoop out cookie dough and place on a Teflex sheet. Roll each cookie into a ball and flatten down to form a flattened circle.

Cookie Center

Combine all ingredients (except for raisins) in a small food processor and add just enough water to form a dough-ball consistency. Scoop out enough dough to roll into a large pea-sized ball. Take 1 raisin and add it to the ball while rolling out. Place each ball on top of the flattened round cookies from above, and then pat down so the base and center are gently joined. Refrigerate overnight on a Teflex sheet.

Cookie Marinade

Juice the orange with the Tribest® CitraStar Juicer. Brush the orange juice on each cookie with a pastry brush (brush the cookies so they glisten, but not so much that they become soggy). Slice the rind into very thin slivers and garnish each cookie. Remove each cookie from the Teflex sheet with a spatula, and place each on an open-grid dehydrator shelf. Dehydrate under 110°F until desired consistency.

Frozen Grapes

Prep: Freezing time

Grapes

Freeze grapes in freezer, and they make a quick tasty snack. I always have grapes frozen in my freezer and when I feel like something sweet and refreshing, I just pop a few in my mouth.

Sliced Cinnamon Apples

Prep: 7 minutes

1 apple, sliced and cored
Cinnamon, to taste

Vanilla, to taste
Agave, enough to cover apple

Place apple in a small glass dish, sprinkle with cinnamon and vanilla to taste, and cover with agave. Make sure the apple is coated in the entire cinnamon, vanilla, and agave mixture. Dehydrate at 105°F until warm.

> **WORDS FROM LISA:**
>
> This dish is a raw take on a baked apple or apple crisp that my Mom made when I was growing up.

Sliced Cinnamon Tomatoes

Prep: 7 minutes

1 large or 2 medium, tomatoes, cored
  and sliced
Cinnamon, to taste

Vanilla, to taste
Agave, enough to cover tomato

Place tomato in a small glass dish, sprinkle with cinnamon and vanilla to taste and cover with agave. Make sure the tomato is coated in the entire cinnamon, vanilla, agave mixture. Dehydrate at 105°F until warm.

Sliced Cinnamon Pineapple

Prep: 7 minutes

1 or 2 slices fresh pineapple
Cinnamon, to taste

Vanilla, to taste
Agave, enough to cover pineapple

Place sliced pineapple in glass dish. Cover with cinnamon, vanilla and agave mixture until well coated. Place in dehydrator at 105°F until warm.

WORDS FROM LISA:

If you enjoy all three of these sliced cinnamon dishes (pages 318–319), guess what: it all tastes good together, too.

Un-Hot Chocolate

Prep: 5 minutes

    1 cup raw almond milk
    Raw cacao powder or carob powder, to taste

Combine the raw almond milk with raw cacao powder, and warm in a little pot on top of your oven (remember to keep the temperature below 118°F). You can also warm the Un-Hot Chocolate in the small warming luncheon crockpots to keep the temperature low. Finally, you can blend the ingredients in a Vitamix® long enough so that the drink warms. Who said you can't have hot chocolate?

Stuffed Dates

Prep: 15 minutes

    ½ pound soaked pitted large Medjool
        dates, drained, and dried
    1 tablespoon cinnamon

    ¼ teaspoon ground cloves
    ½ teaspoon nutmeg
    ¼ teaspoon ground ginger

Slit dates lengthwise to make an opening for the filling. Be sure to remove the end cap if still attached. Place softened, slit dates on a plate and set aside. Combine together with the cinnamon, ground cloves, nutmeg, ginger and walnuts. Stuff dates with the filling. You can eat as is or heat in dehydrator at 105°F until warmed.

Orange Stuffed Dates

Prep: 15 minutes

½ pound soaked pitted large Medjool
    dates, drained and dried
1 cup raw cashews, soaked and drained
1 tablespoon raw honey
1 teaspoon alcohol free vanilla
1 teaspoon orange juice

Pinch of orange zest
Water, enough to make the filling
    creamy, blended smooth but not runny
Orange zest sprinkled on top for garnish
    (optional)
Raw cacao shavings (optional)

Slit dates lengthwise to make an opening for the filling. Be sure to remove the end cap if still attached. Place softened, slit dates on a plate and set aside. Combine the remaining ingredients in a Vitamix® high-speed blender until creamy texture. Add a little water at a time. Once you get to the desired creaminess, stop. Stuff the dates with the orange cashew cream filling. Garnish with orange zest and/or raw cacao shavings.

Fig Christy

Christy Parry

Adapted from Janice Inella's recipe in Jill Samter's book, *A Complete Guide to Optimal Health: The Road to a Brighter Life.*

Prep: 30 minutes   **Dehydrate:** 24 hours

2 cups black mission figs, soaked to
    soften (save soaking water)
3 cups pecans, soaked (if desired)

1 tablespoon alcohol-free vanilla
1 tablespoon pumpkin seed oil
1 tablespoon raw honey

In high-speed blender, blend soaked figs and soaking water (use more water, if necessary, to blend until thoroughly mixed).

    Place the remaining ingredients in a food processor, adding the fig and water mixture. Process until mixed well.

    Spread on a dehydrator sheet to desired thickness, and dehydrate until desired texture (about 24 hours at 112°F).

Crème Fruit Bowl

Prep: 15 minutes

1 banana, sliced

1 cup berries of your choice: blueberries, strawberries, and raspberries (one or a combination)

1 apple, cored and cut into bite-size pieces

¼ cup seedless grapes

Orange juice (enough orange juice to cover fruit mixture)

Raw almond powder (optional)

Raw cacao nibs, (optional)

Cashew Crème, as desired

Slice banana and fruit and place in bowl. Juice enough oranges to produce orange juice to cover the fruit. You can use any fruit combination; these are just some of my favorites. If you are making for a family, you can make a large bowl for or make individual serving sizes for your friends, family, and neighbors as well. Sprinkle raw almond powder on top of fruit.

PART III

Appendix & Resources

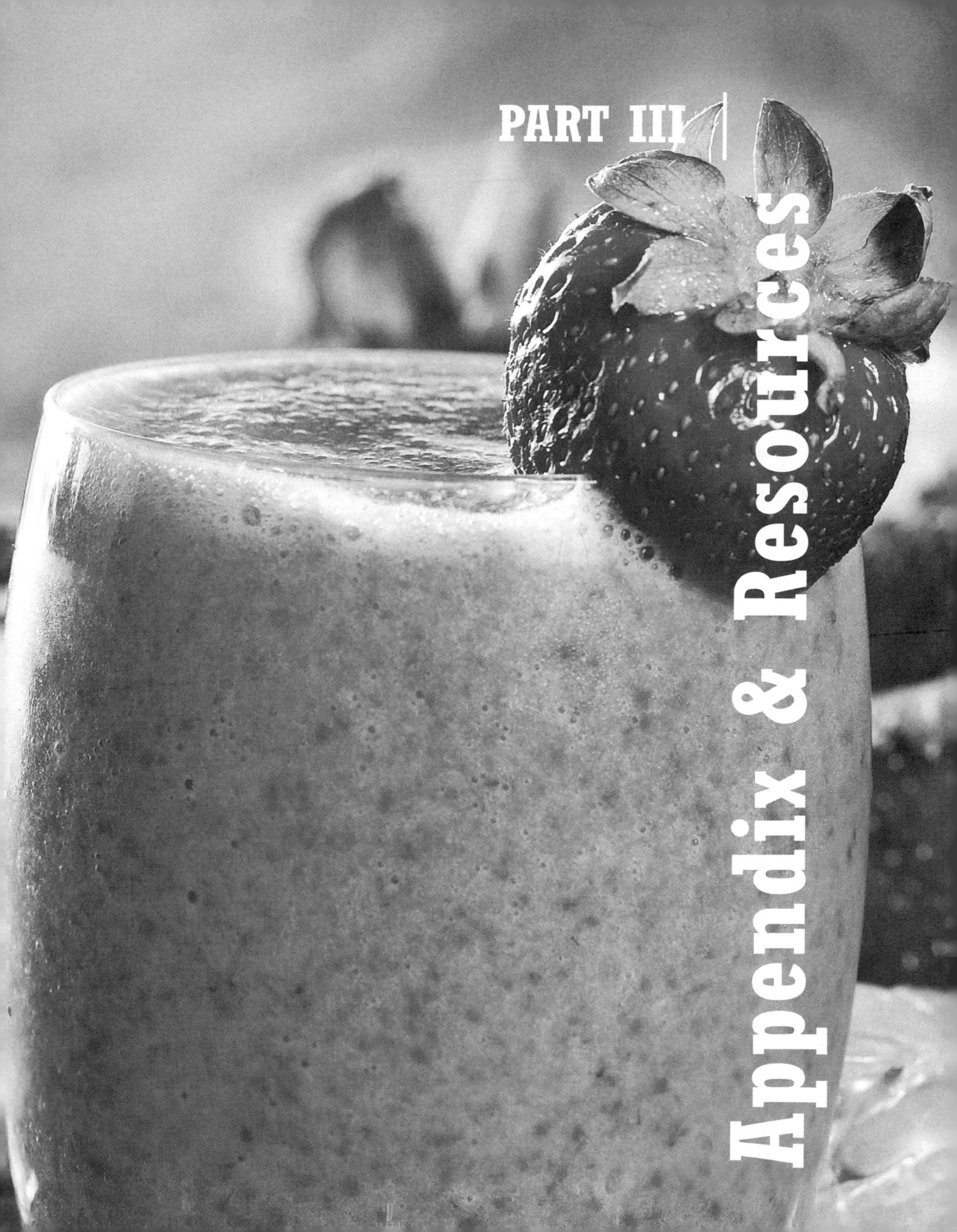

Conclusion

Living a healthy, predominantly raw lifestyle for 25 years has profoundly changed my life. There is not one aspect of my life that has not been fine-tuned; I have gone through a refining fire, which has allowed me to be the best that I can be at this moment. And why do I say *this* moment? Because tomorrow will be an even better day; I will continue to grow emotionally, physically, and spiritually.

Those who have heard me speak know that I believe living a healthy lifestyle is not for the faint of heart. But if you would prefer to stay stuck, and never grow to reach your own heights, then eating and living a healthy lifestyle is not for you. I pray that, by the time you have reached the end of this book, you are so excited about transforming your life that you are inspired to head to the kitchen and begin growing right away!

Have you ever noticed that when company comes to call, or when your family gathers together, they do so in the kitchen? To me, the kitchen is the heart of the home. Isn't it fitting, then, that the heart of the home also has the greatest transformative effect on the heart of your life? I don't think something like that happens by chance.

Take things one step at a time, and you can transform your life. You don't have to incorporate everything you learned in *The Complete Book of Raw Food, Volume 2* today. Start by just eating healthy organic whole foods. Eliminate processed foods. Start drinking a smoothie each day for breakfast and, once you have that under your belt, incorporate a new dish or two each month, maybe even each week! Don't stress yourself out; that defeats the purpose of living a healthy lifestyle. Join a meet-up group or a CSA, or take a class at a raw restaurant. Attend talks at healthy markets, visit wellness expos, participate in raw potlucks; let these experiences serve as counselors to help support you on your journey. You don't have to do this by yourself.

Start drinking more water. If you don't currently exercise, start moving; walk up the stairs instead of using an elevator. Park across the parking lot. Walk around the block with your spouse, your friend, even your dog. Join a gym. Hire a personal trainer. Do what *you* have to do to get yourself moving. I watched my Mom, Dad, and sister all go through long, drawn-out health challenges. My hope for each and every one of you is that you learn to live a healthy lifestyle. Remember to look at how you go through every transformation or change in life; that is how you will go through this life to the end. Through growth, prayer, and counseling, I work to make it through the challenges of life and grow with grace. When my time comes, I want to meet it head-on, like I have everything else in my life.

Denial doesn't work, whether it be emotions or food. Thinking that over-eating and an unhealthy lifestyle isn't going to affect your health is living in denial. I've heard a lot of people voice concerns about giving up their favorite things. "Do I have to give it up?" they ask. And the answer is, no; you don't have to give up anything. But the question remains: what about your quality of life? Are you numb and asleep, or are you alive and vibrant? Incorporating predominantly raw foods in your diet and making healthy lifestyle changes will transform your life.

Living dynamically starts one forkful at time, one push-up at a time, one prayer at a time. How do *you* want to live your life?

I choose to Live Dynamically!

—Lisa Montgomery

Meet Our Chefs

DEREK BATMAN

When working with clients at different ability levels, Derek Batman tries to deliver a simple message: "Emotional attachment to food makes us believe that food is meant to provide psychological comfort, rather than fuel, which is fully its purpose." It was not until a best friend and later his mother were affected by life altering diseases that Derek began to truly appreciate the importance and benefits of the raw and organic lifestyles. It is much easier to tell someone that their food choices will affect their athletic performance than it is to tell someone that their food choices will literally determine how profoundly their disease will affect them; that it will change the quality and duration of their life. Derek relays that message to his clients in an attempt to help them see past the surface benefits—past the effect that eating clean will have on their superficial physical features—to the intrinsic values that their nutrition provides them: mentally, physically, and spiritually. Many of the recipes that Hardbat CrossFit uses and recommends follow Paleo guidelines, which promote raw and organic vegetables and fruits, nuts, seeds, berries, and naturally raised and fed meat and poultry.

Derek Batman
Hardbat CrossFit
70 Aleph Dr, Newark DE 19713
(484) 256-0465
info@hardbatcrossfit.com

DR. ERIC BENEDETTI

Dr. Eric Benedetti describes his goals in pursuing raw food and a healthful lifestyle: "To be attached to nothing. To have the ability to control my mind. To love God and my family, both in word and deed. To obtain the highest professional expertise as a chiropractor and to teach the world my core health beliefs. To educate companies and children on the power of the body so that they may have the blessings I have so enjoyed. To create an oasis of health within my office. To be debt-free in my home and office so that I am free to create and a slave to no one!"

DAVE BIDDISON

Dave Biddison was born in Louisiana, but spent the majority of his childhood and young adult life in northern Pennsylvania, where his parents taught at a state university. A lifelong musician, Dave has co-created music with his brother for over 30 years. He plays with him in their current band, The Llama Dalis, which produces music with an eclectic, highly addictive, danceable sound (www.llamadalis.com).

Dave is the assistant manager for the Café inside Kimberton Whole Food's flagship store, a locally owned, independent natural foods store that serves as a community hub for people with shared values centered around sustainability and integrity (www.kimbertonwholefoods.com). There, Dave has designed the store's popular all-organic smoothie, juice and coffee bar program. He lives within walking distance of the store with his beautiful wife and daughter, who get to visit him almost every day for a smoothie and a chai latte! He loves it when people light up and smile with whatever creation he delivers to them. If they dance, that's even better!

ANNMARIE CANTRELL

Annmarie Cantrell, M.Ed., is a former early intervention educator who has worked with young children with special needs for nearly 20 years. In 2001, after becoming interested in using food as a tool for healing oneself, she went through the culinary program at the Institute for Health and Culinary Arts. She then began a career as a chef and wellness educator, helping people work their way through dietary mazes to find their way back to *real* foods; food meant to nourish their bodies, minds and spirits.

She is particularly passionate about the health of children in this country and works closely with the parents of children with allergies, autism and ADHD, helping them heal by cleaning up the diet and the environmental factors that influence their diagnoses.

SHERYLL CHAVARRIA

(Raw Can Roll Café)

Sheryll has been on a natural healing path for the past 30 years, becoming a vegetarian at around age 20. Throughout her journey, she has experienced a plethora of natural food lifestyles. Eventually her journey culminated in entering the raw foods arena, which brought dramatic changes to her health. Soon after, she was introduced to the importance of colon hydrotherapy, which truly transformed her life. She then attended St. John's Academy in Maryland, became a certified colon hydrotherapist, and opened a cleansing center.

Residing in Eastern Pennsylvania, Sheryll integrated her Colon Hydrotherapy Center with the art of massage, and created a deep cleansing and rejuvenation educational program based on the teachings of Dr. Ann Wigmore. She opened a Wellness Center called Pure Body, shortly after which she opened a raw food café called Raw Can Roll Café to complement the Wellness Center.

Presently, she has moved and merged both Pure Body and the Café into one location on the Main Line, making a total wellness, holistic no-frills center for all. It's all about feeling great! She feels very blessed and thankful to have been given the opportunity to serve others.

CHILI SMITH FAMILY FOODS

Chili Smith Family Foods has its roots in northern California, where the Smith Family has been in the restaurant and ranching businesses for many decades. Betty and Ed Smith came from San Francisco to the valley in the mid-1900s, and opened their first restaurant in Chico in 1961. Over the years, other locations were added to this small chain, known for serving good quality, reasonably priced food by a friendly staff. A large family business, by working hard to supply healthy food they have learned the value of hard work and honesty from the small communities they serve.

Chili Smith Family Foods has grown from making chili and soups to providing almost thirty varieties of dried beans in several convenient packaging sizes, and now ships them all over America and some other places in the world. Their beans are all-natural, grown to high standards and tested herbicide and pesticide free.

They are now exploring methods to provide finished and fully cooked beans—not canned, but fresh—to the people who are interested in feeding their families and customers the finest gourmet heirloom beans on this planet!

Chili Smith Family Foods
(800) 434-2929
(916) 524-7071
www.chilismith.com
Sacramento, California

BRENDA COBB

www.livingfoodsinstitute.com
(800) 844-9876
Living Foods Institute
1700 Commerce Dr. NW
Atlanta, GA 30318

WILL EDDY

Will Eddy has demonstrated the Vitamix machine for more than 10,000 hours since 2008, and is a two-time recipient of the company's coveted Barnard Award. He has helped to steer the Vitamix demonstration department's enormous growth in the northeast region of the United States, training numerous top demonstrators and taking inside roles in creating lucrative relationships with BJ's, Wegmans, and Whole Foods Market. Born in Wiesbaden, West Germany in 1985, Will is inspired and driven by the rapidly accelerating pace of technological progress, and believes the best is yet to come. He now resides in Austin, TX.

More of Eddy's original recipes and videos are available at www.willeddy.com

EAGLE SKYFIRE

Eagle Skyfire's father is Salasaca, of the Quechua, Inca, and her mother is a Spaniard. She jokes that she is the product of two enemies that made love instead of war, and that because of this, she has had the privilege to enjoy the richness of both cultures. Strong spiritual gifts run through her mother's side, while powerful shamanic gifts (including that of being a seer) run through her father's side. She has also been adopted by the Tuscarora of the Iroquois through her uncle, Ted Silverhand, who taught her the ancient art of "seeing" in the Native American tradition. Growing up, she learned from many Native American medicine teachers throughout North, Central, and South America. She is now a recognized tradition keeper, shaman, and priestess for her people.

She currently teaches classes and workshops on several topics, such as Native American spirituality, traditional shamanism, intuitive development, and how to consciously create your divine contract—to name but a few. She also facilitates retreats and leads her apprentices on vision quests. She is presently writing books, and has recordings on these subjects available. People whom she has taught say that she has helped them grow spiritually, develop their psychic gifts safely, and dramatically transformed their lives for the better.

KATIE GROVES

(Creative Kitchen Crew, Raw Can Roll Café)

Katie started working at the Raw Can Roll Café when they first opened in July of 2012 as a new vegetarian interested in nutrition and food. Since working at the café, she has used many of the resources available to educate herself about the raw and vegan lifestyles, leading her to become vegan in the fall of 2012. Going vegan has furthered her dedication to good health, and has helped her to become a better athlete and student.

Katie is 17 years old and entering her senior year of high school. She is a competitive rower and is passionate about health and wellness.

MARINA GRUBIC

Marina Grubic has been an ethical vegan since 2005, and has been an enthusiastic promoter of the vegan lifestyle both in her native country of Serbia and also in England, where she volunteers as a speaker and promoter. When she started learning about natural hygiene and species-specific diets, not only did she embrace the low-fat, raw vegan diet, but she also started to spread the word.

Marina has finished the "Plant-Based Diet" course at Cornell University, translated *The 80/10/10 Diet* by Dr. Douglas Graham into Serbian, interned with Dr. Graham at his fasting event in Costa Rica, worked as a kitchen chef at the Fresh Food Festival in Denmark and has overseen numerous workshops, speeches and retreats.

Marina continues to promote species-specific diets, spreading the word about the fruit-based diets that she believes are a solution for a peaceful, healthy and vibrant world.

You can see Marina's free video at her YouTube channel "Inspire Me to Be Healthy," www.youtube.com/channel/UC8-d2dy971dXrh3ePcA_pEw/videos.

Order Marina's recipe book at: www.amazon.com/dp/B00EGSUCAO. Marina is also the author of *Raw Winter & Holiday* which can be ordered at www.amazon.com/dp/B00HP823DC.

KAREN HANDMAN

After moving to the northern Sacramento Valley in 2006, the Good Faith Organic Farm team got involved with olives. After discovering how olives were made, they immediately stopped eating olives; the once "superfood" olive of old, prized for its digestive qualities, had been reduced to a "fast food." It was now just a lump of dead salty fat.

In order to get the olives they really wanted, the ones called "fresh" olives in Europe, they realized that they would need to go into the olive business for themselves. Soon, they discovered the health benefits of slow-cured olives, processed without the use of lye or heat canning.

The Good Faith Organic Farm olives are from the old groves of northern California. Grown, harvested and distributed by small family farmers; no synthetic fertilizers, pesticides or herbicides—of any kind. No lye, chemical ripening agents, colorings or preservatives. Sea salt cured over 6–18 months. Naturally occurring enzymes and amino acids.

SUE HESS

(Farm at Coventry)

Susan Hess is an herbalist and native weed wrangler who resides in northern Chester County, PA. She enjoys sharing her experience and knowledge through community herbal education workshops and her twelve month "Homestead Herbalism" course. Her website and blog showcase Susan's photography, as well as her herbal product line and educational offerings. In her spare time, Susan enjoys researching traditional healing methods, photography, writing, gardening and cheese-making. Learn more at www.farmatcoventry.com.

BRENDA HINTON

Brenda came to a life of living food preparation in response to a critical health threat, and attributes her recovery to careful nutrition. A life-long "foodie," Brenda wanted to provide the best possible food to herself and her husband Mike. To do so, she enrolled at Living Light Culinary Academy, where she studied until she was hired as an instructor (Brenda doesn't do things halfway). In addition to developing the tools marketed by Rawsome Creations, Brenda writes a monthly newsletter and consults with people who, like her, seek to keep their food as pure and unprocessed as possible.

Brenda is politically active in the movement to label GMOs and otherwise keep our food honest; she understands that this effort puts her and her associates in direct opposition to the mainstream diet of packaged food-like products. She "walks her talk" by maintaining a fruitful kitchen garden at her home at the Gatehouse in Saint Helena, California.

ANGELA HORN

(Professional Licensed Massage Therapist, Raw Can Roll Café)

Angie's passion for holistic/natural health, along with her desire to be of service to both the human and non-human world, has been evolving over the past decade of her life. Incredibly drawn to the realm of holistic/natural health, Angie began researching various aspects of this realm to expand her knowledge. Her interest and passion continued to grow, as her inner-guidance and spiritual path led her to study the field of massage therapy at the Lansdale School of Business, at the National Academy of Massage Division. Now a professional, licensed massage therapist, Angie feels that learning the field of massage therapy has brought forth in her an immediate sense of fulfillment on a holistic level.

Another hat Angie wears is being part of the dedicated team at Raw Can Roll Café. Along with her vested interest in natural health, and a plant-based/raw food lifestyle in particular, she has settled into a niche at Pure Food and Body and is utterly grateful to be part of such a wonderful and significant mission.

KEN IMMER

(Graw Foods)

Former butcher/charcutière turned "ecstatic living activist," when Ken Immer dropped traditional French cuisine for a yoga mat, everything in his life changed. He had found his purpose; having spent many years steeped in the culture of sensual pleasures that is the restaurant industry, he was not about to give up the amazing satisfaction that delicious food can offer. However, his newfound zeal for health and wellness seemed to demand that this obsession come to an end.

Upon discovering that most of the vegetarian/health food readily available to consumers was mediocre at best—and very foreign to most people—Ken decided that there must be a better way, somehow related to the entire body and soul connection. After many, many hours in the kitchen, experimenting with all sorts of new ingredients and techniques, poring over books which were previously relegated only to special dietary needs and "tree huggers," Ken found that he could actually use his fundamental knowledge of cuisine to dissect these recipes and extract the essence of robust health, applying his skills in food preparation to preserve flavor and texture while maintaining nutritional integrity. This new plant-based diet surrounded him with fresh ingredients, which eventually drew him to the raw food movement and ultimately gave birth to the Graw Bar—the core of the new cuisine he was establishing. The creation of this delight was proof enough that there is a whole universe of healthy ingredients out there, just waiting to be combined in new ways that allow you to continue to enjoy food while changing your body chemistry and improving your overall health.

Chef Ken currently oversees production and day-to-day operations at the facility; he is also an adjunct instructor at The Culinary Institute of Charleston, teaches yoga one day a week at a local community center, and travels around the Southeast promoting Graw Foods products and teaching cooking and lifestyle classes.

JANICE INNELLA

Janice Inella's passion for food started with the aromas and tastes of the dishes prepared in her Italian grandmother's kitchen. The creative energy that Grandma Rose and her Great-Grandma Josephine put into their fabulous dishes and presentation; these traditions have manifested in her kitchen today, save with different ingredients.

Her passion for healthy foods and a healthy lifestyle experienced a revival in her early thirties. While touring the country as a union hair dresser and make-up artist with the Broadway shows *Cats* and *Phantom of the Opera*, she began experiencing some health issues and sought alternative relief. But it wasn't until she was in Chicago for an extended period of time and working long hours that she was introduced to a woman who taught a Macrobiotic cooking classes. This was her first lifestyle change. The result was her learning how a healthy food lifestyle could support her on the road while touring. She was taught how to make healthy choices for the first time in her life. Relief was at hand!

Her next awakening was when she settled in southern California. It was the late 1990s, and she was in her mid-forties, feeling a bit toxic from all the years on the road, working with special effects make-up. Working in Los Angeles as an Aesthetic, she was introduced to raw, living foods, a relationship that would continue on into the future:

- 2002: Certified as an instructor/chef in raw Living foods
- 2003–4: Took over Buddha Garden Café in Los Angeles and changed it to a raw food Café
- 2004–5: Raw living food stands—Ardmore Farmer's Market in Ardmore, PA, and Fresh Grocer Super Market in University City, PA
- 2006–7: Goddess Gatherings in the Philadelphia region, introducing and teaching women about raw living foods and lifestyle

Janice, along with her husband Steven, is now the proud owner of the Essene Market and Café in Philadelphia, and is currently in the process of upgrading the 43 year old healthy establishment to meet with today's standards, as well as including her raw recipes on the menu.

Janice A. Innella
"The Beauty Chef"
Essene Market and Café
719 S. 4th St., Philadelphia, PA 19147
(215) 922-1146
jinnella@essenemarket.com

KAREN IZZI

Karen Izzi, PhD. CZT, has been a wellness practitioner and stylist for more than twenty-five years. She believes the healing power of our food choices contribute to our overall well-being. Currently a Fine Arts major at WCU, her poetry and non-fiction appear in many anthologies, newspapers and magazines nationally. Karen is the author of a cookbook, and several anthologies. She is the creator of several natural health newsletters. Karen continues to contribute locally in Chester County, PA, where she currently resides. She teaches the creative healing art of Zentangle. Like many artists, she has six cats that also enjoy natural foods, sewing, art, reading and writing.

ARNOLD KAUFMAN

There isn't a raw foodist in southeast Pennsylvania who hasn't eaten at Arnold's Way. Arnold's Way has been a staple for raw foodists for over 20 years. At 65, Arnold Kauffman, owner of the world famous raw vegan café, shares what he has learned over 20 years of exploring ways to enhance our health and well-being through diet and exercise. Kauffman has been raw vegan since 1998, consuming mostly fruits and greens, and exercises almost daily. A self-described "lean, mean fighting machine," but known as one of the most loving, gentle human beings, Kauffman once operated a junk-food business and, after finding inspiration when and where he least expected it, closed the business to open Arnold's Way in 1992.

Located outside of Philadelphia, Arnold's Way has evolved from a vitamin and herb store into a vegan café, and then a raw vegan café. Kauffman has educated thousands in eating raw foods, helping many to transition to mostly or wholly raw lifestyles. He has also helped many to reverse health challenges by creating optimum healing conditions for their bodies. Kauffman shares his wisdom and explains his daily routine in his book, *The Way of Arnold*. Arnold also wrote *14 Days of Fasting at Tanglewood* and *Seven-Point-Seven*. Arnold is also a father of four and a grandfather of nine. Two more books, *Arnold's Way Childproof Recipes for Everyone* and *Johnny Nucell*, were written in honor of these special children.

MATTHEW KENNEY

Chef, author and entrepreneur, Matthew Kenney is the world's foremost expert in raw cuisine. His impact extends far beyond the walls of his restaurants located in Santa Monica, California; Belfast, Maine; and Miami, Florida (Winter 2013). Kenney's passion for raw cuisine is apparent in his dedication to education. Santa Monica and Miami both include culinary academies adjacent to the restaurants. Kenney has given two high-profile TED talks and frequently lectures as a keynote speaker at food and philanthropy events around the globe. He has authored 10 cookbooks, including: *Raw Food Real World*, *Raw Chocolate* (Gibbs Smith, March 2012), *Everyday Raw Detox with Meredith Baird* (March 2013) and *Plant Food* (Winter 2014). Matthew Kenney Culinary Academies train professional chefs, as well as novices and enthusiasts, in both fundamentals and advanced techniques of raw cuisine. As a classically trained chef who developed a distinct raw-foods lifestyle brand, Kenney also shares his expertise with consumers on the iPad app, Matthew Kenney's Raw Express, complete with 12 full-length videos and more than 50 recipes that can all be prepared in less than 30 minutes. Furthermore, Matthew Kenney Academy Online launched as the world's first classically structured online course focused on raw and living cuisine and currently offers a variety of plant-based courses.

The Food and Wine Best New Chef and twice-nominated James Beard Foundation Rising Star Chef has garnered the attention of critics as well with the most recent opening of M.A.K.E. in Santa Monica, CA. in October 2012 which is described by Los Angeles Times restaurant critic Jonathan Gold as "intellectual food."

For more information, or to schedule an interview, please contact Vanessa Kanegai or Max Block at Wagstaff Worldwide
vanessa@wagstaffworldwide.com
max@wagstaffworldwide.com
(323) 871-1151

LARRY KNOWLES

(Rising Tide Sea Vegetables)

Rising Tide Sea Vegetables sustainably harvests seaweed (on the Mendocino coast of Northern California) for cooking and snacking. Their motto is, "Healthy for you, healthy for the planet." Since 1981, Rising Tide has been fine-tuning the techniques involved in wild crafting (gathering by hand in the wild), drying, and storing sea vegetables.

Today, Rising Tide is one of a few operations that harvest seaweed along the Pacific Coast, offering a full range of local and imported seaweed products. For more information, visit them at: www.loveseaweed.com

BETTI-LOU KRAMER

Betti-Lou Kramer has worked at Whole Foods Market for 20 years and is currently the Whole Body Team Leader in the Plymouth Meeting, PA location. Dedicated wife, mother of two and grandmother of three, Betti-Lou enjoys traveling, spending time with her family (especially her grandchildren) and gardening.

Betti-Lou Kramer
Whole Foods
Plymouth Meeting
(610) 832-0010

TERRINA KRAMER

Terrina Kramer is Betti-Lou Kramer's youngest daughter. When she was young she always loved watching her mom create healthy recipes, and now enjoys creating her own. Terrina currently works for Vitamix and loves both her job and the products she represents.

WENDY LANDIAK

Chef Wendy has travelled the world to bring the taste of the exotic to your doorstep. Unique combinations of spices are her signature. Chef Wendy has cooked for leaders, artists, entertainers and food connoisseurs. Cooking for Deepak Chopra in the '90s was one of her first introductions to Ayurvedic cuisine and since then she has traveled to India, become a member of AAPNA, and has conducted seminars on the combination of Raw and Ayurvedic cuisine. One of her most recent cooking expeditions was (a packed house) for the acclaimed Dr. Joel Fuhrman at Whole Foods Market.

Chef Wendy has studied raw cuisine with the acclaimed David Avocado Wolfe in California. She has also studied with the acclaimed raw food Chef Cherie Soria at Living Light in Fort Bragg, California. She continues her raw studies daily with her neighbor Arnold at Arnold's Way in Lansdale and at Pathways for Change in Emmaus.

Currently, she is working on opening her new restaurant Shankara and operating Balasia Catering (for all your catering needs, specifically: yoga schools, chiropractors, massage therapists, naturopaths, nutritionists, all heath care providers, and anyone interested in the best food ever), the VECO wedding group (an all vegan Eco-conscious wedding company), and The Honey Underground, a weekend supper club.

ELAINA LOVE

Elaina Love is a professional Raw and Vegan Food Chef, Instructor and Lifestyle Counselor. She began teaching and creating healthy foods for the public in 1998. Her unique style of creating extremely healthy, delicious cuisine keeps her busy lecturing, catering, teaching culinary courses and creating new books. She is the owner and director of Pure Joy Culinary Academy in Ubud, Bali, which focuses on a low glycemic, high raw and plant based food lifestyle program. Elaina's outreach includes raw food, low glycemic, gourmet culinary certification courses, detox and cleansing certification courses, and healthy lifestyle products.

With a passion for sharing knowledge attained through her years of experience, Elaina has counseled people throughout the country to bring about positive changes in their lives. Her teaching and support empowers people to lose weight and gain energy and health by making positive lifestyle choices and incorporating more plant based food and superfoods into their diet. She is well known for making phenomenal food that leaves people wondering how they can feel so satisfied yet so energized.

Elaina was the co-owner of Café Soulstice in The San Francisco Bay area for 2 years and now consults with other restaurant owners and cafés worldwide, coaches individuals on upgrading their lifestyle, is the author of several recipe books including the *Elaina's Pure Joy Kitchen* series of recipe books, *The Pure Joy Academy Culinary and Holistic Lifestyle Manual*, *The Pure Joy 5-Day Detox*, and *Raw and Beyond*, which she co-authored with Victoria Boutenko and Chad Sarno. She has several raw, vegan DVDs and is the creator of the Amazing Nut Milk Bag, which is sold worldwide.

Elaina enjoys eating a high raw diet, being a flexitarian and creating a personalized diet based on her own personal needs and activity levels. She enjoys fasting often and eating a pretty clean and light diet—for the most part.

www.ElainaLove.com (blog)
www.PureJoyAcademy.com (courses)
www.PureJoyPlanet.com (store)
www.facebook.com/PureJoyAcademy
(480) 788-5581
info@purejoyacademy.com

KARMYN MALONE

Karmyn Malone has been passionate about creating healthy and delicious raw recipes since first learning about the raw food diet back in 2005. She created the child friendly raw recipe book *Feed Your Tike What He Likes*, based on the favorite recipes of her son Andrew and her daughter Rainbow. You can learn more about her by visiting http://karmynmalone.com.

CARLY MARTIN

(Creative Kitchen Crew, Raw Can Roll Café)

Carly joined the Raw Can Roll crew, excited to be part of a community where love, food, and service collide. She has been a vegetarian for three years and finds herself loving the exploration of many different food lifestyles, for which Raw Can Roll is a perfect fit.

Beyond the health aspect, one of the major factors that drew Carly into these different food lifestyles (raw/vegan included) is the care and awareness for the environment that is such a huge part of eating in this way. It is not only body healing, but earth healing as well.

MELISSA MILES

Melissa Miles is an Environmental Biologist, Conservation Planner, Permaculture Designer/Teacher, Urban Farmer, and author. Melissa has been serving as the Organizer of the Eastern Pennsylvania Permaculture Guild and the Director of the Permanent Future Institute, a regional center for regenerative design consulting and education located in the Philadelphia metropolitan area for the past six years, where she consults with private and institutional clients, working to create more productive and resilient landscapes. Melissa teaches and lectures at various institutions in the southeastern Pennsylvania region on the topics of small-scale organic farming and gardening, permaculture, agroforestry, animal husbandry, sustainable land management, homesteading, appropriate technology and various other subjects.

Melissa is the founder and farm manager of Two Miles Micro-Farm (a one-acre, certified naturally grown, urban micro-farm), growing healthy, local food for the farm's CSA members and supplying restaurants in the Philadelphia metro area with lesser known wild and cultivated perennial vegetables and honey. In addition, she is the co-author of the upcoming book, *Dragon Husbandry: The Why and Wherefore of Biogas Systems* (Chelsea Green Publishing, available 2014), on the subject of small-scale, integrated anaerobic digesters.

Melissa Miles
Director
Permanent Future Institute
Regenerative Design, Consulting and Education
permanentfuture@gmail.com
(484) 949-1600

NATURAL ZING

Through three decades of research and consulting with numerous nutritionists and vegetarian specialists, Natural Zing has gathered "the best of the earth:" products that help you develop your *own* natural zing! They continue to search for and only offer the highest quality foods the earth can provide—living, vegan, organic, or wild crafted foods that result in improved vitality.

Natural Zing is a family owned business that is owned and managed by the same founder that started the business in 2003 after changing to a raw, vegan diet a couple years earlier: Jeffrey Rose manages the operation with the same passion with which it was started those many years ago.

Leading the specialty food sector, Natural Zing offers over 1,500 raw, organic, and vegan selections that are "good for you and the Earth™." They pride themselves on offering reasonable prices, fast delivery, and knowledgeable customer care representatives. For more recipes and raw food ideas please visit www.NaturalZing.com and their blog, www.Naturalzing.blogspot.com, or call (866) 729-9464.

NATALIE NORMAN

Natalie Norman is a passionate raw food culinary artist and teacher who strives to make eating raw food not only *easy* for you, but *delicious* and *fun*, too. She is an attorney and an Advanced Raw Food Nutrition Educator, who received her certification from the world-renowned Living Light Culinary Institute, where she studied with top educators and experts in the science of raw food nutrition.

In addition to recipes, Natalie provides nutrition education and lifestyle support designed to facilitate your transition into a raw, plant-based lifestyle. Having gone through her own health challenges in the past, including weight gain, skin and joint problems, and decreased energy, Natalie knows firsthand how daunting it can feel to embark upon a new journey towards health and start a different lifestyle. Natalie firmly believes that a raw food diet can help the body heal itself while providing you with abundant energy and mental clarity.

Connect with Natalie online at:
www.natalienorman.com
Twitter: @natalienorman

CHRISTY PARRY

To support your goal of eating lots of raw fruits and veggies every day, consider two fun and effective catalysts for better health. Juice Plus+ is an easy way to get more fruits and veggies into adults and kids every day because it contains 24 raw, juiced, nutrient-dense fruits, veggies and berries—with their thousands of naturally occurring micro-nutrients—in capsules or tasty gummies. For more information visit www.christyparry.juiceplus.com. Check out the Children's Health Study tab—your child may be eligible for free.

Tower Garden is an exciting and abundant way to grow your own tasty fruits, vegetables, greens and herbs right outside your door (or inside in the winter). It's fresh and local; good for you and the environment, and there is no weeding!

For cool videos and information, visit www.christyparry.towergarden.com. See the Chicago O'Hare Airport towers that serve the airport restaurants; a chef in New York growing produce on his roof; or a time lapse video showing how quickly the produce grows.

Please contact Christy with your questions or to place an order. She gives great customer care!

Christy Parry
(610) 293-0612
Juice Plus and Tower Garden:
www.MySunny.JuicePlus.com
Juice Plus+ and Tower Garden: Eat and grow your way to better health!

BROOKE PRESTON

While training for a figure competition (an event similar to body-building), Chef Brooke Preston was placed on a high-protein diet, which included as much as three pounds of buffalo meat per day. As she began to develop thyroid problems, she noticed that younger competitors, those who had competed in one or more competitions, were all on thyroid medications. Curious about the link between diet and hormonal imbalance, Chef Brooke researched nutritional alternatives to thyroid medicine, ultimately discovering the power of living foods in healing chronic illness. Rather than filling her doctor's prescription for thyroid meds, she immediately switched to a raw food, plant-based diet, and shortly thereafter was completely healed of her thyroid imbalance.

For many years, Chef Brooke has worked as a health-conscious personal chef and caterer on a personal mission to bring families together for home-cooked, nourishing meals. With her newfound interest in a living foods diet and lifestyle, and a desire to bring whole, living foods to a new level, Chef Brooke decided to enroll in the Living Light Culinary Institute – the world's premier organic, raw, vegan chef training school. Aiming to bring the value of raw food to the public with a supportive, educational bend, Chef Brooke worked to better understand the tools and techniques of creating beautiful cuisine in a raw, vegan, nutrient-dense form.

Chef Brooke especially enjoys equipping people on their transition to a raw vegan lifestyle through offering raw foods preparation classes and 30 Day Raw Challenges at her restaurant in Sacramento, California and also through remote classes and coaching online through www.thegreenboheme.com. She is currently working on a recipe book of customer and staff favorites from her healthy café, The Green Bohème!

KAREN RANZI

Everyone wants their children to be super healthy, and Karen Ranzi has the recipe. She is an author, speaker, speech pathologist, holistic health coach and raw vegan chef. Karen has authored and published her groundbreaking book, *Creating Healthy Children through Attachment Parenting and Raw Foods*. Karen travels throughout the United States and abroad, delivering her impassioned message about raising healthy families. She has presented for universities, schools, health institutes, and associations. For the past 15 years, Karen has helped thousands of individuals and families to reach their health potential. In June 2012, Karen was the keynote speaker at the "Health Congress: Flowers of Life" conference south of Moscow, organized by the Russian Association of The Raw Food Movement and Naturopathy. Her two upcoming books are titled *Raw Vegan Recipe Fun for Families* and *How I Healed*

25 Years of Cystic Acne in Three Months. Karen writes about raising healthy families for Get Fresh Magazine, Eternity Watch Magazine, Vibrance Magazine, VegWorld Magazine and Super Raw Life Magazine. She has been interviewed on numerous radio and TV programs as a featured guest, including several episodes on Dr. Gary Null's Progressive Radio Network, Main Street Vegan Radio with Victoria Moran, Interviews with the Raw Vegan Masters with Steven Prussack, The Conscious Parenting Summit with Matthew Monarch, The Conscious Foods Summit, and is currently seen on 14 cable networks on The Living Healthy Show.

RHIO

Rhio is a singer and author, as well as an investigative reporter in the area of health and environmental issues. Her best-selling book *Hooked on Raw* is about living a life more closely aligned with Nature by adopting a raw/live food lifestyle. The 358-page book covers many of the reasons for making these healthy lifestyle changes, as well as more than 350 raw recipes in all categories. CNN and American Journal aired stories on raw foods featuring Rhio. She is considered an expert in the area of raw and living foods and lectures on both the raw/live food lifestyle and the genetic engineering of seeds/plants. Rhio hosts an internet radio show called Hooked on Raw which can be heard worldwide at: www.RawEnergyRadio.com. Rhio's Raw Energy website: www.rawfoodinfo.com also provides extensive information on the raw/live food lifestyle, as well as organic agriculture, environmental, human rights, civil rights, globalization and economic justice issues.

Rhio is also a talented singer, and her singing voice can be heard in an upcoming movie entitled *The Last of Robin Hood*. The song is called "Some Say."

TIFFANY ROBBINS

Tiffany has always been conscientious about what she eats. Growing up in the Seventh Day Adventist Church taught her to read labels on food packages at an early age. She knew what monoglycerides, diglycerides and Red #40 were when she was seven years old. She first learned about living raw in 1993 or 1994 from Vernon Dawson, of the Voice in the Wilderness Mission, the first of many teachers she was to have in her raw journey. She would go in and out of phases where she would eat raw foods, and phases when she practiced vegetarianism and veganism.

She has studied with several raw food chefs and teachers such as David Wolfe, Arnold Kauffman of Arnold's Way, Eddie and Lillian Butler of Raw Soul, Mamma K, Dr. Aris Latham, Amy Levin, Russell James and a few others. She has spent hours reading raw food books and watching videos and attending lectures. She now teaches raw and living food preparation classes. From time to time, you will find her raw pizzas in Atiyolas' Spirit First Foods under the label "Rawdelish." An enormous shout out to all the raw food chefs, restaurants and stores that carry raw foods; may one day the raw food restaurants outnumber the drug stores!

SAMANTHA ROSENSTOCK (MANAGER, LEAD MARKETING AND EVENTS COORDINATOR, RAW CAN ROLL CAFÉ)

For as long as she can remember, Samantha has had two consistent passions in life. The first is food: growing up, her mother was always baking; the house smelled of banana bread, chocolate chip cookies, and carrot cake. It wasn't until Sam got older that she realized the reason her other had made baking a top priority; it was not simply because she had a passion for it, but more so for the joy and happiness it brought to people's faces when she came to them, arms bearing her special treats.

Sam's second passion is talking; to put it simply, she never stops, never runs out of things to say. As a little girl, she always had something to say, and she always made sure she was heard. After a failed attempt at a college degree in speech pathology, she sat down as a junior in college and re-evaluated her life. She realized the importance of following her passions, as it meant she would be doing what she loved. She thought about the passions in her life that had faded, the passions that were current, and then the two passions in particular that were still following her—food and talking.

Now, a recent college graduate from the University of Vermont, doing the two things she loves; talking with people and preparing food. She loves the joy emulated from her customers' faces as they try the food for the first time, surprised at how good it makes them feel. The best is to see the shock on their faces at the realization that the products are made fresh, using local ingredients, and are raw, vegan, *and* gluten free. Samantha loves the idea of communicating with other local businesses about partnering up. If living in Burlington, VT has taught her anything, it is the importance of good neighborhood relations. She hopes to work with other businesses on the Main Line and embody that community feel between the residents and local businesses like the Raw Can Roll Café and Pure Body.

BARBARA SHEVKUN

Barbara Shevkun is a raw vegan recipe developer extraordinaire, educator, author of the Living Cookies eBook and other publications, all-around kitchen geek, and the creative force behind her raw vegan blog, www.rawfullytempting.com. Barbara is currently working on her recipe book, Raw Pizza. Barbara strives to take the fear out of trying something new and has a knack for creating and writing recipes in an easy to follow format, complimented by mouth-watering photos that give her readers confidence to create their own raw delights with ease.

Shevkun's presence is quickly growing in the raw, vegan and healthy eating communities. Her creations are amazing and her signature Chocolate Kale Chips were even featured on Oprah.com. She was invited to compete, and won 1st place in Chef Andrea Beaman's "Unlock the Taste of Summer Tour Cook-Off" with her award winning Champagne Mango Cream Sauce and Zucchini Pasta.

Barbara Shevkun is available for demos, hands- on workshops and private raw food prep coaching. See her blog for more information. Check out the Rawfully Tempting Raw Café for an amazing line of nutrient dense, raw, gluten free cuisine that explodes with flavor.

NATALIE SHULTZ (GRAW FOODS)

Natalie Shultz comes from the quaint little town of Winchester, VA, about an hour outside of the D.C. area. Joining the growing team at Graw Foods in February of 2011 as CMO/EVP of Sales and partner, her savvy business instincts, efficiency practices and background in sales and marketing made her a natural choice. She believes that, in order to be successful, first you must believe in what you do, because if you don't, who else will? Second, over-deliver: people never expect it and always remember it. Third, everyone is selling something, so you had better be the best!

After joining the executive team at Graw Foods, she is now responsible for directing sales and moving into new markets, as well as guiding the marketing and branding of the company through its growth phase. She is thrilled to call Charleston home now and looks forward to growing yet another successful business!

ADAGIO & JINJEE TALIFERO

Adagio Talifero, 9, is being raised as a raw vegan and loving it! He enjoys inventing new recipes, and is always happy to talk to people about the benefits of the raw diet. Sometimes they have to stop him from "helping" people on the street as he tries to teach them why they should not eat cooked food! You can find out more about Adagio's raw family at http://thegardendiet.com and http://jinjeetalifero.com.

TRIBEST CORPORATION

Tribest Corporation, located in Anaheim, CA is a leading designer, OEM manufacturer and marketer of a broad range of branded, high quality small appliances for healthy lifestyles. Tribest is an innovative leader in the Juice Extractor, Dehydrator, Blender and Sprouter business and continues to bring the best products oriented towards the health and well being of their customers. Tribest brands are sold and recognized worldwide and have gained a solid reputation in providing the latest developments in natural health. The Green Star juice extractors are reputably the world's finest juicers, and continue to win numerous international awards. Some of Tribest's other renowned products include the Sedona Combo raw food dehydrator, Tribest Personal Blender, Freshlife automatic sprouter, and Dynablend Horsepower Plus super power blender. For more information, please visit www.tribest.com and www.tribestlife.com.

ULTIMATE SUPERFOOD

An industry pioneer, Ultimate Superfoods, Inc. (USF) specializes in pristine foods and health forming products from the most mineral-rich, nutrient dense micro environments on earth. Like their customers, they aspire to a bold future of vibrant nutrition, longevity, and well being for generations to come. Emerging humbly from the epicenter of Southern California's Superfood movement in 2003, USF sources, directly imports, and internationally ships an array of high quality raw foods, ingredients, and health empowering products to customers around the world. The award winning Ojio and Ojio Sport brands developed by Ultimate Superfoods have won international acclaim from celebrity chefs, professional athletes, and modern consumers alike.

ANTANAS VAINIUS

Antanas Vainius is a Nourishment Expert and BodyMind Coach with a life-long passion for nurturing our evolutionary potential. He guides people toward rediscovering the true power of nourishment, one that creates a solid foundation for the body and mind to thrive. He has taught and lectured internationally, produced, written and directed the critically-acclaimed indoor micro-greens instructional DVD "Grow Your Own Greens," and is currently working on his new book on deep nourishment secrets.

Antanas has been involved in growing wheatgrass and other indoor greens for over 20 years with Loreta's Living Foods. During this time, he has been experimenting with using these living plants as a dynamic tool for his own growth and healing. He has been following the raw/living food movement for as long as he can remember; indeed, most of us begin as living-fooders, receiving life-giving, deeply-nourishing breast milk, until something happens, and we become exposed to foods that do not have their vitality intact. Antanas' journey has been one of learning how to reconnect with the source of life, while supporting others in doing the same by offering them deep body/mind nourishment.

Email: BMNCoach@gmail.com
Website: www.antanasvainius.com.

DR. SCOTT AND RAECHELLE WALKER

Scott and Raechelle Walker have "grown up" together since high school. As athletes, they have always known the power of a healthy lifestyle. Chiropractic therapy, nutrition, and exercise have been at the core of their relationship. Both graduated from Life University; Scott as a doctor of chiropractic and a Certified Chiropractic Sports Physician; and Raechelle as a Sports Health Specialist and massage therapist. Since then, they have been on a mission to promote healthy living and are committed to raising their son and daughter naturally.

They can be contacted at spinewalker27@yahoo.com.

BRUCE AND MARSHA WEINSTEIN

Bruce and Marsha Weinstein, both from the suburbs of Philadelphia, are the creators of Awesome Foods. They started Awesome Foods in September of 2005 to provide raw, organic, right-carb foods to the public. They have owned a health food store, Nature's Harvest in Willow Grove, PA since 1992. They started to eat mostly-raw during the summer of 2003 and noticed the improvement in how they felt right away. As they shopped for raw foods, they noticed that many of them were made with dates, honey and other very sweet ingredients. They were inspired to make foods that were really healthy for people and tasted awesome. Thus, the idea for Awesome Foods was born, and they opened Awesome Foods for business.

Most of the food they make is unsweetened. However, their sweet items are made with coconut nectar, agave nectar, carob powder or mesquite powder as the sweetener. Coconut nectar is very low on the glycemic index and is low in fructose. This means that it does not cause a strong insulin reaction, unlike dates and honey, which are very high on the glycemic index. Their new fruit and nut bars are made with dried prunes, apricots or figs, which are also lower on the glycemic index.

LANY WENKE

Lany Wenke works as a personal trainer for Fitness Trainers, Incorporated, located in Malvern, PA, and is looking to go back to school in the fall of 2014 to get her Doctorate in Physical Therapy. Physical and mental health has always been her priority: Lany believes you are what you eat. The food she eats affects her mood, energy and overall demeanor. She has realized just how important it is to put health food in her body in order to get her through her busy days.

Lany first became interested in eating raw in June of 2013, when she began personal training for Lisa Montgomery. Amazed by her great skin and unending amount of energy, Lany was interested to know her secret! As soon as Lisa shared her books with her, she was hooked. When she started eating raw, she began to realize so many positive changes: she had more energy and wasn't as sore after her workouts; she stopped getting daily headaches and dips in energy, and even lost ten pounds! Eating raw has made her into an overall happier person.

MITCH WHITE

(Graw Foods)

Mitch White spent the first half of his professional career in the tennis industry. After attending Virginia Commonwealth University on a tennis scholarship, he transferred to Purdue University and then went on to play professionally and coach for many years, serving as director of tennis at the prestigious Chantilly Golf and Country Club in Chantilly, VA. In 1992 he launched a tennis management company called Topspin Unlimited, based in Washington DC, which was acquired by a competitor in 1996. From 1996–1998, he was partner in the sports facility development company ISG.

After many years of travel throughout Asia he founded Simon and White LLC in 2006, a consulting company which specialized in helping U.S. based businesses expand into Asia, with emphasis on South Korea. Marquee clients included companies like Carfax and Johnny Rockets. In 2008 Mitch was asked to help launch DMBCi, the sports based interactive technology division of DMBC-the Digital Media Broadcast Company. The division was responsible for the broadcasting of live sporting events on an internet based interactive platform to subscription viewers.

After successfully helping launch DMBCi Mitch was approached by gRAWnola (now Graw Foods) to help lead the growth of the company, initially as an investor and then as the CEO and partner. Mitch helped turn the company into a strong regional presence in the South and attained an average YOY growth rate of 75 percent since taking the position in 2009. He's grown the company from two products and a single market focus to 13 diverse product offerings and multiple new markets and revenue streams. "My goal is to make Graw Foods one of the leading health based snack food companies in the U.S., utilizing our expert knowledge of food science, unique manufacturing methods and explosive growth of food consumers looking for healthier snacks that taste great."

He has been a member of several prestigious organizations, including YPO and Capital Clubs, and has been a guest speaker on numerous of panels. Born and raised in the Washington DC area, Mitch lived in Charleston from 1988–1990 while competing on the professional tennis circuit, and in early 2011, he left Washington, D.C. to once again call Charleston home.

LAURA WRIGHT

Always into alternative paths to health, Laura began the raw food vegan path three months prior to discovering she had chronic lymphatic leukemia (CLL). She then began sharing her health journey by making videos at www.youtube.com/user/StarFlower99654.

Life's next journey includes moving in with elderly, ailing parents and preparing healthy meals as well as other alternative therapies to give them a quality life in their golden years which will be video documented on her channel.

Today, Laura is celebrating 9 months of being in remission and is starting a new channel that incorporates many healthy recipes from various eating plans called Dare2EatDifferent also on YouTube.

TONYA ZAVASTA

Born in the former Soviet Union with two damaged hips, one leg shorter than the other, Tonya ached just to walk normally.

The raw food lifestyle offered the answer to *all* her problems, inside and out. She'd just been looking for a way to get through multiple surgeries without becoming an old, sick, unhappy woman. But the results far exceeded those modest expectations. Eating 100 percent raw for sixteen years, she has found her bones actually respond like the pliable, developing bones of a teen. The raw food lifestyle creates a certain elasticity even in mature, developed bodies—more than medical science admits. As she became younger, so did her entire body, her skeletal system included. It seems the longer she stays raw, and the longer she practices what she calls Quantum Eating—her own form of anti-aging lifestyle—and diligent exercise, the better her results get!

Tonya Zavasta is a leading raw foods expert, lecturer, and author of seven books on the 100 percent raw food lifestyle. With her math/science background,

Tonya's creative thinking reaches from quantum physics and cellular biology to the most advanced anti-aging practices. Her books *Your Right to Be Beautiful, Beautiful on Raw* and *Quantum Eating* show you how to radically improve your health and appearance through the raw food lifestyle. Tonya, now in her mid-50s, is walking testimony to the power of raw foods to reveal the natural beauty within us all.

www.beautifulonraw.com
www.facebook.com/BeautifulOnRaw

Resources

I'd like to share with you some of my favorite resources that I have found through the years.

EQUIPMENT

What follows is a list of the best products I use in my raw food lifestyle. I was going to do a Top 10, but couldn't narrow it down; they're all too wonderful!

Top 21 Raw Kitchen Must-Haves
1. Vitamix® 5200 High-Speed Blender
2. Tribest® Greenstar Elite Jumbo Twin Gear Juicer
3. Tribest® Slowstar 2-in-1 Juicer and Mincer
4. Z Star Manual Z710 Juicer
5. Tribest® Personal Blender
6. Tribest® Citristar CS-1000 Citrus Juicer
7. Cuisinart® DLC-XPN Classic 20-Cup Food Processor
8. Tribest® Duet Water Revitalizer
9. Strawberry Fields Naturally® Megahome Water Distiller
10. Tribest® Sedona Dehydrator GSE-5000
11. Ball® canning jars and lids
12. Knives: Kershaw® and Zwilling J.A. Henckels®
13. Paderno World Cuisine® A4982799 Tri-Blade Plastic Spiral Vegetable Slicer
14. Tribest® GlasLife airtight glass storage containers
15. Zak® mixing bowls (made out of recyclable materials)
16. Pyrex® glass mixing bowls
17. Cutting boards
18. Tribest® Mandoline
19. Coffee grinder (for grinding nuts and seeds)
20. Assorted kitchen tools (zesters, peelers, graters, etc.)
21. Nut milk bags

Vitamix High-Speed Blender (www.vitamix.com)

By now you know that the Vitamix® is my preferred high-speed blender. I take my Vitamix® with me, even when I travel. I made the mistake once when, as a family, we spent Christmas at a condo in Florida. The condo had a blender, so I didn't take my Vitamix®. The blender supplied with the condo could not even blend watermelon meat! It's worth taking your Vitamix® with you, so you don't get caught short. And these days, it seems that all hotels have a small refrigerator, so you can hit the local grocery store and purchase your smoothie ingredients and salad fixings, allowing you to continue eating healthy when you're away from home.

Tribest (www.tribest.com)

Not only do I use Tribest's quality tools in my kitchen (such as the Greenstar Elite Juicer, Slowstar Juicer, CitriStar, and Sedona Dehydrator), they are also products of the highest quality, supported by a fantastic sales team.

Fante's Kitchen Shop (www.fantes.com)

Run by the same family for generations, Fante's Kitchen Shop is located in the heart of the Italian Market in southeast Philadelphia, Pennsylvania. They have over 10,000 kitchen tools and a reliable online ordering system. Whatever I am looking for, regular kitchen tools or the obscure, they always have them.

Rawsome Creations Nut Milk Bag (www.rawsomecreations.com)

Rawsome Creations makes my favorite nut milk bag, which can be purchased on their website. These nut milk bags are made by hand in Bali, Indonesia for Rawsome Creations. A portion of Rawsome Creations sales support Ibu Robin at the Bumi Sehat Birthing Center (www.bumisehatfoundation.org) and Yayasan Widya Guna Orphanage near Ubud, Bali. So, not only are you buying a good product, you are supporting good causes!

INGREDIENTS

The Date People (www.datepeople.net)

The Date People in Niland, California are my resource for dates. They have their own date farm, on which they grow an assortment of dates.

Rising Tide Sea Vegetables (www.loveseaweed.com)

Rising Tide Sea Vegetables® in Mendocino, California has been my resource for sea vegetables for years. They provide a variety of sea vegetables and their quality is impeccable.

Good Faith Farm (www.goodfaithfarm.com)

Good Faith Farm in Flournoy, California grow their own heirloom organic olives. What is great about Good Faith Farms is the people you talk to on the phone are the actual people who grow and harvest the olives.

Loreta's Living Foods (www.loretaslivingfoods.com)

In southeastern Pennsylvania, Loreta Vainius has been growing sprouts and wheatgrass, and teaching classes for over 20 years. You can either buy your sprouts and wheatgrass from her, or you can take one of her classes and learn how to grow your own sprouts and wheatgrass. Loreta was my very first raw teacher. She set me up with my first juicer and my first Vitamix® and spent countless time answering my many questions. If it wasn't for Loreta teaching me the fundamentals about raw foods, I wouldn't be where I am today. Thank you, Loreta.

The Sproutman

Murray Tizer is the original Sproutman. He has been growing and selling his wheatgrass and sprouts since 1978. Murray sells his wheatgrass and sprouts through distributors. You can find his products in markets like Essene Market & Café, Whole Food Markets, Kimberton Whole Foods locations, and Millers to name a few. If you don't find The Sproutman products in your market, ask the produce manager to bring them in.

Chili Smith Beans (www.chilismith.com)

Chili Smith Beans in Sacramento, California is a great resource for heirloom beans. What's great about Chili Smith Beans is that you can not only eat them; you can take the same bean, plant it, and it will grow. You can go to Chili Smith's website to purchase the beans, find recipes for each of their beans, and watch informational videos about beans, including how to use them and how to prepare them.

Sun Organic Farm (www.sunorganic.com)

Sun Organic Farm in California is one of my go-to places for pure vanilla. Sun Organic is a 15+ year old mail order retailer of certified organic food ingredients. They gather over 350 different organic food items and offer the freshest and most nutritious foods for their customers in the United States and around the world.

Mushroom Mountain (www.mushroommountain.com)

Mushroom Mountain is *the* place to go when you want to purchase mushrooms or grow your own mushrooms. You can purchase mushroom bags, logs that already have the spores implanted in the log, or you can start from scratch by purchasing your own spores. The products come with directions.

Ultimate Superfoods (www.ultimatesuperfoods.com)

Located in California, Ultimate Superfoods is an amazing resource for ingredients and advice. The products are high in quality and the employees actually live the healthy lifestyle. You can purchase small quantities or buy in bulk. By buying in bulk, you save money. I like not having to go out when I start to create a raw dish, so it's nice having the ingredients on the shelf.

Natural Zing (www.naturalzing.com)

Natural Zing has everything you need to live the raw food lifestyle. Some folks aren't as lucky as we are in my area, where we have resources to purchase the ingredients that I like to have on hand. Located near Baltimore, Maryland, you can buy small quantities or in bulk. The folks at Natural Zing are so helpful and courteous. Natural Zing was gracious enough to share some of their favorite recipes so you can get to try them and get to know them.

Essene Market & Café, Kimberton Whole Foods, and Whole Foods Market

The Essene Market & Café (www.essenemarket.com), Kimberton Whole Foods (www. kimbertonwholefoods.com), and Whole Foods Market (www.wholefoodsmarket.com) are just a few of the healthy markets available.

One Lucky Duck (www.oneluckyduck.com)

One Lucky Duck is one of my favorite mail order providers. Their Rosemary Quackers and Cheese-y Quackers are delicious, and their cookies and ice cream are to die for as well. If you want an elegant, gourmet raw meal, be sure to go to One Lucky Duck, located in Pure Food and Wine in New York.

Miller's Natural Foods

Miller's Natural Foods is a natural food store in the heart of Lancaster County, Pennsylvania. They also do mail order. People come from all over, up and down the East Coast of the United States, to go to Miller's. Part of the fun of going to Miller's is that it's in the middle of farms. If you don't know how to get there, you wouldn't find it by just passing their door.

HERBS

The following are resources to purchase dried herbs, as well as knowledgeable resources on using herbs.

King's Herb Nook

King's Herb Nook in Honey Brook, Pennsylvania carries live herb plants (season appropriate) and dried herbs. They also carry a lot of their own homemade herb products.

Horizon Herbs (www.horizonherbs.com)

Horizon Herbs in Williams, Oregon, is another great resource for dried herbs.

Mountain Rose Herbs (www.mountainroseherbs.com)

Mountain Rose Herbs in Eugene, Oregon carries a wide variety of dried herbs and products to help you incorporate herbs into your lifestyle. You can buy small quantities as well as bulk.

Permanent Future: Melissa Miles

If you live in southeast Pennsylvania, and are interested in permaculture, you will come to know the name Melissa Miles. Melissa is not only a walking encyclopedia of permaculture knowledge, but she is also interesting and funny. She teaches you how to incorporate permaculture techniques into your everyday life. Many folks hire her to incorporate native plants onto their properties. Melissa also runs a CSA and sells her produce weekly to a five-star Philadelphia restaurant. She can take economical ingredients and combine them with the tools on hand to create a solution to a challenge. Melissa is currently writing her book in her spare time.

Eagle Skyfire (www.eagleskyfire.com)

Eagle Skyfire is a Native American Shaman, and has great wisdom. She has the ability to share the wisdom of her ancestors and make it applicable for real world living today.

WATER

Below are a few of the water systems that I use in my house.

Regency II Water System

I use this system in my kitchen. It uses reverse osmosis and adds pH, while removing any debris from the water.

Tribest Duet Water Revitalizer

I use the Tribest® Duet after my water goes through the Regency II2 water system.

Megahome Water Distiller

I just recently purchased a Megahome water distiller from Strawberry Fields Naturally. Strawberry Fields Naturally is an online website where you can purchase tools and products for your healthy lifestyle. When you make recipes like kefir water, kombucha, and beet kvass, the recipes call for distilled water. The owner of Strawberry Fields Naturally swears that his health improved a lot by drinking distilled water.

GARDENING AND SEEDS

Below are my favorite heirloom, organic seed sources.

Baker Creek Heirloom Seeds (www.rareseeds.com)

Baker Creek holds the annual National Heirloom Seed Expo in Santa Rosa, California, which is an amazing event to attend. I went this year for the first time, and I was in seed heaven.

Comstock Seeds (www.comstockseed.com)

Comstock is a 200 year old company. One of the major advantages of ordering from them is that they carry watercress seeds and native heirloom organic seeds.

High Mowing Organic Seeds (www.highmowingseeds.com)

This company carries organic seeds.

Seed Savers Exchange (www.seedsavers.org)

This company carries heirloom seeds.

Gardener's Supply Company (www.gardeners.com)

Gardener's Supply is my go-to place to purchase innovative tools and supplies. The sales staff is friendly and knowledgeable.

Spray-N-Grow (www.spray-n-grow.com)

Spray-N-Grow in Rockport, Texas carries products that are safe for people, plants, and pets.

RAW SCHOOLS

Today, we are very lucky that we can take raw cooking and uncooking classes from the chefs of raw restaurants such as Jenny Ross's 118 Degrees restaurants in California (www.118degrees.com), or Sheryl Chavarria's Raw Can Roll Café (www.purefoodandbody.com) in the Philadelphia, Pennsylvania suburbs. Raw meet-ups and potlucks have popped up across the country and around the world, as people help support each other in living a healthy lifestyle.

Some other raw schools include:

- Matthew Kenney Cuisine located in Santa Monica, California (www.matthewkenneycuisine.com)
- Cheria Soria's Living Light Culinary Institute of Raw Foods in Fort Bragg, one of the forerunners to raw food schools (www.rawfoodchef.com)
- Brenda Cobb's Living Foods Institute in Atlanta, Georgia (www.livingfoodsinstitute.com)
- The Natural Gourmet Institute in New York, New York, teaches raw food classes, as well as other forms of healthy cooking (www.naturalgourmetinstitute.com)
- The Institute for Integrative Nutrition in New York teaches all the healthy ways of eating and living, so you can decide which way works best for you (www.integrativenutrition.com)

Hippocrates Health Institute (http://hippocratesinst.org)

Hippocrates Health Institute in West Palm Beach, Florida was founded by Ann Wigmore and Viktoras Kluvinska, the grandfather of raw foods. Many doctors send their clients to Hippocrates when they don't know what else to do with them. Hippocrates has science behind them; they can run tests on the patients when they arrive to find out exactly where their health is and then plan a course of action for each and every client. I have not yet attended Hippocrates, but I have spoken with many who have, and their response was that they learned a lot to help them live a healthier life.

Index